Advanced Redesign

How to Maximize Your Profits

in Your Interior Redesign, Redecorating and Home Staging Business

Barbara Jennings, CRS/CSS
The Academy of Staging and Redesign

Table of Contents

Advanced Redesign

Chapter 1
Basic Redesign vs. Advanced Redesign

Welcome to **Advanced Redesign**. Whether you've already been trained in re-design business techniques, strategies and ideas by me in my basic tutorial called **Rearrange It!**, or whether you've already been trained by someone else, or whether you haven't had any training at all, I hope and trust you will find your excursion into this more advanced approach a worthwhile and profitable adventure.

For those of you who may have jumped into this training with no background whatsoever in re-design, or staging of homes for that matter, I strongly encourage you to acquire my basic training manual called **Rearrange It** (http://www.decorate-redecorate.com/rearrange.html). This manual will concentrate on many of the tactics and strategies that top professionals use to catapult their businesses into six and seven figure incomes. But to apply these strategies to your redesign business, you should first be grounded in the basic tactics and strategies of starting and growing a redecorating business. Then the concepts you will learn in this manual will serve as an extension of what you're already applying and doing in your core business.

Ok, let's move on.

What's the difference between the basic re-design concepts in **Rearrange It!** and **Advanced Redesign**? I know what you're thinking . . . what else could there be? Well, in short, plenty. Let me explain. Basic Re-design really only covers the main concept of going into a client's home, taking the furniture and accessories they already own, moving them to new locations based on solid interior design concepts, collecting the flat or hourly fee, and leaving a hopefully happy client behind.

Now that's pretty simple stuff when you stop to think about it. And if that's all you're interested in doing, you don't need to read any further. But if you're serious about maximizing your time and effort and getting all you can out of your new or established re-design business, then grab a cup of coffee and a snack, get your notebook out, get a pen, and let's get to work getting you filled to the brim with exciting ideas and strategies to help you grab all the profit there is out there that can possibly be related to re-design by any stretch of the imagination.

Having said that, bear in mind that I'm not telling you that you have to do all of these strategies to be successful. You certainly don't. You probably won't have time, to tell you the truth. But look them all over carefully and pick the ones that you feel you are best suited to incorporate into your business and go for it.

Nor am I claiming to cover each of the ideas I will present here to the fullest and most exhaustive extent possible. That would be ridiculous. There just isn't space and I don't want to insult your intelligence. Each of the related business strategies, services and products could easily warrant a book of its own, I think. But that is not my purpose here. My purpose is to tantalize you with so many ideas, concepts and strategies for how you could really capture all of the profit out there for a re-designer, that it will blow your mind wide open.

When I've done that and made you kind of dizzy with the greater possibilities, then I will have done what I set out to do in this manual.

Bear in mind, however, the basics of operating, growing and managing any of these business strategies are so similar or down right the same, to repeat it for each strategy would be redundant to say the least. You would simply hate me for getting you all bogged down - and quite frankly I wouldn't blame you.

Some strategies might not appeal to you. Some of you might be in a region that is saturated in a particular concept, but other concepts are wide open to you. Others of you might have some logistical problems (like transportation or storage) that might preclude your participation. But keep an open mind and remember: it's your business. You can specialize in whatever you want and you can tweak any of the strategies to suit your needs.

You might also discover along the way, that an idea or strategy that I present might lead you to adapt it into some off-shoot. Feel free to tweak these ideas any way you choose. Nothing is written in stone. Adapt them. Expand them. Play with them. Experiment. Discard what doesn't work for you. When you find something that works for you, go with it. Work it to death. Combine things. Do whatever you need to do to gain your fair market share, **so long as it is legal**.

Support, Bonuses and Contact Information

I want to reassure you that I will be available to you to help you apply the concepts in any way I can. Here's how.

SUPPORT AND QUESTIONS
Due to SPAM, we periodically have had to change our email addresses. So for the current methods of contacting us, please visit http://www.decorate-redecorate.com/about.html or http://www.decorate-redecorate.com/support.html . Just look for the appropriate links on the page. If you don't receive a response within 24 hours, please resubmit your request. Chances are we never received the first one. The up-to-date phone number is listed at the bottom of our Home Page as a back up. Please note that all technical support issues are handled by email, not by phone.

If you purchased this training from my website, you may write me with regard to any concept or problem that is unique to your situation and I will be happy to help you **personally**. This personalized help is one of the most valuable parts of your purchase, so please take advantage of it. In the meantime, I truly wish you the best with your new redesign/staging venture. If you purchased this training from another source, you will have to become a client of mine to qualify for free, on-going mentoring help.

BONUSES
The Home Staging 8-Page Check List of services, that should greatly help you determine a quote for your services, is printed out for you at the back of this manual.

The Business Forms are also printed at the back of this manual.

ADDITIONAL SUPPORT PRODUCTS
Take a minute to look over the list of additional ways we can support you in growing your business at the conclusion of this book. We have many additional training products and tools of the trade. Most of these are exclusive products. By investing in some of these, you're sure to grow your business much faster and to greater heights.

A Review of Common Basic Strategies to Add to Your Redesign/Staging Services

Below on this page you're going to find the most common re-design add-on strategies promoted by me in **Rearrange It!**, but also similarly taught by other programs. If you're already acquainted about these, whether you're using them or not, please read this section anyway. Consider it a refresher course.

I want to make sure you are well grounded in the most basic services that typical re-designers around the country are offering. These are very common sense approaches to re-design and easy to incorporate into your host of available services. If you haven't been doing any of them, perhaps now is the time to do so. They are pretty simple and most require no further investment, because you are merely maximizing your **time**, for which you receive a fee. So look them all over and see how you can incorporate them now or in the future into your business.

Paint & Color Consultations

A good way to get "in the door" to a client's home for a very affordable fee, is to offer a paint and color consultation service. I just got a call yesterday from a local lady wanting help in selecting the colors for the exterior of her home. So there are people who are seeking this type of service. Enterprising re-designers are happy to accommodate this type of client, because it's the perfect way to start out "small" and then up-sell the client into more services once you are there in the home and have established rapport. For a discussion on effective up-selling, finish this section and move on as I'll cover it more thoroughly in a later chapter.

I've said many times, the best time to help a client make decisions and understand the full range of services you offer is when you are standing right there in their entry or living room. By this time they have met you, they hopefully like and trust you, and are completely open to what you have to offer them.

But you better know what you're doing when it comes to color. Color is very tricky because it is affected so easily by lighting conditions and by surrounding colors. Colors will surprise you, as they never ever look the same as they do on the small color chip you get from the paint store or a fabric swatch. You might quite easily find that pastels will look much lighter than expected. They might look brighter than expected. Darker shades might easily become overwhelming in large doses. Warm colors tend to advance towards you, while cool colors tend to recede. But guess what? Not always. It just depends - and it depends on so many other factors. So color, even in the hands of a pro, can be tricky.

This is not the time or place to teach you about color. I have already put an extensive section regarding color and paint in **Rearrange It!** (http://www.decorate-redecorate.com/redecorate.html). Please re-read that section or acquire your copy if you have not done so already.

I will say this, however. You must know that all colors are divided into two distinct Color Keys: warm colors (with yellow undertones) and cool colors (with blue undertones). It is often difficult, just by looking at a color (believe it or not), to tell which Color Key it belongs in. This can be problematic and I see professionals making major mistakes ALL the time because they do not pre-determine the Color Key of the choices they are combining together in a room, on a fabric, on furniture, etc.

You used to be able to get a Fan Deck (a color selector most paint companies create, where the samples fan out for easy reference) that was divided into Color Key I and Color Key II. It's not available any longer, unfortunately.

You see, even neutrals like white and black have their warm side and their cool side. All warm colors will blend with other warm colors; cool colors will blend with all other cool colors; but warm colors will not blend well with cool colors. It's that simple.

You can visit the paint department of your favorite home decorating store. Usually paint manufacturers set out their paint chips with colors going from cool to warm. Obviously the colors closest to the crossing point between cool and warm are very difficult to ascertain. They have either such little yellow in them or such little blue in them, it's almost as if they could be put into either color key. But in reality, every hue and every tint or shade of every hue belongs in one color key or the other. So the closer you get to the middle of the sample display, the more that color can cross between one Key and the other, so the less risky it is when mixing with colors that are definitely in one Key or the other.

Be sure to purchase at least one fan deck and take with you on appointments. When at a client's home, if you want to check the warmness or coolness of the carpet, the paint color, a background color in the wallpaper, or anything else in their home involving color, you can find a chip in the fan deck that comes closest to the color. When you've done that, just check to see which color key your chip falls in and you'll be pretty certain you have assigned the right color key to your client's colors. It's as simple as that.

I don't know of any interior designer, decorator or re-designer who has ever taught this method of color verification except me. If you run across someone using it, chances are they learned it from me or someone connected to me.

For additional tips on color or choosing colors, please visit my website's sitemap. I have a list with hundreds of free tips, but specifically on color too. Here is the link: (http://www.decorate-redecorate.com/master-sitemap.html).

Now, having said that, let me also repeat: color is tricky. Even the best can be fooled. So a word to the wise: test, test and test some more. Never advise a client on getting a specific color, or group of colors, without also telling them to buy a small quantity of the color first and test it on an area of the place they are considering before committing all out to the final choice.

Testing is the best way for anyone to be absolutely certain that what they have chosen is the right color and that they will be happy in the long run.

If actually painting a large area is out of the question, there might be alternatives to consider. For instance, I once had a client who had white walls throughout the home, but all of the wood on the furniture in the living room and dining room was black. Above the fireplace was a beautiful mirrored wall sculpture on a white background. There was so little contrast that the power of the mirrored sculpture was lost and fell flat. I suggested to my client that she paint the wall above the fireplace black, then re-hang the sculpture on the black background. I had a border rug made in the colors of the room to anchor the seating arrangement. Reluctant to actually paint the wall, even though a small section, my client took large black construction paper and stapled it to the wall, covering the wall completely with the black paper. Then she hung the sculpture. It was so amazingly beautiful she then instantly painted the wall black.

So this is just another example of testing first before making a commitment. It is so important.

Summing it up, offering a Color Consultation, whether it is for picking out paint colors, wallpaper, fabrics - whatever - is a smart additional service you can offer to advance your re-design business. If it appeals to you, do it.

General Interior Design Consultations

Offering a more encompassing design consultation is **not** advised unless you have had a sufficient amount of interior design training, either by taking formal design classes at a college or university ending in a degree in interior design. This is far more risky because there are some areas of expertise that can easily become very involved, that one needs licenses for, that need a contractor and so forth.

Just because you are creative and know how to move furniture - that does not mean you are qualified to offer a full fledged design consultation service. Because of the liability issues that one can face on this issue, I am recommending that you do not offer this service. But for those of you who are willing to devote the time and effort to getting formal training, here are some tidbits to help you on your way.

Professionals in the interior design field furnish the interiors of commercial, industrial and residential buildings and homes. They must be up on federal, state and local codes and able to wear many hats.

Quick Start Steps

1. Understand that as an interior designer you will need to know more than how to decorate a space. For example, you will need to fully understand flammability and toxicity standards, be able to easily read a blueprint and know how to communicate with engineers, architects and clients.

2. Obtain a bachelor's degree in interior design from a college whose design program has been accredited by the Foundation for Interior Design Education Research (FIDER). Check out FIDER's Web site for a list of approved programs.

3. Include computer-aided design (CAD) courses in your electives. As a designer you will be expected to know how to use computers to create your space designs.

4. Apply for internships through your school. Your contacts might lead to a future job.

5. Contact your state's regulatory agency to confirm its licensing requirements for interior designers. State-by-state information is located in the National Council for Interior Design Qualification (NCIDQ) Web site.

6. Spend a year or two working in the field for someone else after graduation, prior to taking and passing the NCIDQ qualification exam. It is a prerequisite to your receiving a license. Take the exam even if your state does not require licensure. You will need to pass it to be accepted in professional organizations that are key to the success of designers.

Suggested Tips
Subscribe to interior design and architecture magazines for the latest trends.

A Warning to Heed

Designers work irregular schedules, at the convenience of their clients and projects can be sporadic. Strong communication and professional skills are required.

Holiday Party/Special Occasion Decorating

There are many times during the course of a year when holidays or special occasions require a homeowner to want to do some special decorating. Here are a few of the types of holidays and events that such decorating needs might arise for: Easter, Christmas, New Years, Thanksgiving, birthdays, Super Bowl party, wedding, bridal shower, baby shower, party for boss, wedding anniversary party, valentine's day, assorted children's parties, open house - you get the idea.

A great way to offer this type of service is to be sure to take photos of all parties that you decorate yourself for your own family or extended family.

Once you have a sufficient a portfolio put together, decorating for hopefully a wide variety of holidays or special occasions, then you're ready to add this specialized service to your list to offer to clients. The reason I emphatically tell you to make sure you gain specific experience doing this type of decorating for yourself, family and friends without charging a cent (other than to cover the cost of materials) is because holidays and special events (in particular) are very emotional times for people. More than at any other time of the year, these events form serious memories and photo opportunities that can **never** be replaced. So the clients have a very specific vested interest in the desire that they have perfect outcomes.

I don't want any one to get in over their head and damage a service and have a very irate client and possible small claims law suit facing them. So unlike some of the other ideas that I am presenting here, you need to be particularly careful when offering services that are uniquely tied to emotional times in people's lives. If you get it wrong, there's no way to rectify it to their complete satisfaction.

Once you are ready to offer the service and you have someone eager to hire you, then it is best to set an appointment and go to the home to discuss all of the arrangement and decorating details. Do not try to do it over the phone. Go to the home and discuss the decorating of the following areas: outside entrance to the home or location, the inside entry, the main room of the party, any specific focal points in the room, any adjacent rooms or areas that are needed, the decorations needed for the table (if a sit down affair), any and all serving table decorations, decorations for apparel of hosts and/or guests, etc. In short you need to construct a form to take with you that outlines or has a checklist for all things you should discuss so that you don't inadvertently forget anything important.

Whenever you agree to provide a service that involves a lot of specific details, such as a party decorating service, you want to have a contract in writing. I've said before and it bears repeating. Whoever draws up the contract is responsible in the event there are any ambiguities. So legally, should there be a dispute later and it winds up in court, all ambiguities will go against the party that drew up the contract. For this reason, it would be advisable to consult an attorney in drawing up your contract.

Decide in advance whether you want to charge a flat fee or an hourly rate. I see that a lot of re-designers are charging an hourly rate. I think this is a problem. Whenever I see someone charging an hourly rate, my first thought is that they are pretty inexperienced. The reason for this is that experienced re-designers have a very strong knowledge of how much time any one of their services will entail. To that rough idea they can easily add an extra hour or two to cover them in the event of complications. So giving a flat rate is easy for them.

Inexperienced decorators do not know how many hours something will take, so they feel better charging an hourly rate. But clients tend to be leery of paying someone an hourly rate as there are too many ways for the time log to get padded. My advice is that if you're going to charge an hourly rate for any of your services, that you add a "not to exceed" time frame. In other words, say that the service normally averages between 5-8 hours, but you will never charge for more than 8 hours. This way the client can hope for a 5 hour charge but knows it will not exceed 8 hours. You need to make people feel comfortable with buying your services. An open-ended hourly rate is never going to make anyone but your mom feel comfortable.

Exterior Holiday Decorating Service

And don't forget about the exterior of homes. How about offering a holiday decorating service for the exterior, as well as the interior. Using the decorations that your client already owns, or by selling them special decorations that you have selected just for a custom design of lights, plants and other decorations, you can go in before the holidays and put up all of the exterior lights and decorations. You could offer a basic design, a moderate design (such as you see pictured here) or a really deluxe design (where the lights  cover the roof and all of the plants and so forth. Naturally you would charge according to the number of lights or the time it takes to create and implement a design.

After the holidays are over, your service should also include removing the decorations as well. I know of one enterprising exterior decorator who charges $350 for the service. You must know a good deal about lights and all of the electrical safeguards one must take to handle thousands of Christmas lights. Do not offer this type of service unless you are very knowledgeable about electrical requirements and make sure you have worker's comp insurance. You'll obviously need an extension ladder, hammer, hooks, extension cords and so forth. Check with your city as to whether there are any special licenses required for doing this type of service.

Home Decorating Shopping Services

Love to shop for decorating items? Turn your passion into another service and offer a decorating shopping service. Others are doing it, so why can't you?

Quick Start Steps:

1. Get some experience by shopping with or for a friend or relative. Remember that you're not buying something for YOUR home, but for theirs. This means that you have to be in tune with what they like, what they dislike, their colors, their style and so on.

11

2. Do your research. If you want to decorate someone else's home, you must know a lot about that person's home, so you must first visit the home and do a complete walk-thru, with their permission, of course. You should discuss with them the furnishings they feel they need, where they would put what is purchased, what shape it should be, it's height, it's width, it's color and the budget they have to work with.

3. Take notes; do not rely on memory. Better yet, take a digital camera or other camera and take pictures of the room(s) you are decorating. It's amazing how one's memory of the size and shape and colors can "change" once you are out in the stores. Don't rely on your memory - it will deceive you. Take thorough measurements of the space you will have, even doing a line drawing on graph paper to guide you. Collect color samples if your client has them available: paint, wallpaper, window treatment fabric, pillow from sofa, etc. Take them with you.

4.  Make a list of places you will visit. Get your local Business to Business Yellow Pages, or do a thorough search on the internet in your area for unique stores, especially wholesalers. You should pre-develop a relationship with showrooms where you pre-register your business. Most will require a business card and a resale license. Some will also require a copy of your letterhead. They want to make sure you are legitimately in the "trade". Trade showrooms have a unique and individual way of pricing the merchandise so that you will know the cost for you to buy, but your client will not. Some showrooms will price the merchandise by the suggested retail price. Others will not. Know that there will be some clients who, after knowing where you shop for designer products, will try to shop there on their own without you. So be careful about which stores you take your client to visit.

5. Organize your skills and portfolio. Start with colleagues from your previous profession, friends, relatives and neighbors. Target busy men and women whose professions dictate a love of style and leave them little time or energy to worry about their homes.

6. Draw up a written contract that spells out exactly what your service includes, and what it does not include. It should state what budget you have been given, your hourly or flat fee for services rendered, and any other particulars to the agreement between you and the client. It doesn't have to be real involved, but it should be specific enough to represent your intentions. Any ambiguities, in a small claims court, will go against whoever drew up the contract, so be sure that your paperwork protects you.

7. Get on the phone or send e-mail. Look for busy people - that's why they will be attracted to your services. It's up to you to tell them all about how much time you will save them and how you know just the right places to shop on their behalf.

Additional Tips

Know your client's budget and respect it. Always offer your clients a variety of options, but avoid exceeding their budgets. You'll establish a bond and trust with your clients and keep them coming back for your services. Be sure to shop where you can return merchandise that doesn't work out without being penalized with a restocking charge. At first you may bring some things that will not be suitable for your client and you will have to return them. But you'll learn. The more careful you are on the front end, to take appropriate measurements and really zero in on the types of things your client already has and loves, the better you will be and the less time it will take to achieve their complete satisfaction.

Get referrals from your satisfied clients the moment you are done. If you wait, you're less likely to get any. Get them while the client is the most happy with your service.

The Detailed Steps

With the fast-paced, high pressure professional lifestyles of today, more and more people have limited time to do their personal shopping, much less their home decorating shopping. Holding down a full-time job, raising children, and maintaining a household doesn't seem to leave enough hours in the day to get everything done. That's why many people are now opting for services that will handle these matters for them. Men are especially interested in these services, because most men hate to shop anyway.

Within the past decade shopping services have emerged as a rapidly growing cottage industry with the potential for highly profitable large-scale operations. It's a service that appeals to a busy, above average income clientele. And an enterprising re-designer providing this kind of service can make substantial profits. This service can be used to generate clients or it can be used as a natural back-end service to a re-design appointment.

Shopping for other people is not necessarily a difficult task. As stated earlier, the re-designer usually meets with clients in their home to determine their needs and compile a list of items to be purchased within the client's specified price range. Recording the appropriate measurements needed in advance is critical to a successful shopping service. Then the shopping begins. After the client's items have been purchased, the shopper and client meet again. The client looks over the purchases, and once satisfied with the shopper's selections, pays the bill. Most of the "work" involved with a decorating shopping service, is in the shopping itself.

Start-up costs for a decorating shopping service can be relatively minimal. There's little need for expensive equipment and hardly any initial investment in inventory. The biggest expense a home-based decorating shopping service encounters is usually the method of transportation used by the shopper. Since most of a personal shoppers time is spent shopping, an efficient running, low-mileage car or van is essential to get to the many shopping locations. I have a PT Cruiser, which allows me to transport most accessories, even artificial trees, quite easily. Naturally, if you're shopping for furniture and you don't have a van, you'll have to have it delivered.

Start your business as a part time, home-based operation. Beginning the service at home allows a new re-designer to maintain a full time job while devoting ten to twenty hours a week to being a decor shopper or re-designer or whatever.

Once a profitable client list has been established, and depending on the market size, the service can expand to a full time, multi-employee business with substantial yearly earnings.

Reminder Business Overview

Before starting up any new business venture it is essential to determine if the business is right for you. You must have the right temperament as well as the facilities and an adequate market for your service. Understanding these and other factors involved in operating a decor shopping service before you "take the plunge" will enable you to be prepared for any eventuality. It's also a good way to insure success and profit.

Shopping can be a tiresome, demanding and frustrating undertaking. Obviously if you want to be a decor shopper, you must enjoy shopping. Most of the people who utilize a shopping service simply don't have time to shop for themselves. And some just don't like to shop. If you are not fond of shopping for yourself, you especially won't like doing it for others, even if they pay you. You can draw from previous personal experience to help you determine if you would enjoy shopping for others.

Once you've determined that you have the ability, and would be happy shopping for other people, you'll need to focus on the "business" side of operating a decorating shopping service. And that means you will have to be certain that there is a market for your service.

Generally, a decor shopping service cannot rely on clientele with average or below average income. You'll need a "pool" of clients who can afford to pay for someone to shop for them. Many re-designers have found that people with incomes of $80,000 or more are their best sources of clients. You'll need to do some research before you start up to determine if your market can support a decor shopping service.

The success of a decor shopping service depends largely on the quality of the service. You must offer professional service and quality merchandise, and often the kind that is not readily available at low-end retail stores or chain furniture stores. This type of service requires that you know the best places to shop, be familiar with brand names, and that you work within the client's price range. The most successful decorating shoppers have established good connections with wholesalers and retailers and know where to get the best merchandise and the best prices. They usually have their wholesale discount and credit account already set up with their sources.

You'll also need to be creative. Many times a client will need a gift for someone - let's say, an artificial floral. The client gives you a description of the person and their home decorating colors, and then it's up to you, the decor shopper, to find the gift to fit that person. This requires not only creativity, but an understanding of people as well.

Another important factor to consider is how you will advertise and promote your service. This is especially important when you are starting up. You'll need to make your service known to your market area. You should investigate all the available avenues of advertising and determine what's best for you. Establishing a realistic advertising budget and implementing an effective advertising campaign will mean more business and bigger profits. Refer to **Rearrange It** for more on this subject.

Equipment

Starting a decor shopping service at home is the ideal way to begin or to add to your re-design services. No large facility is needed for storage or equipment. One room can serve as office space for administrative purposes, such as bookkeeping and record keeping. You should also have an answering machine for your telephone, a typewriter or computer and printer if affordable, and various office supplies.

Furnishing a home office can be relatively inexpensive. A desk, chair, filing cabinet and bookshelf are the only basic items needed to begin. Purchased new, these items will cost from $500 to $700, depending on your taste and where you shop. You may be able to find good quality used items for much less. Many yard and garage sales have adequate furniture for a home office and at very good prices too. Later I will discuss furniture refinishing.

If you don't already have an electric typewriter, you can get a good one for $200 to $300. You shouldn't go overboard here -- a typewriter that produces professional looking documents is all that is needed. A computer is an optional expense that can wait until the business has expanded. Once the business is "booming" investing in a computer can bring a high degree of organization and efficiency to bookkeeping and record keeping and enable you to create your own business cards, letterhead, brochures, flyers and such.

The most important piece of "equipment" a decorating shopper will need is a vehicle conducive to shopping and transporting décor items. Transportation is also the biggest expense this type of service will likely incur. Since well over 50 percent of a personal shopper's working time is spent on the road, to and from shopping excursions and consulting with clients, an economical and dependable method of transportation is a must.

Most people operating home-based services use their own cars. This alleviates the necessity of buying a new car, or leasing a vehicle. If your car is in good working order and gets good gas mileage it makes sense to use it for your business. The government will reimburse you, via tax deductions, for the driving and other expenses incurred as part of the business. However, your personal auto insurance will not cover items that you carry that are part of your business, so you should consider switching your policy to a business policy. As your business grows, you might consider up-grading your vehicle in order to transport more and bigger pieces.

Many decorating shoppers also invest in a small camera. This is a relatively modest investment that adds an extra service to your business. A camera will allow you to take pictures of items you think particular clients may be interested in, just in case they are not returnable, will have a re-stocking charge attached if returned or you just are not real certain the client will like it. Your clients will appreciate this extra service because it allows them the opportunity to see, and approve an item before it is purchased. It's a good way to build an on-going and trusting relationship with clients, increasing the chances for repeat business. Repeat business is very, very good.

A good instant camera is sufficient for a personal shopping service. You can get one for about $50 and it is well worth the investment. The best, however, is a digital camera because you don't have to wait for film to be developed and you can print off the photos yourself and put in a nice presentation for the client. Camera phones can also be used, though the quality isn't very good usually. I personally use a wide angle digital camera for shots of the rooms I have done and another camera with a zoom lens for close-ups. But these types of cameras can be pricey, so starting out, you can get by with less quality until you can afford to invest in better equipment.

When starting your service, it is important to remember to "live within your means." There's no need to get several pieces of expensive office furniture, or buy a new car. Be sensible and get only the basics. Your total investment in equipment and office furnishings and supplies need not exceed $1,000.

Inventory and Pricing

Since a decorating shopping business is service oriented, you won't be selling a specific product. That means there's not a lot of initial inventory as there would be if you were starting a retail business. If you purchase wholesale merchandise for your clients, it is important that you maintain a good relationship with dependable suppliers of inventory. Some of them, well actually many of them, have some kind of minimum order to purchase. Depending on the product needed, you might not be able to shop for the product from a wholesaler, but will have to purchase at retail. Hopefully you'll be able to get a slight discount. Be sure to ask for one.

Karel Exposition Management is the nation's largest producer of regional furniture and accessory markets. This weekend I'm attending a furniture and accessory trade show in Long Beach, not far from my office. It is open to the trade only and I have to register each time I go, showing proof that I am actually in the business. Proof is required in the form of two of the following: on company letterhead, I must fax to them my resale license, personal name on business card, copy of ad in yellow pages, business license or copy of a wholesale invoice showing I've done business in the trade - that type of thing. You might check to see if they have a regional show in your neck of the woods. It could be a great source for products. Visit http://www.kemexpo.com or email them at info@kemexpo.com.

The better your connections with reliable suppliers is, the better your chances of getting those special items for your clients at a good price. Even though you might not be selling a product, you will always be selling a service. And you'll need to take just as much care in pricing your service as you would a line of products. Most decorating shoppers use one of two common methods for pricing their service:

1) Set a fee based on the total price of the merchandise - say 25-50% of the value.

2) Charge an hourly rate and sell the merchandise at your discounted cost (this makes lots of prospects nervous, however).

Whichever pricing method you choose must bring in enough income to cover any overhead you have, your time and labor, and leave you with a reasonable profit. This requires knowing what the market will bear, as well as how much you desire to make your service personally profitable.

Most home-based shopping services initially institute a fee based on the total cost of the merchandise purchased. This fee should be a percentage of the purchase price. The percentage will vary depending on the market area, the type of clientele and the total price of merchandise purchased. It's up to the decorating shopper to determine an appropriate percentage. Be sure your client agrees to pay all delivery costs, however.

Generally, the larger the total price of merchandise purchased, the smaller the service charge. For example, if you charge a service fee of 20% on a purchase of $500 or more, your minimum fee will be $100. For a smaller total purchase of merchandise -- say, from $200 to $500, your service charge could be 25%. That would leave you with a minimum fee of $50 and a maximum of $125. All of this must be evaluated against the time you feel it will take to find the merchandise, buy it and deliver it, factoring in how much you feel your time is worth. Don't forget to factor in the wear and tear on your auto and your gas expenditure.

This type of pricing makes good business sense if you do a lot of pre-shopping from the internet, newspapers, catalogs and by phone. That way, you've located your merchandise before you actually go shopping. This will save you time and result in a higher degree of profit on your labor.

Hourly billing for this type service usually works best if your service offers a good deal of consultation as well as shopping. In most cases, decorating shoppers who also feature home interior consulting as part of their service, charge an hourly fee. If your service is in a market that has the potential to support a home consultation as well as a decorating shopper, you may consider billing clients by the hour.

Many re-designers who also offer consulting as part of their service charge as much as $45-150 an hour, depending on their background and expertise and the market. The rate you set depends on how much you feel your time and efforts are worth, and how much the market can afford. You'll need to make a profit, but you'll also need to be affordable and competitive. If you limit your service to shopping -- no consultations -- then an hourly rate may not be realistic. Sometimes you may only be shopping for $50 worth of merchandise and charging an hourly rate of $30 to $40 will not be appreciated by the client.

Your rate should be such that every client feels it's worth the time saved to pay you to do their shopping. For shopping services only, a service fee based on the total price of the merchandise is more practical, and ultimately more profitable than an hourly rate. This way it doesn't matter as much if you are paying retail or wholesale. Actually if you are buying at retail prices, you will actually earn more because your percentage is calculated on the total price of the goods purchased.

Getting Clients

Any decorating shopping service's client list depends, in large measure, on the variety of shopping and consultation offered. As pointed out earlier in this training, some decor shoppers also serve as re-designers or interior decorators, giving advice as well as selecting accessories or furniture to show the client.

Generally, if you are located in a market of less than 100,000 people, there will not be much demand for decorating shopping services. That's why you should be located in or near a relatively large population base with an abundance of working people, and a variety of stores. The services offered in such a market can be varied to cater to specific client needs.

If shopping for home decor accessories is your forte, your client list will most likely be comprised of women. Your ability to consult with these clients -- to advise them and select appropriate accessories will go a long way in determining your success as a decor shopper and consultant. In many cases, men are becoming more open to the idea of getting help in selecting their home decorating products. You just have to work harder to convince them that they need to decorate.

When you are shopping for home decor *gifts*, most of your clients will be men. Many of these will be husbands who know what they want to get their wives but don't have the time to shop for themselves or have little, if any, idea where to shop. It'll be up to you to track down these items, usually in a limited amount of time.

Other clients on your gift shopping client list will include executives who need to get gifts for their clients and employees. It is essential that they know what the home decorating colors are of the people they wish to gift, however.

In most cases, these clients will also be men. As a rule, it seems that men prefer to have someone else shop for gifts rather than spend the time themselves going from store to store. So a decor *gift* shopper can usually count on men as a good source of clientele for this type of service.

Your client list will also include some elderly people, or physically disabled people who aren't able to do their own shopping. This type of client, while not a major source of your income, could be a steady source if they have large extended families to gift.

One major source of income for many decorating shopping services is the corporate client. This type of client may take a great deal of time and effort to land, but the results will make it worthwhile. That's because corporate clients normally make large volume purchases, and if they are pleased with your service will be a source of repeat business. They usually have larger budgets as well. One client I serviced had over 50,000 employees to gift every Christmas. Just a $1.00 profit on each one makes a very nice profit for minimal work.

There's no doubt you'll have to work hard to get corporate clients. It requires a rather comprehensive study of your market in order to be familiar with all the potential clients, followed up by an impressive and convincing sales presentation. But if you can convince many of the businesses in your market that you can save them money, time and hassle by doing their home or office gift shopping for them, you'll have a valuable client list with a high profit potential. So you should be determined and persistent when pursuing these clients. These people all live somewhere and are good prospects for re-design services.

In the most basic of terms, a decorating shopping service's clientele depends on the types of services offered as well as the market's need. The client list will include busy professionals -- both women and men, corporate clients with business gift needs, and senior citizens who are unable to do much shopping for them selves. Your market will dictate which segment of potential clients you should rely on. You'll need to know the kinds of people in your market area and what they need in a home shopping service. Your service should cater to those needs.

Advertising Your Services

Even though your talents as a re-designer or shopper may be formidable, you won't get much business for any service you offer if you don't let people know your service is available. That's why it is essential to develop an effective advertising and promotion strategy.

Since decor shopping services have traditionally been offered just by full service interior designers, it is not as uncommon as re-design, but still needs to be advertised and explained. These people need to know what a decor shopping service is and how it can be of benefit to them. It's up to you to let them know what you offer and how you can save them time and get better merchandise. The success of your service depends on how effectively you "spread the word" about what you are doing.

Determining the best advertising campaign for your service will require some research of your market to understand the best way to reach the widest segment of potential clients. First of all, you'll need to have a good idea as to who your potential clients are, and how many of them there are. You'll also need to offer them something that isn't already available and then convince them to take advantage of your service.

This "pre-marketing" research doesn't necessarily have to involve a great deal of expense. One good and inexpensive method of obtaining information about your potential market is to conduct your own survey. Discuss your decorating shopping idea with all of your contacts -- business and personal. You can also get a sampling of opinion by going through the phone directory and calling as many people as time will allow. Be prepared to ask specific questions that will allow you to obtain usable information. Some questions worth asking include:

1) Would the person pay a service to do their home decorating shopping? If the answer is yes, you should then find out if they would use the service on a regular or repeat basis.

2) What kinds of shopping would these potential clients pay a service to do? Try to get them to be as specific as possible about furniture, accessories, gift giving, and so on.

3) What's the potential client's idea of a reasonable service fee? You may have to do some prompting here. That is, you may have to suggest something like 20 to 25 percent of the retail price. You should soon get an idea as to what the market would be willing to pay.

This isn't a scientific survey, but it should enable you to better plan and instigate your advertising campaign and make sure your services are reasonable, affordable and competitive. You'll have a good idea as to who your potential clients are and what they would expect from a home decorating shopping service. The next step is to come up with an advertising budget you can afford and then find out where your advertising dollars can best be spent.

You'll have to use your own judgment as to how much you allocate as an advertising budget. However, you should keep in mind the importance of advertising to the success of your service. Many businesses, both small and large, budget anywhere from 1 to 5 percent of their projected gross sales for advertising and promotion. You should have at least some idea of projected gross sales from your pre-start-up research. Sending out press releases, on some newsworthy angle of your service, will get you more bang for your buck - it's absolutely free and pulls better than advertising. Getting press releases printed by the media is by far the best approach, but it takes time to develop. And remember that the benefits can be short lived, so you need to be prepared to take the article or piece, duplicate it and use it to promote your business separately.

The important thing to remember is to be reasonable. Don't spend more than you can realistically afford. You'll need to be as financially solvent as possible until your business is bringing in a healthy profit. At the same time, you don't want to undermine what an effective advertising campaign can do to help your business.

Once you have decided how much you can afford to spend on your initial advertising campaign you'll then have to select the media which will bring you the best results. Generally, for a home decorating shopping service, advertising in newspapers, the yellow pages, and by direct mail can be helpful.

A less expensive, but more time consuming, means of advertising is through personal contacts. This form of advertising usually works better in small markets, but can be effective in larger markets as well. You'll need several hundred professional business cards to pass around. Impressive business cards are not at all expensive and are a good way to get your name and service known. Office supply stores, like Staples, Office Depot and Office Max offer great bargains on business cards. You'll also need to set aside a good bit of time making personal calls on prospective clients. This is an excellent way to let people know that your service is available.

When calling on a prospective client you must be well prepared. This means being able to explain your service in a clear and professional manner - like having an "elevator speech" - a concise description of what you do and how it will benefit people that can be said in one minute or less. Let your prospective clients know exactly what your home decorating service offers and how it can be of benefit to them. And before you leave, make sure they have your business card as well as any brochures or flyers you may have detailing your service. Ask them to consider your service, then follow up your elevator speech with a phone call a couple of weeks later. Don't let them forget about you and the service you are offering.

Newspaper advertising can be marginally effective for a home decor shopping service that gets most of its clients from the immediate community. Again, this type of advertising may work better in smaller to moderate markets. Most newspapers charge reasonable rates for display and classified ads and reach a high concentration of potential clients. Be sure to test. Don't expect too much. Most people prefer to hire consultants and shoppers from referrals or meeting you personally in some manner first.

Another means of advertising your decor shopping service is in the yellow pages. Make sure you choose the most appropriate category for your listing or advertisement. You can have an illustrated quarter page spread or simply a one line listing with the name of your business, address and phone number.

The yellow pages can be one of the most effective methods of advertising at your disposal for many types of businesses. But be careful and test it first. While it is good for one year, you cannot cancel it for a partial refund if it isn't producing. You'll have to be careful and get your ad in before their deadline ends, otherwise you will most likely be waiting an entire year before you can advertise in the yellow pages. However, online yellow pages are another vehicle. There are no deadlines to meet with online advertising unlike the large delivered books. More and more people are hunting for services online rather than hauling out those heavy books, so it is something to consider.

Other forms of advertising you should consider include; direct mail, which allows you to distribute information about your service to a selected group of potential clients in the form of newsletters, flyers and brochures. All of these methods of advertising can be effective and are relatively inexpensive. Knowing your market is the determining factor, along with your budget, as to the type and amount of advertising you do. It should be obvious however, that the more advertising you do, the better your chances of reaching the greatest number of potential clients. And that is, along with convincing those potential clients that your home decorating shopping service is the best in the market, what your advertising campaign should strive for.

Potential Earnings

To some degree, a decor shopper's business is not seasonal. But no one can predict how much business you will get. There are so many variables, not the least of which is you and the talent and dedication you bring to the equation. Other factors include the time devoted to the business, proper marketing and setting fees that bring the best return for services rendered.

Many home-based home decorating shopping services, operating part-time, have reported extra earnings of as much as $1,000 per month. This type of profit is usually realized by shoppers who take advantage of the service's low start-up costs. In the beginning, these services are equipped with little more than a telephone and an answering machine. Advertising is done through some personal contacts, fliers posted on bulletin boards, and business cards. These part-time shoppers use their own cars for shopping excursions, which average about twice a month. Some of these shoppers get as many as five individual clients in a month's time. The result could be a handsome profit that more than covers the initial investment.

If you are planning to get into the business on a full-time basis, you'll need to make a larger initial investment. If, instead of a home-based service, you plan to utilize a commercial office and at least one helper, your start-up costs will be substantially greater than a home-based, part-time operation. You'll likely need more than one vehicle for shopping trips, and your advertising campaign will need to be more extensive. My advice always is to start small and work your way to the big time.

This type of operation could mean an initial investment of $7,000 to $10,000. No doubt that's a sizable investment, but once the service has become established, you can realize earnings of $50,000 and more per year. If an investment of several thousand dollars is beyond your immediate means, beginning a decor shopping service part-time, at home, will allow you to get into the business with a good chance to expand to full-time in a year or so.

Summarizing

Because of the low start-up costs and high profit potential, a home-based home decorating shopping service can be the ideal business for many people, particularly combined with a re-design business. But, in order to be successful there are several key factors prospective shoppers should understand.

(1) Shopping can be a tiresome and frustrating experience. If you don't like to shop for yourself, you won't like shopping for other people and your business will not succeed.

(2) If you are not located in, or do not have reasonable access to a fairly large market, a decorating shopping service may have a tough time surviving. Before you start up, analyze your market -- know who your potential clients are and how many of them you can realistically count on to pay for your service.

(3) Knowing the best places to shop for the finest quality home furnishing merchandise at the most reasonable prices, is essential. You'll need this expertise to convince clients that you are, indeed, the best person for the job. It's something you'll have to demonstrate in order to get new, as well as repeat business.

(4) This is a personal service. You will be shopping for other people's home decorating needs. In order to do this properly, you'll need to get as much information from your clients as possible. Let your clients

know you understand what they want, and that they will be well taken care of. You'll need to be a good listener as well as a good communicator.

(5) Your service fee should be realistic -- both for you and your clients. You will, of course, need to make a profit. But you'll also have to work within your client's means. If your fee is too high for your market, potential clients will usually find the time to do their own shopping.

(6) A well planned advertising campaign can mean the difference between breaking even and making substantial profits. Develop an advertising budget that will allow you to make your service known to the majority of potential clients in your market. At the same time, concentrate on getting free publicity through press releases.

(7) Adjusting your service to fit the needs of your market will mean greater profits. If you specialize in re-design, you may be overlooking other potential avenues of income, such as described in this training manual. You should be as versatile as your time, resources, and the market will allow. A decorating shopping service can be a personally rewarding and highly profitable venture. It is not, however, a means to "overnight" wealth. It will take a good deal of time and work to make your service known and understood, and to build a client list substantial enough to return big profits. But, if you like to shop, and you are good at shopping for other people, a home decorating shopping service could be the ideal business for you to offer all of your re-design clients.

Relocation & Move-In Services

Working with relocation clients can often be more time-intensive and may yield a lower profit margin because you may have to pay a referral fee. But I've found that selling in the relocation niche can be rewarding and it can lead to other services and sales. Approximately 1.5 million employer-assisted relocations take place each year, according to the Employee Relocation Council, so there is a need for help no matter how extensive or little your involvement.

Working with relocation clients can add a nice percent to your sales volume annually if you pursue it properly. Plus, relocation referrals can make your phone ring more regularly than other types of services.

I've also enjoyed meeting people relocating from other parts of the country or world and making them feel at home in my community. Those smiles and thank-you letters sent to you by families who have moved 2,000 miles make the relocation niche personally rewarding as well. My most recent relocated client moved to Southern California from Montana. While their furnishings often reflected the lifestyle of the northern woods, it was fun to help them make their furnishings work in their new, more high-tech home.

If you don't already work with this important niche, here are some things you should know about the relocation business before you get started.

- **The only constant is change**. Corporate and government relocation is a growing segment of the real estate industry. Corporate mergers, reorganizations, and job promotions fuel the need for companies to move employees from one location to another, around the country or the world. With dual careers, school-age children, and multigenerational households, moving can impact more than just the transferee. The increasing complexity of moving employees has helped fuel

- **Change brings stress.** Imagine you have been promoted to a new position in a far-away city. For the transition, you have to retain your current job responsibilities in your current city as well as take on new ones; find a home in your new city and sell your current one; and commute weekly between your old and new city. While you're working in your new city during the business week, you're living in a hotel room or studio apartment. Your spouse or partner has a great job he or she really doesn't want to leave, and your kids love their friends and schools. The new job is a good step professionally, but you're not excited about moving to the new city. These factors all play a role in a transferee's mind and can create stress for transferees and their families. So it takes a unique type of personality to not only help the family cope with the stress, but the anxiety of making all of the old furnishings (or at least as many as possible) work in the new space.

- **Real estate practitioners and re-designers play an integral part of a transferee's move.** While the transferee will have relocation coordinators who counsel and coordinate the transferee's move by e-mail or telephone, you and the real estate agent might possibly become the only people involved with whom the transferee will interact with in person. Being the only face-to-face contact can be both rewarding and challenging. You also can be the only person transferees know in their new community.

  Educating the transferee about your community, real estate market, shopping malls, utility companies and schools are important benefits you can provide in a brochure or flyer that you give them. By helping them to transition smoothly into their new community, you can make the entire experience a little less stressful for transferees—and you may acquire a client for life in the process. When you have a host of services you can provide, including the arrangement of their furniture and accessories (even including the unpacking of boxes), there is no end to the amount of value-added services that this type of client will likely need and appreciate.

- **Relocation requires special knowledge and paperwork, however, if you're going to attempt to be more involved than the final furniture arrangement type service.** Most relocation and brokerage companies request that you complete some type of training in relocation procedures, policies, and administration. The training can run from a half-day to a week.

  You will learn the relocation chain of command, required relocation documents, and how to interact with transferees and relocation coordinators. You should enjoy completing paperwork, as relocation requires another level of records than your typical services will entail. Good organizational skills and the ability to communicate professionally are essential to work in this niche successfully.

- **More than likely you will pay a referral fee for relocation business.** With most relocation clients, you will pay a percentage of your fee to the person or company that put you and your client together. Referral fees vary but typically fall within the 20 percent to 40 percent range. The advantage is that you didn't have to do anything to generate the client and this client could be extremely valuable to you once they know of the total number of services you will offer to them. Some part of a fee is better than no fee at all and many smart entrepreneurs know that they often make more money on products and services that they "back end" than on the initial sale.

You should look at relocation redesign as another form of prospecting. The referrals and business relationships from relocation can lead to non-relocation business once they are satisfied with your services. The relocation business knows no season.

Serving Blended Families

Now let's discuss the unique dilemma of helping a client settle when the furnishings are coming from two different households, where the styles, colors and taste are quite different. This is the ultimate challenge and you've got to be confident and experienced enough to handle it or take a pass. Unlike the other services mentioned in this chapter, I have yet to see any re-designer trained by any other group or person offering a rearrangement service to blended families. This is a very specialized niche market that has great possibilities for those that want to tackle it.

Let's say the husband has a set of furnishings and so does the wife. This would be the norm. They had former lives and families, and all are now moving into one home with far more than they have room to keep. This can be a real challenge, particularly if they have differing tastes in home decor. The re-designer may be uniquely called upon to be an "objective 3rd party adviser". It is wise before beginning to clarify your role and get each party to agree to carefully consider your recommendations and emphasize that your goal is not to please one spouse at the expense of the other one. You need to carefully hear the desires and wishes of both parties (preferably not the children of the adults in the situation).

Once you know the desires of each adult and you've had a chance to look at all of the furnishings that you can consider, and you know which things are favorites and which are not, then you can proceed - but do so with caution. I once had clients who had been married for some time but who had diametrically opposing views on what should or shouldn't be. It was even embarrassing to me at times because they would verbally fight with each other in my presence. They had this sort of love/hate relationship thing going on. But happily both considered me to be the expert and believed I had their best interest in mind, so they listened to my advice and followed it. This might not always be the case.

Sometimes merging two families into one home will entail having to look at the furnishings in two different residences, neither being the home they will ultimately reside at. More than ever, it is important to have a digital or other type camera with you. Go to each home and take pictures and take plenty of notes and measurements of the major pieces of furniture each "pre-family" cares the most about. Do not try to rely on memory. Then go to the new residence and do the same thing.

Ideally all of the furnishings for you to consider are already at the new home and maybe some preliminary decisions for placement have already been made by the husband and wife. Make a list of all of the furnishings that **must** stay, what may be discarded, what must stay in a particular room, what can be moved if necessary, what is loved by both spouses, what is loved by one but not the other, what is hated by both spouses. You get the idea. This one can be tricky and may need great diplomacy for a winning outcome.

From all of the pictures and data, the desires and hopes of your clients (both husband and wife), then you treat this type of re-design like any other. If you have done your job right and listened carefully to the desires of both parties and the needs of the newly enlarged family, you should have two happy campers when you are done.

It's important, if possible, to get some background on the former lives of the individual parents. Are there any divorces in the past for each spouse that could affect not only their feelings about the decor, but the feelings of the new mate? Was there a death of a spouse or a child in a previous family of one of the spouses that could affect choices of furniture and/or accessories now? Many people in a blended family do not take the time or effort to discuss their true feelings about the other person's possessions which they brought into the new relationship. They are usually busy with dealing with relationship issues of the present and the future, especially when children are involved. So the topic of possessions brought by both families may very well have never been discussed. In this type of situation, the re-design plays a very unique and important role in helping all sides to feel comfortable and at peace with the new space as well as the furnishings brought from a household belonging to someone else.

So don't be afraid to include this type of service in your marketing efforts. Sometimes it's the really small niche market that pays off the best these days. Promote yourself as a specialist in this area.

Serving Families Who Are Downsizing

Is it time to downsize, de-clutter and simplify?

At some point in everyone's life, they usually come to a crossroads where they need to ask themselves this question. Perhaps it's when the kids move out to go to college. Perhaps a divorce or death has occurred in the family. Perhaps relocation is contemplated because of a job change or an adjustment is necessary for financial reasons.

Perhaps it's just time to slim down - to have less stuff. But one of the most difficult tasks many people have is making the decisions necessary to downsize or de-clutter their home. I don't know about you, but I face that dilemma too. It's hard to get rid of things. I'm always wondering if one day I'll wish I still had it. Why? Because there have been many times in my life that I have felt that way. I totally regret getting rid of many of the fine furnishings my grandmother had: an old antique sewing machine with the peddle action table, several beautiful chests of drawers and a vanity table, a beautiful mahogany desk. I just didn't have room for them and they weren't my "style" at the time, so into the garage sale they went and were sold for a fraction of their true worth. My bad.

Well, you just have to do what you have to do at certain times in your life and not look back.

Many people find themselves in this predicament, not knowing what to sell or give away and what to keep. And they would love to have someone detached come in and help them make these decisions. The rule of thumb seems to be that if you haven't worn it or used it in the last 6 months you should get rid of it. Well, easier said than done, right? But what a great opportunity, business-wise, to offer a de-cluttering, downsizing consultation service to people. Start subtracting and organizing your own possessions, and see what happens in your own life. You might be surprised. Can you see yourself doing this for other people?

Some people decide to downsize because they are just too busy with their creative activities to take care of the responsibilities of a large home. I interviewed a couple who had made the move from a big house to an apartment 25 years ago. Still quite young at the time, their only reason for making the move was to enjoy a simpler life. They never regretted their decision. Every time I have to look at my own large front and back yards, I think about downsizing, even though I enjoy having both. But just as you should love shopping before offering a decorating shopping service, so you should love to sort and organize before you offer to do it for someone else for a fee. Chapter 12 deals with this more fully.

There are several ways that "stuff" can be disposed of: given away to friends and family, sold in a garage sale, donated to charity, or simply removed as a courtesy by the re-designer (an option that could be quite profitable, which will be discussed later). As a corporate art consultant too, I was often asked by companies who were purchasing new art from me, to take away old things they wished to discard or to have artwork reframed to match the new images being purchased. At no time did those companies ever request that I bring back the old frames, many of which were in mint condition. Those frames then became part of my inventory and I was able to use many of them in other ways to benefit future clients or for my personal usage. Something to think about.

SOME USEFUL TIPS TO RE-DESIGNERS AND CLIENTS ALIKE:

1. Do most of the packing yourself, but hire the best professional movers you can find. Use reputable movers, even if more expensive. Some people have had their possessions stolen or held hostage for higher unexpected fees by unethical movers that advertised lower rates but turned out to be dishonest once the service was performed. Make sure your paperwork states thoroughly what is being transported for you, that the company is fully insured, has provided you with good references, that they carry workman's compensation for their employees and have liability insurance. Be sure the contract states that there are no hidden fees and that any estimates shall not exceed a specific amount, the pick up and delivery dates.
2. Carry by hand as many of the valuables and breakables as possible. Let the professionals pack artwork, mirrors or other valuables that must be shipped.
3. If possible, relocate to a place where there are family or friends, social connections, and activities which your family enjoys.

HOW ONE RE-DESIGNER DOWNSIZED A FAMILY'S HOME

This is the story of a re-designer who helped one family who moved from a four-bedroom, three-story home with an attic, basement, and garage, to a two-bedroom apartment. The process took 3 months to complete.

The re-designer started in the basement and worked her way up. By making three piles of stuff -- what to take, what to sell or give away, and what to throw out -- she was able to keep everything organized as she worked. This made logical sense to the homeowner and kept all from getting confused.

The homeowner's late husband had been a pack rat who loved garage sales and had many collections. Fortunately the re-designer and the wife weren't in love with his collections. His collection of telephone insulators went to the telephone museum, and his collection of old radios was sold at an auction held by the local radio club. Everything else sold at her garage sale.

TIPS TO GIVE THE HOMEOWNER OR ASSIST THEM IN DOING:

1. Go with relatives or friends to look at apartments, condos or town homes. Not only can they help the homeowner decide, but they might spot problems that would be missed otherwise.
2. Find a new apartment before starting to downsize so that the homeowner or re-designer can measure the floors and create a plan to scale. This way they will be sure which furniture will or will not fit.
3. While organizing for the move, make sure to have someone around who can carry out the trash. There will be a lot of it.

For clients that are worried about how to let go of the memories say, "You just have to make up your mind you are going to do it!"

Attitude can make all the difference in the ease and success of a downsizing project - your attitude as well as the client's. If you approach organization or a move with the **end** in mind -- a simpler, happier, more carefree life -- everyone will enjoy the process so much more.

Whenever anyone downsizes, they will find themselves having to break emotional attachments to their possessions. This is not easy. Be empathetic.

Although letting go seems difficult to do at first, most people honestly won't miss anything left behind. Get them to take the time to carefully assess their belongings and bring only what is meaningful, necessary and irreplaceable. They will quickly learn how little they really need, and how holding on to too many possessions can limit their freedom.

As with any business service mentioned already, or in the rest of this training, the key to being successful is to let people know over and over again what you do and how it can benefit them. Do that effectively and there is no limit to the number of valuable services you can offer to increase your business revenue. All of the services and products I write about dovetail nicely together. Pick and choose what is best for your situation and what you feel you would love doing as a business.

Workshops & Speaking Engagements

A business consultant works with the management of a business to improve the profitability of the business. As a re-designer you are most emphatically also a consultant in the finest sense of the word. Consultants tend to be very highly paid individuals. Some consultants charge $100 per hour. So do established re-designers. Corporate consultants charge $1,500 per day for their services, and still others work on an annual retainer fee of $12,000 to over $30,000 per year from any number of large corporations. These are not realistic fees for a re-designer, but all too often, in the redesign field, consultants either charge way too much for their expertise or way too little.

When a consultant has developed name recognition, their ability to command higher fees goes up and so it should. But there is a limit and one's fees should always be evaluated with the fees charged by other well known talents in the industry as well as other unrelated industries.

The field of consultants is continuing to grow. In fact, independent consulting is one of the fastest growing businesses in the country today! Re-designers would do well to position themselves in this market.

As a consultant you need to become an expert at recognizing problems and shaping solutions to those problems. The need for problem solvers for business problems and personal problems has never been greater. The ever changing moods of the buyer, plus the myriad of crisis situations faced by people almost daily, have created this "seller's market" for the alert re-designer.

Be careful not to be an over-enthusiastic entrepreneur who rushes headlong into a business in which you have little or no experience. Many such dreamers invest their life savings in questionable projects without even considering the idea of bringing in a competent business consultant to analyze and evaluate their plans. So please evaluate carefully all of the strategies and tactics that I lay out for you to make sure there is a "good fit" before you jump in with tons of investment dollars, if any are required.

Even experienced people are prone to overrate their own ideas. The dream of the end result, and dedicated enthusiasm toward the attainment of one's goal are the prime prerequisites for success; however unmerited enthusiasm and misdirected dedication can be very costly as well. Unless it is based upon solid research, it may cause people to chase headlong after nonexistent rainbows. So be careful.

It is not necessary for you to have owned or operated a successful decorating business to become a success in interior re-design. Nor is it imperative that you have been in management or have held a titled position. You will, however, need the ability to sell yourself, and to acquire an up-to-date understanding of the area in which you intend to market your products and services.

Isolate Your Strengths

The first step is to make a honest evaluation of your own training and experience. You might be an ambitiously creative individual with a flair for color and design who was never recognized for your abilities. You might be especially good in such areas as sales, marketing, scheduling, expediting or productivity. Know where your strengths and your weaknesses lie.

There are consultants for people who redecorate their homes, who need help acquiring more furniture and accessories, who need to re-locate and downsize all at one time, who need help getting ready for a party, who need more accessories that are unique and creative and custom, who need help organizing their stuff. The important thing is to choose an area in which you've had some experience; an area that you have spent some time learning about; and of course, an area of work that you enjoy. That is why I say all of the ideas presented here are not right for everyone. Besides, there isn't enough time in the day to do all of them and do them justice.

You also must face your fears. Almost everyone is afraid of the responsibility involved with one or more ideas. They claim they don't have the experience or the knowledge. Some are just plain afraid to promote themselves.

Getting Your Business Organized

The point is, most people don't realize how much expertise they really have, or the probable marketability of their training, knowledge and experience. The important thing is to look over your educational strengths, combine that with any special training or on-the-job experience, and then offer your expertise to help others with their problems along the lines you know best. It may not be a re-design project - it might be some other aspect of the interior design field. That's ok. A friend of mine has expertise in how to design and install a sprinkler system in your yard. Usually what you love is what you're good at, so go with that.

You don't need a big, fancy executive type office in order to get started, especially if you start your consulting business on a part-time basis. A spare bedroom, a section of the basement, or even a corner of the dining room will do very nicely.

Instead of going to the expense of paying for a business phone, use your residence phone and train all members of the family to answer it in a business-like manner during normal working hours. Save copies of all the sales letters you send out, and of course, all job proposals you submit. Set up your file system with your final plan in mind, and you'll save a lot of time as well as frustration. Get the kind of file folders that hang from the sides of the file cabinet's drawers, allowing you to position the file folder title anywhere across the top of the folder.

Then as you add clients to your file, you can keep them in alphabetical order without a jumbled-looking file drawer in which you have to search for each title. It's also a good idea to keep your active accounts in one drawer, your "hoped-for" accounts in another, and master copies of all letters, proposals, contact information and records in still another drawer. You'll also need business cards. Your nearest quick print shop can usually order these and help you in selecting wording and design.

Be Wary of Expensive Advertising

Today I visited a website that boasts of being one of the internet's most prominent sites for helping people start businesses. They have a fine reputation and I checked them out. Their Google rank is 6 out of 10, which means they are getting a decent amount of traffic to their site overall, but not nearly as good as they want you to believe.

When I checked the page ranks of my competitors already listed there, those pages didn't have any rank at all, so that told me that the critical pages I would want people to visit on their site were not worth the $850 per month fee their sales rep was trying to convince me was a good deal. So you have to be careful.

Another indication to watch is whether there are a host of businesses advertising there. In the decorating area, there were only 4 businesses listed. All of them sell very expensive training programs or services. If this was a good place for businesses like mine to advertise, the page would have been flooded with listings. I passed on the idea.

If you do use broadcast advertising, the commercial is very important. Really concentrate on this, and use lots of common sense in writing the message. Even if you engage the services of an experienced broadcast copywriter, make sure the message speaks to your potential customers, and convince them that you can help solve their problems. Recognize that your target market for interior design is always the above average income homeowner, particularly women.

It's not good practice to quote or even discuss prices in either your advertising or on the phone when people respond. Always get name, address and telephone number, then explain your services in general. Set up an appointment to look over their home, analyze their needs, and make a verbal or written proposal to solve their problems. It's easier for you to tailor your quote after you see their home. and it's much harder for them to say "no" to you in person than it is over the phone.

There may be a number of factors involved in establishing your fees, but starting out with the lower end of the scale is recommended until you line up 50 regular clients My suggestion for fees for start up ventures would be $50 per hour, possibly $75. Don't price yourself out of the market. By the same token, don't charge so little you aren't regarded as professional you have the opportunity to speak before a gathering, whether large or small, you should set up a display table or vignette. Set up a large conference room table on one side of the room, visible by everyone. Rent or buy a skirt for the table. Staples has inexpensive table skirts in about 3-4 colors for $15.00 that you just stick on to the perimeter of the table with the double sided tape that comes already attached. Of course you can buy more elaborate ones for around $100 that are really nice, but don't do that unless you plan on getting lots of speaking engagements.

Over that place a nice white or black table cloth. Use a plain color so that the focus goes to what's on the table and not anything else. On the table, create a beautiful vignette to instantly prove your ability to design.

Ideas: small chair, throw pillow, end table, lamp, plants, flower arrangement. Add a framed picture leaning up against the chair. You could drape a throw or long fabric over the chair in a coordinating print. Place a large sign with the name of your company (or your name) on it. The sign should be large enough to be easily read from the back of the room. Next to the vignette, place your literature: business cards, brochures, appointment forms, basket for drawing, etc. This should all be done early, before people start arriving.

Create a brief form to fill out and offer a free drawing. Have the forms passed out to entire group before you start and have someone pass a basket at some time to gather them. This is an excellent way to get their names, phone numbers and addresses. The form can include such things as: request for CD slideshow, request for appointment, request for ...... you get the idea.

Pull one entry out at the close of your talk and give your gift to the lucky winner so they know it was a real drawing. The key then is to follow up with each person a few days later and find out if they have any needs, any questions or any referrals. This is called "education based marketing".

For your program, include humor whenever possible. I worked with slides and a projector (olden days) and overheads. If you have Powerpoint on your computer, you can create a Powerpoint presentation and connect up a laptop - that would be ideal. We offer two PowerPoint Presentations currently, one on Home Staging and one on Redesign. Recently a stager wrote me that she used the staging presentation for a small group of 10 real estate agents. They were so impressed with the concept they exclaimed, "When can you start?" as soon as she finished. You do not need to have PowerPoint on your computer to use these presentations but it is easier if you do. More details later.

If you are creating your own presentation, however, the more "before and after photos" you can show the better. People love those. If lacking "before and after photos" that really sizzle, create bird's eye views of rooms (layouts), showing the "before" arrangement and then an "after" arrangement. You will keep the audience in the palm of your hands with great visuals.

The Essence of Your Talk

Start by briefly introducing yourself and giving a very short bio about you. It can include your education, being trained by me, years in the business, whatever you feel will help you establish instant credibility for yourself. Then give the audience a quick overview of what you're going to talk about and how it will benefit each one of them. Introduce your "drawing" and get it started while you continue on.

Explain the "before and after" pictures you will show and talk about each one and how it helped the family, how it made them happier, and how it made their home so much more beautiful, enjoyable and functional. Weave experiences and challenges that you have solved into the talk whenever possible.

When you have finished the "show and tell" portion, end with a series of benefits that people commonly receive from hiring a re-designer to work with them. Remember, people won't be interested at all if they do not see it benefiting them in any way. Don't give them a list of "features", but talk about real specific issues and the impact it has had for others. This will help them make the transition to their own home and their own unique issues they'd like to have resolved.

Relate your services to that of a non-judgmental "nurse" or "nanny" coming to solve their most pressing decorating challenges - hopefully doing it with what they already own at no additional cost to them. Become the "Decorator 911" for your area. It's very powerful!

For instance, one of my clients was a middle aged couple who had been school teachers. The husband, now retired, had cerebral palsy and had to walk with his legs extended slightly out to each side. Walking sideways was not an option for him, so he needed any arrangement I would create to incorporate extra wide traffic lanes so he could navigate the room easily. This was a dilemma for both of them that I solved quite easily and they were thrilled. When you can weave in a story like that into your talk, it really helps your audience realize that a professional re-designer just might be able to resolve some pressing issues they have struggled with for years. They make the mental transition all by themselves. The story builds wonderful credibility for the re-designer and makes the whole presentation far more personable and interesting too.

If "home staging" is the theme, then your job is to demonstrate good selling techniques as well as anything else. Be sure you differentiate between the focus of "redesign" and the focus of "staging homes to sell". There is a big difference in preparing a home to live in and a home to be sold.

Presentation Slides Available for You

I have developed two really cool slideshow presentations which I use to make redesign or staging presentations to groups. They are both Power Point Slideshows, but you don't need to have Power Point on your computer or laptop in order to show them. Each show comes with a fully written script to go with the slides. You can make your own or consider getting mine. See end of book for details.

The goal is to sell your services. You do that by touching the audience's emotions. People buy for these reasons: they trust you, they like you, they need something, they want something, or you have reached them emotionally.

- Sharing of information and your vignette = they trust you.
- Your smile, your tone of voice, your giving attitude = they like you.
- When you SHOW them what a difference a redesign can do for them and how much it is needed and appreciated by others = they start to want it.
- When they WANT it, they will buy it from the person they now trust and like, assuming it is affordable.

Make it appear more affordable by comparing the typical charge to how much they spend on getting hair and nails done, doing lunch, renting videos, etc. Break it down to a few dollars per day. Then it doesn't seem like so much. Compare the beauty of a beautiful home that is fully functional and well organized and pleasing to the eye, and that pleases family and visitors and brings more relaxation to everyone to spending money on things that do nothing to better the well being of the family.

When speaking to a church group, perhaps you could find ways to bring in Proverbs 31 from the Bible. If you look at the chapter, the perfect woman is described as one who will benefit her family - not herself - but her entire family and bring honor to her husband at the city gates. Hiring a re-designer is a step in benefiting the whole family, not just one individual.

A Call to Action

Regarding price, if you offer credit card purchasing, tell them. If not, tell them to get a cash advance and pay it off over time. I've always found that when someone really wants something, they will find a way to afford it. Give them a special discount if they book a redesign that day. Offer an additional gift or discount if they give a referral or two that also books a redesign. You can work it many different ways. Be creative but be sure to include a "call to action". There is where many people fail. They never tell the prospect what to do next to make it happen. If you don't call them to action, and put some kind of sense of urgency to do so immediately, they will never follow through.

How many times have you meant to buy something later and never did? How many times have you told someone you would return to get it, and you never did? How many times have you laid a brochure on the desk or table, meaning to order something later, only to wind up throwing it away without ever placing the order? We all do it. So it is imperative that you call them to **action** right then and there.

Lastly, never worry about how much you give away. What goes around - comes around. I've been called twice recently by magazine reporters in search of an article for their magazine and requesting an interview. I love it! Do I hold back on any of the information? Absolutely not. Give them a great article full of great tips, and you've not only taken an opportunity to "give back" to society, but that reporter/writer will love to come back and write more articles about you and what you do. You just can't buy that kind of exposure! The people who read the articles will view me as some sort of "expert", just because I'm being quoted in a major magazine. And no matter how much information I give them, it's only going to help my business and not take anything away from it.

Just yesterday I got a call from a young gal interested in doing redesign as a business. She asked several questions about my training program, but what she really wanted to know was "Why would anyone go around teaching other people what they do? Aren't you just creating a whole bunch of competitors for yourself?" What this young gal fails to realize is just how many millions of people there are in this country! Has she never stopped to think about why shopping malls are so successful? Aren't all of those stores competing with each other? Do you think for one moment they are concerned about competition from the other stores? No! Because they realize the importance of togetherness. The "group of stores" attract the buyers to come in droves.

The more people who come into the business, the more the benefits of the service become widely known and accepted. The more they become widely known and accepted, the less advertising and convincing each re-designer needs to do on the front end. The less you have to do on the front end, the easier it will be to turn a profit. It will be mega years before one every needs to fret about competition. By then you should have achieved your goal that your business be well entrenched as **the** place to go.

Generating Clients Thru Direct Mail

There's still another very important method of finding new clients, and that is via Direct Mail solicitation. This is done either by postcard or sales letter mailings. For a mailing list of local homeowners, check the yellow pages of your telephone directory, under the heading "Mailing Lists." Tell the advertiser the kind of mailing list you need---if they don't have it, ask them for the names of suppliers who might be able to meet your needs. Make sure you are buying a recently "cleaned" list. Require the provider to give you a sample list to try out. If they refuse, don't trust them.

Alternately, you could compile your own mailing list of prospects most likely to be interested in your services. Mark the names you want and pay someone to input these names onto a computer disc for you. You can get peel-and-stick address labels at a nominal cost and print them on your computer. Microsoft Word has a pretty good program for address labels, but you should know that the moment you slap a label on an envelope, you're going to increase the chances of your mailing being tossed in the trash and never read at all. However, putting your list on computer from the start will save you thousands of dollars and countless hours of work. Data storage software programs will allow you to customize your mailings very easily.

Your postcard solicitation should basically be an elaboration of your printed advertising. You can purchase the following postcard from us in quantities of 100 to a set. They are beautifully printed with a high gloss coating. The back is left blank for you to personalize in any way you wish. See the end of the book for details on postcards we have available if you choose not to make your own, including a quick start promotional pack, variety packs, folders and business cards. You can see a few examples of the appeal of postcards, which are less expensive to send out than other types of mailers and literature.

Home Staging Helps You Sell Faster for Higher Profits!

Home staging is the least expensive way to out-distance the competition when selling your home. Hailed by real estate agents everywhere, let us help you gain that competitive edge quickly and easily.

CALL US TODAY. STAGING WORKS!

A direct mail solicitation sales letter simply uses more words than the postcard, reads smoother, and forces the reader to respond as you direct her. Your sales letter can be any length needed to tell your story and achieve the objective. To be successful, though, it must embody and follow the "AIDA" form: A=Attention I=Interest D=Desire; A=Action on the part of the reader.

PROPOSAL
HOME STAGING & REDESIGN

Another point to remember when writing sales letters: Always appeal to the needs and wants of the person who's going to be reading the letter. She will start reading to see if your services can benefit her. She is looking for answers to her most pressing decorating problems. Keep these elements in mind when you write a sales solicitation letter. Letters can be professionally presented in person, as well, using beautiful folders such as you see pictured here. In a visual business, it's important to have literature and stationery that is nicely printed and classy.

People receiving sales letters are somewhat more responsive to a letter that is typed as opposed to one that is typeset. But the typed letter must be "letter perfect" and not of a different or unusual style of type. As a decorator your letterhead should be simple while still conveying to the reader a sense of class. Your paper should be the best quality you can afford---not flamboyant, but sending a subtle message of success. Direct mail surveys show that slightly better numbers of responses are received when a light beige or off-yellow paper is used.

Basically your letter should do what the postcard does for you---move the recipient to call you and allow you to set up an appointment to discuss her needs as your client. Whether you're writing an advertisement or a sales letter, it's important that you have the objective clearly in mind---what you want the reader to do. With this in mind, you needn't use the "hard sell" approach quite as forcefully as someone asking for money on the first contact.

All that's left is meeting with the prospect, listening to her problems and hearing what she wants, then doing whatever is necessary to please and satisfy her. This means selling yourself to the prospect--- assuring her you know what you're talking about, and that you can make her home more beautiful and more functional at the same time.

There you have it--a plan that can lead you to success as a Redesign Consultant. Remember, though, no amount of research, reading, listening or investment can make you successful until you do something with the ideas. Action on your part is the absolute ingredient that must be added, and that's up to you. Your future is in your own hands.

Referral Cards and More

You might add a referral card to your arsenal. Here is an example how coordinated literature works for you. We combine a beautiful, colorful folder with matching letterhead and a matching referral request card. It reminds people, gently, that we are never too busy to handle their referrals and that we appreciate getting this type of business from them.

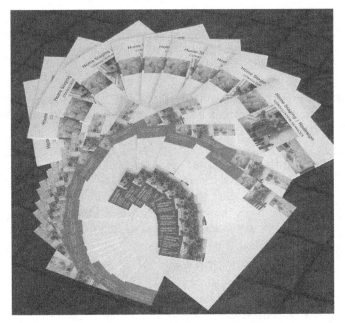

Redesign/Staging Business Forms

I've had a few requests for re-design business forms. I thought they were pretty simple to do on your own, so I did not include them in **Rearrange It!**. But it was also because displaying forms in a digital format is really difficult and time consuming to create if you want a quality reproduction.

At any rate, I have put together some basic forms for you to use. You will find them in the back of the manual. Use them. Don't use them. The choice is yours.

More Specifics on Suggested Fees

The fees you might consider charging will have to be balanced according to the area of the country or globe where you are located, your own personal talents and experience, your comfort level, the ability to pay by your target market, the level of value that you're able to convey to prospects and the amount of competition you have in your area.

Just as an overview, for purposes of discussion here, the typical way re-designers define their basic redesign and specialty services goes something like this:

Consultation: - The time for a client to discuss their wants, their likes, their dislikes and decorating dilemmas in one room or the entire home. Re-designer will focus on furnishings, colors, window treatments, whatever the client wishes to make their home what they want it to be.

One Day Redesign: - Based on the client's taste and desires, re-designer will rearrange the furniture, re-hang art, re-accessorize the room using the client's own furnishings. All will be accomplished in one day or less.

Decorating Shopping Service: - After discussing needs of the client, re-designer will provide the legwork necessary to shop for all of the appropriate items needed to complete the look. Re-designer can shop independently or accompany client.

Real Estate "Ready to Sell" Services (Chapter 16): - Utilizing a detailed checklist, re-designer will do a walk-thru with client who wishes to sell their home to analyze how seller can alter the decorating so as to show the home more effectively and assist the seller in achieving a quicker sale for top dollar. Re-designer will suggest ideas and tips to seller to make the home look spacious and appeal to broadest number of prospective buyers.

Home Transition/Relocation Services: - When clients transition from a larger home to a smaller one, or combine two households into one, decorating dilemmas always arise. Re-designer offers advice on what stays, what goes where, how to blend furnishings, how to pair down when there is too much, and how to arrange furnishings in new space.

Holiday/Special Occasion Decorating Services: - Re-designer ascertains the theme or nature of the party, then decorates the home accordingly using the client's decorations (a lower fee) or bringing in new or borrowed decorations (higher fee).

Meeting Presentations: - Re-designer offers expertise to groups or associations for a fee, which usually generate additional clients for the re-designer and assists the group to provide quality programming.

But to give you some guidance, here are the fee schedules of two completely different re-designers who offer additional services than just redesign.

- **RE-DESIGNER #1**
- Initial Consultation - $75.00 per hour
- Color Consultation - $75.00 per hour
- Shopping Services - $50.00 per hour
- Average Size Room Redesign - $250.00
- Home Resell Consultation - $100.00
- Home Resell Services - Fees Vary

- **RE-DESIGNER #2**
- Initial Consultation - $90.00 per hour
- One Day Redesign - $300-$500 (call for estimate)
- Personal Shopping - $90.00 per hour
- Real Estate Resell Consultation - $125.00
- Home Transitions - $90.00 per hour
- Holiday/Special Occasion Decorating - Fees vary
- Meeting Presentations - Fees vary

These examples are pretty typical in the United States, however, let me tell you about a situation that arose just today. A woman visited my website and called me to inquire about information she needed before purchasing **Rearrange It!**. She was naturally concerned about how she should price her services and felt that the rates she had discovered being advertised by re-designers over the internet were way too expensive. She quoted me some rates she was thinking of charging that were seriously too low, in my opinion. Upon further inquiry, I found out that she had spent the greater portion of her recent 10 years volunteering for an organization that helps people get out of debt. I could immediately see that she was transferring the financial hardships of her normal clients in that business on to the prospects she hoped to serve. Don't make this mistake. When I pointed out to her that her target market for re-design was not low income prospects or people with serious financial hardships, it was a light bulb moment for her. She hadn't realized that she was mixing up the two types of services and had fixated on the wrong target market for re-design.

Your target market is middle to above average income homeowners or renters. The rich don't need you. They have full service interior designers at their beck and call. The poor can't afford you, no matter how well you excite them about your services. I'm not saying you won't occasionally get a client in one income bracket or the other. I'm just saying the vast majority of clients will come from middle income to above middle income wage earners - generally speaking, people making in excess of $80,000 per year. That's where you need to concentrate your energy.

You must price your services in such a way that is affordable to a certain level of clientele, but not so low as to totally devalue you and your time and expertise. If you don't value yourself and what you bring to the equation, no one else is going to value you either. You may have to experiment a little. But when you know you've arrived at a rate commensurate with your area and professionalism, stick to it. Charge what you deserve to be paid even if the prospect doesn't spring for it. Don't grovel for the job. By the same token, don't gouge - be fair. If you do that you should be very successful.

Advanced Redesign

Chapter 2
Why Do Some People Get Hired and Others Don't?

Developing a successful redesign business is not difficult - not when you stop to think about how simple the concept is. So why is it that more people do not become outrageously successful? The answers are simple. Most people are not willing to do the things that outrageously successful people are willing to do.

Outrageously successful people take chances. They are risk takers. They recognize that the success of their business will probably necessitate a degree of risk. They think outside the box. They are willing to experiment. They test their ideas and keep testing them until they find a winning idea. They tend to be creative people, assertive people, organized people, tenacious people - people who believe in themselves and won't quit.

But they also have a few other important ingredients.

You Must Be Likable

First of all, they are likable people, like my Diamond Trainee, **Kristen Noble** (DreamHomeImpressions2.Com). Now before you claim this is not an advanced strategy, let me say that I'm amazed at how many people never consider this all important aspect of their business venture. Stop to think about it for a minute. How many people have **you** ever hired to do anything for you that you didn't like? Chances are the answer is **no one**. We do not hire people we do not like. Not in big business, not in small business, and certainly *not* as consultants. So if you do not have a likable personality, at least likable to most people, you better not consider a people business or a sales business - people will not hire you as a rule.

Well, what do you mean "likable"? If I'm not that likeable now, how can I become *more* likeable. Well, everyone is going to have their own definitions of what "likeable-ness" is, but here are a few of the definitions I would give it. Sometimes it's easier to think about what you *don't* like in a person than what you do.

I don't like braggarts. I don't like people who are always "tooting their own horn", so to speak. Now this is different from people who are just showing confidence. Being confident is not the same as being a braggart, though some people confuse them. Braggarts are actually very insecure people. That's why they brag. They feel a desperate need to tell everyone they meet how special they are. They are so self-focused. They never pay any attention to anyone else, nor to the needs of other people.

Let me give you an example. I have someone in my family who would periodically call me up. He lived in another area code, so the telephone call was a toll call for him. As long as the conversation centered on him, his business and his family, or his problems (since he usually only called me for relationship advice), he would gladly talk for an hour or two. But invariably, the moment the conversation shifted to someone else, he suddenly was out of time and had to get off the phone. Now, because he was paying for a toll call, that was a little bit understandable and just an irritant. But then there were the times when I called him *on my dime*, and the same response would happen. He had no time whatsoever to talk if the subject was not centered on him.

He would often brag about his business and how successful he was. But he would get quite irritable if anyone else experienced success in their business. More times than I can tell you, he demonstrated that his only genuine interest in anyone else extended only so far as his personal and business interests.

Is he a likeable person? Not after his style became evident. His motivations were self-serving and he had no idea he was so transparent.

To put it simply, to be a likable person you must always put the other person's well-being and success ahead of your own. You must refrain from extolling your virtues, experiences, successes - unless, of course, asked to do so. In my sales letters on my website, I do spend some time advancing my background and expertise. But I always try to concentrate first on telling prospects what benefit they will derive first from trusting me as their guide, teacher or mentor.

I genuinely care about people. I genuinely care about my clients. They will find me a source of encouragement, on-going training and help long after the "sale" has been made. I am here for the long haul. That's sometimes pretty difficult to convey just with written word. With an internet business, no one ever meets me to see my smile and hear the tone of my voice.

So the first thing you need to understand, is that people will **not** hire you to do a redesign or anything else for them if they do not like you.

You Must Be Trustworthy

Elizabeth Young (StagingConcepts-Redesign.Com) is one of those really reliable, trustworthy professionals, another Diamond Trainee, who is building her business step by step.

But how many times have you ever decided to do anything with anyone that involved money, on a business or personal level, whom you did **not** feel (at the time) was someone you could trust? Once? Twice? I bet the answer for most of you is **never**. I mean, you'd feel stupid, right, if you gave money to someone you didn't trust and they took your money and never gave you what you paid for or did what they promised they would do in exchange for the money?

I love court TV shows. I just love the law. Maybe I should have been a lawyer or something, because I just love watching court cases. But I'm too emotional. I lie awake all night if I'm upset. I know I don't have the temperament for it. But I love watching Judge Judy and People's Court.

But if you've ever watched those shows, you'd be amazed at the number of people who loan money to friends, relatives and co-workers without ever getting anything signed regarding the fee nor when and how it is supposed to be paid back. Why? Because at the time, they had a measure of confidence that the person's word was good. Sadly they found out the other person's word was worthless.

Well, it is even more important in business that your prospects feel they can trust you. I can almost certainly guarantee you that trust will not be built by you bragging about yourself up front - your education, your expertise and so forth. Nah, nah, nah. Don't do it. You don't have to.

Your genuine interest in the other person and your personal confidence is what will make people trust you. Confidence, coupled with a professional manner of presenting yourself, will instill the right feelings in the other person. Did you know that most people make up their mind in 4 minutes or less about whether they like you, trust you and want to ever have relationship with you again? That's right. We all do it. We make up our minds very early on in a relationship as to whether we like and trust someone. We spend the rest of our evaluation process deciding whether our initial first impression was the right one or not.

So it should go without saying that if you don't make a good impression in the first 4 minutes of contact with a prospect, you are fighting an up-hill battle to gain their trust and friendship. So what does this say to us as re-designers? Simply this. Invest your whole being into learning about the prospect and listening to them, getting them to talk to you, appreciating who they are, appreciating what they do for a living, appreciating their home and their family. It is so important. Forget about trying to earn a redesign fee. If you're focused on getting a fee for yourself or talking about yourself, you're not going to get hired, in most cases. And you won't even know why because they will never come out and pointed say, "I don't like you. I don't trust you. Therefore I'm not going to hire you."

No, what they will do is give you any reason they can think of to get rid of you. They'll tell you they have to talk it over with the spouse, or they have to wait until something else gets done first, or umpteen number of other handy excuses to put you off. They don't want to be rude to you, so they never tell you what the real reasons are.

But no matter what they tell you (and sometimes reasons are legitimate), the truth of the matter probably is, if you don't get hired, that you did not convey properly to them how your service or product would benefit them, and/or they don't like you, therefore they don't trust you either.

So forget about what's in it for you. Forget about appearances (other than to be clean, odor free and appropriately dressed). Forget about talking about yourself. Stop worrying about what you will say. Don't worry about having an exact procedure. Be kind. Be attentive. Be complimentary. Have a sense of humor. Listen with your ears, not your wallet. Praise them genuinely. Be a source of encouragement. Spend most of your time listening. Speak little. When you do speak, be conversational. Don't speak with a "canned" response. Be enthusiastic. Be happy. Laugh. Little by little, you'll have opportunities open up just in general conversation where you can slip in a remark about a previous client's home, a problem you solved or something else that let's the prospect get a **glimpse** of some of your experience. Notice I said **glimpse**. We're not talking about launching into some 5 minute spin on projects you've done in the past.

My associate and I once had a sit-down introductory meeting with the President and Vice President of a large computer company. For years, in addition to redesign, I have owned a successful corporate art consulting business. The appointment had been made by the VP, a nice middle aged woman. The President was an older gentleman. Unknown to us at the time (but not unusual), they had pre-determined to interview 3 different art consulting firms before selecting one. Since I was meeting with a woman who seemed to be interested in decorating, at one point in the conversation, I pulled out a copy of my book Where There's a Wall - There's a Way, and offered it to her as a free gift, saying, "I thought you might like to have a copy of a book on wall grouping design to use at home." She politely thanked me. In a completely unrehearsed, spontaneous moment, my associate chimed in, "What Barbara didn't tell you is that she wrote that book." That's all he said. Now she actually opened the book and looked at it, and almost at the same moment, the President turned to her and said, "Don't even bother interviewing anyone else. I like these people. We're going to hire them. How about if I give you a $10,000 budget? Do you think you can decorate the facility for that?"

Likeability. Trustworthiness. Humility. In the consulting field, whether it is redesign or art consulting, or anything else: People will hire you if they like you and if they trust you. If they don't, they won't. Your education, your training, your expertise, your reputation, your list of satisfied clients, your service, your product - none of it means anything if they don't like you and don't trust you.

Position Yourself as an Expert

Successful entrepreneurs have found a way to not only spread the word effectively about their products and services, and do it consistently, but have over time managed to position themselves as an authority figure in their market. They are viewed as being a specialist in their area of expertise. This does not happen overnight and it does not happen by chance. These people don't try to push anyone into doing business with them. They aren't viewed as "salespeople". Rather, they try to educate people, often for free, and in the process of sharing valuable insight or tips, people view them as experts. Instead of having to chase after prospects to convince them to hire them or buy their products and services, the prospects come to them asking for help.

Successful entrepreneurs also find ways to give back to their communities and to society in general. I've watched several 15-week airings of Donald Trump's "The Apprentice" reality show. Have you noticed how often Donald Trump is involved in attending or hosting events that are strictly for charity? Granted most of us can't do things the way he does, but we can tweak these concepts and downsize them to fit our abilities if we try. If you can afford to host a charitable event, not only will you find it easier to get some media exposure and free publicity out of the deal for your company, but look at the good you can do for others in the process?

In my basic business tutorials I discuss all kinds of methods, approaches, tactics, strategies, principles and concepts for marketing your business – which work for redesign as well as home staging. The bottom line is that you must take action. Don't try to do everything. Pick out a few ideas and tactics that make sense to you and then put all of your time, energy and resources into those few. The key, however, is action. Don't wait. Act now. People who fail do so because they fail to act. And be persistent. No business is built overnight. Be patient and you are bound to succeed. The road is different for everyone, but one thing is a given. Building a business requires tenacity.

Earning a Six and Seven Figure Income

The first step in earning a six or seven figure income is to set a figure as a specific goal. If you aren't specific, you will not likely reach your goal. Then you also need to set a time frame to achieve the goal. Without some kind of deadline (which can always be adjusted as needed), you will probably lack the tenacity and drive to press on until you reach the goal.

While you want to set a specific figure and a specific date to achieve it, your goal must also be relatively achievable. So you don't start out from zero income and say you're going to make $1,000,000 within your first year – not normally. Not to say it can't be done – but it would be unusual to build your business that quickly. Make your shorter term income goals force you to stretch, but make them achievable too. The largest figure will be your long term goal. Give your shorter term goals a deadline for achievement as well as your longer term goal. Write your goals down on paper, date and sign the paper. This will reinforce them into your mind and heart.

Periodically pull out your goal sheet and see your progress. Reset goals where you feel you need to. In the stock market, companies must state their expected earnings for each quarter. Sometime they exceed the expectation and their stock goes up. Sometimes they miss the expectation and their stock usually declines in value. But they always have to predict the future and then measure their progress along the way. So you must do the same.

Advanced Redesign

Chapter 3
Understanding the Sales Process

I've talked over and over again previously about the importance of pitching your service or product from a **benefits-oriented** stance. If the client prospect does not see that what you are offering will benefit them at all, or at least benefit them in such a way as to justify the price you are asking, then they will not purchase what you are selling. You see, if they don't like you or don't trust you (and those kind of go together), they will see **no benefit in associating with you further**. Therefore you won't get hired.

Show Them, Don't Tell Them

But let's say, in the first 4 minutes they decided they liked you and they trusted you, and now they have swung over to taking an honest look at your service and/or product. They now want to know how you will benefit them - how your product will benefit them. They want to know that, in most cases, long before they want to know what it will cost to get it. So you've got to show them how it will benefit them.

Notice I said **show them** and I didn't say "tell" them. You've got to understand something in the sales process that is very important. 95% of people are visual learners. A very low percentage of people are auditory learners. A few people are kinesthetic learners (that means they need to see, touch and feel to learn). That is why you are reading this material. That is also one of the reasons I do not allow my ebook students to print off the ebook. I want all readers to take notes. Readers might not take notes if they have hard copy and they're more likely to do it if they can only access this information on a computer. If they take notes, I can guarantee their retention level will dramatically leap to a much, much higher level than if they merely read the material. For those reading this manual, it's beneficial for you to highlight or underline key points – write in the margins even – I've left you plenty of white space for that.

But just as you are a visual learner, so are your prospects. It is very, very difficult to *tell* someone what a redesign will do for them. It is very easy to *show* them, however. You can show them very easily by utilizing a slideshow CD which shows many before and after pictures, from a wide variety of homes and apartments in all income brackets, and include a host of slides at the end that will easily point out to anyone viewing the slideshow how a redesign service will benefit them.

If you do not utilize this strategy, you are **leaving money on the table**, I guarantee it. People need to see to believe. It doesn't matter if the homes are not in their income bracket. It doesn't matter if the style of furniture isn't what they like. They're going to see immediately that a dramatic improvement was made to the space, no matter what the caliber of home, no matter what the style of furniture, no matter if it is new furniture or old furniture, high-end furniture or garage sale specials.

You need to trust people with the ability to *see* and *understand* and make the mental transition from the homes in the slideshow to their home. Just this week I had a gal call me up, who ordered 6 of the CDs, and ask if she could trade them for something else I offer. The reason was that she wanted to sell her services to people who, in her mind, were in a higher income bracket "who wouldn't be able to identify with some of the furnishings in the slideshow". I asked her where she lived. She told me. I asked her what value of homes she anticipated working on. She said the people would average in the $300-400,000 home bracket. Depending on the part of the county the home resides in, that could be either a low income bracket or a high income bracket. I actually didn't know how to respond to her since the slideshow is represented by homes in **all income brackets** giving it a universal appeal and value. No matter who views the slideshow, they should find homes represented that are in the same income bracket as their own home. This way everyone can relate to the slideshow in some manner.

What matters is that this young trainee was making a glaring sales mistake. She was transferring her own mindset, her own taste and judgment onto her prospective clients, whom she hadn't even met yet. Worse than that, she was actually telling me that she thought these potential clients, whom she hadn't met yet, would be incapable of looking at before and after pictures from a wide range of income levels and styles and be able to make the mental and emotional transition to how much improved their own home could be. Now that's a pretty harsh conclusion to come to about her prospective clients and a very foolish conclusion for the re-designer to make. It was rather insulting to me as well because she criticized the product I offered to help her and criticized it for the very *concept* that made it such a very valuable tool in the first place.

Never, never, never prejudge your clients. This is a huge mistake and it will cost you plenty of profit if you do. I don't care how intelligent you are, how discerning you think you are, you will never ever be able to put yourself into the mindset and wallet of another human being. This was a mistake I made early on in my entrepreneurial ventures.

I started in the art consulting business, just after I had experienced the total failure of a wicker/rattan furniture retail store I tried to launch in one of the worst economic recessions we've had in my lifetime. Thereafter I took a position with a company as an independent consultant, selling mostly custom framed art. The art prints weren't too expensive, but once you added framing to the total, in most cases, at that time in my life, I would not have been able to afford to buy my own products. I figured that if I thought it was too expensive a product line that everyone else would feel the same way. Not true. I also tended to approach people to use my services and buy my products who were in the same income bracket as I. So naturally they thought the products were expensive and that convinced me even further that the price points were out of line. Bottom line: it was very, very difficult to sell products you can't afford yourself because you'll transfer your financial difficulties onto your prospects and somehow they'll pick up on it. You have to be really, really careful not to do that.

What is expensive to one person might be quite inexpensive to someone else. Now it's important to price your product and services properly (more about this later); it's equally important not to prejudge your prospects. Many people, once convinced that the benefits of a purchase justify the price, will dig deeper into their pockets to own something. They will borrow the money, from a credit card or from a family member to get it once they are convinced it will greatly benefit them.

So don't prejudge anyone. You can literally place a CD in someone's hand, show it to them at work, let them take it home to show the spouse, and put yourself in the best possible place to get them to hire you by picking the CD up **at their home**. If you want to service someone in their home, the very best place to be is at their home. You are in their environment. You can see for yourself if they need you or not. You might even be able to make a couple of *free* suggestions initially that will make all the difference in the world to them and seal the deal. Decisions about the home are best made right in the home. So you will find it much harder to be successful at redesign if you do not have a nifty way to get into the homes of people, particularly people you don't know. (Details on these marketing CDs at the end of this book.)

While I'm on the subject of people you don't know, do you realize that strangers will accept you as an expert far more readily than your friends or family? It's that old saying, "A prophet is not respected in his own home town." People who knew you in the past, doing some other line of work or no work at all, find it next to impossible to value your opinion or see you as professional. I don't know what it is. But we're all like that. I just had a call today from a lady in my hometown who found my business in the yellow pages. She wanted to know if I did consultations on exterior paint. I said it was not my focus but that I'd be happy to help her if I could over the phone. I asked her to describe to me what she wanted to do.

She told me she wants to paint her home with a soft white, high gloss black on the shutters, and a red door. She said her friends told her not to go with high gloss black but to use flat paint. She felt criticized and wanted an independent opinion from someone she could trust. Sight unseen, she trusted my opinion merely because I had a business in design listed in the yellow pages. I advised her to use a flat black instead of the high gloss, to go to Home Depot and look at the brochure cards by Behr Paints, who have pre-selected some exterior color schemes (with black, red and white being one of them), and think about not just what she thought she liked, but how the home would then blend into the neighborhood. I then told her to buy a pint of each color she thought she wanted, and actually try it out on the front of her house. Then stand at the sidewalk and see if the home would still blend in with the environment and not stand out like a sore thumb. And before the conversation ended, I suggested she visit my website and browse the free tips pages.

She thought these were good suggestions. She did not take it as criticism because it came from someone she had already determined in her mind was an "expert", even though I told her I was not an expert on exterior painting schemes. What is the difference? She didn't trust her friends to have common sense - not because they were incapable of reasoning as well as she, but because they were her friends and because none of them had a design business listed in the yellow pages.

My point is that once you get beyond family and friends it becomes easier to get clients, in one sense, because you don't have to fight that automatic, built-in refusal to accept you as a bona fide professional. In a sense you are accepted as professional (by strangers) unless proven otherwise. The opposite is true with people who already know you, generally speaking. With people you know, you are accepted as being a novice *unless you prove otherwise.* That is a huge difference in perspectives and something to recognize and accept as being out of your hands to control.

So understanding the difference between how strangers will instantly perceive you and how your friends and family will perceive you is an important concept to get. Many re-designers start out talking to friends and family about their business venture, and either never get beyond those people or get discouraged by those people and quit. This is one of the reasons I made a decision early on in my business to never ever charge a friend or family member for services rendered. Not only is that a good way to lose a friend or damage a family relationship (because you never know what their expectations are in advance) but I just never felt cool about profiting from friends and family. So those jobs have always been complimentary.

But precisely because they are complimentary, allows you to freely experiment without worry. These are the absolute best situations to play with and try new ideas and get all of your fears and doubts out of the way. And it is a perfect way to bless someone you already care about at the same time and in a unique way.

So my advice in this regard is to never charge your family or friends for a redesign. Use the opportunity to gain more experience and, come away with some sharp before and after pictures of your work to add to your portfolio, and with some referrals to start your business or maintain and grow it.

A System of Getting Regular Referrals

When you enter the consulting field, and you are a staging or redesign consultant, you will quickly realize the value of getting referrals from your clients, your prospects, people you know, family, friends, co-workers, other trades people, and so forth. Referrals are very powerful and help to grow your business and sustain your business.

But getting referrals doesn't happen automatically. You've got to take a pro-active approach and put systems into place that help you generate them. Here is one of the best systems you can utilize.

It's a system of sending out regular greeting cards to people you want to stay in touch with. I recently decided to award the refinance of my home to a mortgage broker who consistently sent me greeting cards. His approach was very, very low key. Since it wasn't by email or phone, I never got upset when I received his periodic greeting cards. What he was doing was reminding me, ever so gently, and every so often that he was still in business and ready to help me if I needed him.

So after getting his cards a few times, and when the timing was right, I contacted him to handle the processing of my loan application.

If you will capture the power of sending out greeting cards to the people you want to do business with and people you want to refer business to you, you will go a very long way in building, growing and sustaining your business for the long term.

But I've got a powerful system developed by some very shrewd marketing people who have put together a system that makes sending out greeting cards so easy you can do it faster than doing it yourself. All you have to do is visit **www.sendoutcards.com**. You'll be able to see how the system works and just how easy it is to send out greeting cards for any occasion and purpose to anyone you want to send them to. You'll love this system. You don't have to stock cards, you don't have to have stamps on hand or get them to the post office. It's all done for you over the internet. And you can even customize the cards with your signature and picture if you like. I use it in my own business and have found it to be very helpful, a time saver and very powerful marketing tool.

Up-selling to Your Client

What do I mean when I use the term "up-selling"? Well, it means taking your prospect or client from one place in the sales process to a higher level. Let me illustrate this. Have you ever seen an infomercial on

TV about a product that you decided, based on the benefits described by the salesperson as being valuable to you, and based on the fact that you pretty much liked the presenter and trusted that what they said was true, and trusted that all the 3rd party endorsements were also true, that this was a company or product that would benefit you in the exact way they said it would? So you picked up the phone, called their toll free number, had someone answer the phone where you told them what you wanted to buy. And did they, after writing down your name, address, phone number, credit card number and expiration number then proceed to ask you if you wanted to get two or three for an additional discount? And after you said "no", did they then try to get you to purchase a more advanced version or a deluxe version that did more for a higher price?

Well, if you've ever experienced anything remotely similar, whether from an infomercial, or a telemarketer or whatever, then you have just been involved in a sales technique called "up-selling". You see, savvy marketers know that if you have just decided to purchase a product from them, that while you have your credit card out, or your wallet or checkbook out, you're highly likely to purchase a second item or even a third item too, if they make you an offer geared to let you know that it is a special deal if your order it right then.

Even if they didn't offer you a better price to act then, they know that you're in a buying mood. You already trust them so this is the absolute best time to get you to buy more. They just have to offer it to you. And that's exactly what they do. Sometimes their motive is merely to sell more goods, and sometimes they offer you additional products because they genuinely know they will help you. That's what I do in the course of writing my tutorials. Getting this valuable training is fabulous, but there are a host of other products and services that will continue to aid you in your quest for a successful business, so I want to make sure that you at least know about them in case you feel you want to take advantage of the benefits they offer. So I sprinkle blurbs about them throughout my training manuals. Naturally I would like to garner more of your business, but at the same time, I want to give you the best possible chance to succeed. So we practice the tactics of up-selling, but in a softer approach than others.

I have experienced this many, many times. I often do increase my purchase because of the offer. I rarely do it over the phone, however, because I'm a visual person, plus I don't like to be pressured. Phone sales people usually annoy me. They have their little scripts and canned phrases. No matter what I say, they never seem to listen to what I've just said and they move right on with the next plan of attack. This annoys me further and I invariably wind up getting hostile and telling them either to forget the whole deal or very emphatically that I want just what I set out to purchase, no more and no less.

Well, whether I should get upset with the person or not (they are just doing what their over-zealous boss taught them to do), I fully recognize that I have just been dealing with a company that really knows the value of up-selling and has put into place strategic strategies for getting me to spend more with them while I have my credit card out.

You can make this same "sales process" work for you, but please don't get obnoxious about. Let's say you loan out a CD and make arrangements to go to the person's home to pick it up again and talk about their decorating needs. Some re-designers schedule a brief (free or paid) consultation in advance to "just give some advice". Obviously this type of consultation will not pay at the same level as an actual redesign, but they wait until they are in the environment interacting with the client to present the idea of a full blown redesign. In this case, a traditional redesign would be an up-sell from the original "advice only" consultation. In an actual redesign, you are going to be there longer and you'll actually be helping to move furniture and accessories, in the end giving the client a "finished" room for a higher fee.

But even that's not the end of the opportunity to *up-sell* your client/prospect while you're at the home. There is always the ability to get your client to hire you to re-design the entire home, not just one room, or multiple rooms as opposed to just one room. The higher the economic level of the prospect, the easier it will be to attract them into hiring you for multiple rooms. The way to do this effectively is to offer to do one room at a specified price. Then offer to do a 2nd or 3rd room for a discounted price, so long as they decide to hire you for the additional rooms at the same time.

Why tack on the "at the same time"? Because you always want to place some kind of call to action and put some kind of sense of immediacy on their decision. Stop for a moment and think about your own buying habits. I'm sure you receive tons of junk mail just the way I do. I sometimes receive an offer through the mail that appeals to me. But I often set the literature aside with the good intentions of revisiting the issue at a later time. Sometimes I will save brochures, postcards, discount coupons and such in a special drawer. Sometimes I leave them on the counter. Are you like me?

Well, invariably I have noticed that if I don't act immediately and purchase the product or service when I am first introduced to it, then I never purchase it at all. I know that most people are just like me. So it is an important sales tactic to get people to act now, while the urge to act at all is at its highest point. In other words, act while the fire is hot!

The same thing is true of your prospect. They will be far more likely to hire you for multiple rooms if you are there in their living room offering them a special "deal" than later after you have gone. Everyone likes to get a deal. That's just human nature. So make sure you offer one. You can simply say, "My normal fee to rearrange a room is $_____, however, if you hire me today to rearrange two rooms, I'll do it for $_____ per room. That's a savings of $_____." Be sure to point out how much they will save by acting now as opposed to later.

Don't be pushy or obnoxious about it. As a matter of fact, the more casually you present this option, the better your chances are of getting the higher deal. If, however, the prospect/client feels you are pressuring them into something to enrich your wallet, you'll not only not be able to up-sell them, you risk losing the basic 1 room arrangement as well. So you have to be wise about how you go about offering additional deals to up-sell the project.

Back End Selling

This advanced training is largely all about back-end selling. What does that mean and how is it different from up-selling. Up-selling refers to the front end. A client purchases a product or service from you, and while they are in the process of that, you get them to purchase additional products or services, or upgrade the particular product or service that they already decided to make.

Back-end selling refers to the ability to present offers to your clients at a later date and time. In order to sell your client on the back-end, you have to have their contact information. This is the most important aspect of selling and making on-going profit. It is so important that many businesses are willing to lose money on the front end in order to collect the contact information of a good prospect because they know by past experience that they will make far more money off of serving that client over the year, over the next five years, over the course of a life time than they ever will on the front end.

Many marketers refer to this as the "lifetime worth of a client". Knowing what the average client is worth to you over the course of a lifetime is critical. Did you know that someone that purchases from you one time is far more likely to purchase from you again given the opportunity to do so?

I'm in the internet publishing business. Most of the visitors to my website are just looking for information. This is true of all web businesses. The vast majority of visitors land on the site, stay for a page or two, then disappear, never to return again. And when you understand that most people need to be introduced to a company several times before they ever purchase anything, you begin to understand that collecting their name and contact information is crucial. When you have just that little bit of information in the internet publishing business, you stand an excellent chance of turning that prospect into a client somewhere along the way because you can get them to return to your site. You didn't really think we went to all that trouble to write lengthy newsletters just for the fun of it, did you?

This is one of the many reasons why so many internet businesses create and offer free newsletters. I read somewhere that the average person needs to be presented with your business 11 times before they will make a purchase. I don't know how true that is. I'm sure it's different for every business or industry group. However, I do know that some kind of spaced repetition is a very valuable tactic for increasing sales -- all because each time a person is approached by a company, they become a little more familiar with the products and services that company offers and their trust level usually goes up.

Back-End Products

This is why I offer newsletters. It keeps me in some kind of regular contact with my customers as well as visitors to my site, gives me a way to help them in some small measure and it also allows me to regularly re-introduce myself to them in some way.

In advertising this is called "spaced repetition".

But spaced repetition is not enough to make your business successful. You've got to have actual back-end products and/or services to present to your former clients, current clients and general prospects. It's best to make sure these products and services relate to the main theme of your business. It's also important that these products and/or services have quality and substance. Offer inferior products and services and your client base will deteriorate rapidly.

Chapter 4 will elaborate on the types of products and services that most homeowners need at the point a re-designer usually meets them. The products I have selected are directly related to the decorating industry. More than that, they are products that clients have failed to purchase for their homes in adequate supply, in most cases.

One should have a small arsenal of products and services to offer every client. Some are perfect to offer when you schedule the appointment to meet them at their home. Some are more appropriate to offer AFTER you have been to the home the first time. Others are more appropriate to offer AFTER the re-design has taken place. But in every case, they are great back-end products and services that will dovetail nicely into any re-design business.

10 Killer Ways to Sell Your Back-End Products

If you're not trying to sell back-end products to your customers, you're making a big mistake. It is easier to sell to existing customers than it is to sell to new ones who don't trust your business yet.

Below are ten killer strategies you can use to sell your back-end products to your existing customers:

1. When you ship people the first product they bought, insert a flyer or brochure for your back-end product or service in the package.

2. Give customers a free subscription to a customers only newsletter (more next chapter) when they buy your product. You could include your ad for your back-end product in each issue.

3. Send your customers greeting cards on holidays or on their birthday. Include a small advertisement inside the card for your back-end product or service.

4. After people order your first product from your consultations, send them a thank you and include your back-end product ad on that page.

5. Send customers a free surprise gift after they hire you or purchase from you. You could attach another ad with the free gift for your back-end product or service.

6. Never sell or give anyone any product or service without leaving them with an enticement for something else you provide.

7. Give your customers a free membership into your "customers only" private website you've created just for this purpose. You could include your ad for your back-end product somewhere inside the private site.

8. Contact your customers by phone and ask them if they were happy with their re-design or other product or service. You could tell them about your back-end product personally that way.

9. I recently got invited to my mentor's wedding reception he hosted in connection with a free weekend conference he sponsored "just to say thanks". You can bet there was plenty of front end selling, back end selling, up selling and affiliate marketing going on all weekend long.

10. Ask your customers if they want to be updated in the future when you have new product offers. You could have them sign up to receive e-mail or snail mail updates.

As a re-designer, if you've been to your client's home and had a chance to sit down with them and really discuss their needs for the home, you're already going to know of many different areas you could help them. Timely notes regarding other problems they need to address can pay off handsomely for you. Your business will have a greater chance of surviving when you attempt to educate them about something and then sell back-end products to them that will be things they are interested in or that solve problems they might have. Don't leave all that money on the table by failing to do this.

Referral Selling

On the internet, you'll often hear the term "affiliate marketing". You'll see plenty of links inviting you to sign up as an affiliate. What does all that mean? Well, quite simply, affiliates make money by recommending the products and services that other companies sell. When you register as an affiliate, you are assigned a special code that you insert into the link on your website. When a visitor to your site clicks on that link and goes to another website recommended by you and they purchase something there, you receive a "commission" or "royalty" on the sale.

But there's no reason why you can't set yourself up as a real world affiliate if you don't want to sell certain products or services yourself. While it requires, both on the internet and in the real world, that the other company honestly record a sale as having been triggered by you and then paying you the commission you deserve, it's at least better than not getting any commission whatsoever from a referral you might give.

To be effective as a referring marketer, I think it best to make "soft" offers or recommendations. If you come on too strong, overly enthusiastic, pushy or otherwise not normal in your referrals, you're likely to alert your client or prospect to the fact that you stand to gain financially if they take your advice. So keep your recommendations soft. Try to educate your client or prospect. Encourage them to ask questions of the company you are recommending. Present your case in as objective a manner as you can. And make sure that the products and services you recommend are quality products and services. Never forget that your personal and business reputation depends on it.

Visit the companies and try to make friends with the owner. Do this enough so that they recognize you. Make an appointment with them and work out a deal whereby you can make referrals but feel confident that your people will be properly serviced and that you will be compensated appropriately for the referral.

You could set up referral fees for yourself with all manner of trades people: landscapers, wall paper hangers, painters, contractors, flooring installers, carpet installers - you get the idea. When you are doing a redesign for a client, whenever you see someone in need of a service, hand them a pre-prepared list of vendors that you recommend.

By giving them a list of people, they will be more likely to hang on to it rather than dropping it in the trash. If your list sits around the house for a long time, there's no telling when they might call someone on the list and you could get a commission in the mail out of the blue.

> **IMPORTANT:** Be sure to state clearly on the list that they should mention your name as the referring party. Tell them that by mentioning your name, the company will give them extra special attention or a special discount that they won't get if they fail to mention your name. But don't promise anything that you have not pre-arranged with the service company. You don't want to lie. Since everyone likes to feel they got a good deal, especially one they couldn't get on their own, having a "deal" to offer them works like magic in making sure your name is mentioned as the referring entity.

I am an internet affiliate with a few companies and it's really fun to get a check in the mail I am not expecting. So be sure to set up a system for yourself. Once it is set up, there's no more work you have to do other than hand out your list of "pre-qualified vendors".

Offer Free Bonuses to Get More Business

Once you have narrowed down the options as to the types of services and products you wish to offer your clients, look and see what types of things you could offer as **free bonuses** to sweeten the deal. Think back to the offers you have read on my website. Most of the products I sell come with several free bonuses. It makes good business sense. I love to feel that I am getting a little extra in addition to the product I decide to buy and I know other people feel this way as well.

Look for things of value that you can give that don't cost you any money. While time is money, and smart entrepreneurs know that, when you are new time is the one thing you have plenty of. So what other service can you offer your prospects to make the redesign service more valuable that only involves a little extra time on your part?

How about offering to give 15 minutes of additional design advice on any room in the home at no additional charge? Pretty simple, huh? Easy to do? You bet. How about offering to send them a complete report of the things you have discussed with them during the re-design so that they don't have to take notes or try to remember everything? Can you sit down and type up a 1-2 page summary of the advice you are recommending to send to them? Of course you can.

These are just two small examples of things you can offer to sweeten the deal and help you land a re-design project you might not get otherwise. Sit down with a pen and notepad and just do some brain storming and write down little services you can offer at no charge that only require a little extra time on your part.

Perhaps you can also make a gift to give. For years I have created hand painted all occasion cards. I paint my logo in different hues on the cards and on the envelope. Women just love them!!! They are very easy for me to make. Women often tell me they love them so much they just keep them and never use them. I feel the same way -- and I can go make more any time I get ready. I buy the paper and envelopes from a wholesaler of paper products to the printing industry. So I can literally make a dozen hand painted cards with matching envelopes for less than one dollar. What an inexpensive gift, that takes little time and effort on my part to create, which adds incredible value to the services I offer.

What can you create that is easy, inexpensive and that would appeal to just about any woman? Think about it. I'm sure you'll come up with something! As you begin your business, and generally, have more time than money, be generous with your time and bless your clients with special (even unique) free bonuses.

Guarantees That Have Real Value

I'm quite shocked as I visit the websites of my competitors in re-design to discover how few of them offer any guarantee whatsoever for their training or services. They obviously don't understand the power of a great guarantee. It's called "risk reversal" and it's very important that you offer a strong guarantee.

First of all, a strong guarantee sub-consciously tells prospects that you are very, very confident in your product or service. No one is going to offer a guarantee on a sub-standard product or service. They would be immediately out of business.

Will people take advantage of you if you offer a refund guarantee? Yes, some will, but the vast majority of people are fair minded and won't try to benefit from you without paying you for those benefits. From time to time I have people ask me for a refund for a training product and I can literally tell which ones are genuinely asking because the product couldn't meet their needs and which people bought the product with the full intention right from the start of gaining the value and then asking me for a refund no matter what they received from me. What goes round, comes round and those people usually don't get anywhere in life anyway, so don't let them deter you from using good business practices. Good products carry guarantees.

In over 20 years of doing re-design, I have never had anyone ask me for a refund. My guarantee is that they will be happier when I am done rearranging the room or I will put it all back exactly as I found it and charge them nothing! I totally accept ALL the risk. They go into the business arrangement with total assurance that they will be happier or owe nothing. That's very powerful.

I know I dealt with this subject in **Rearrange It!**, but it bears repeating here. Offer your prospects a 100% satisfaction guarantee -- then work your tail off to make sure they are happy when you are done so you don't ever have to hear those words, "I'd like a refund please and will you put it all back where you found it?"

Getting Rid of Home Odors for Clients

To illustrate the offering of a back end product, consider adding a **Home Staging Sanitizer.** This is a product that helps eliminate: pet urine odors, smoking odors, cooking odors, mildew or mold odors, etc.

I use one myself since I have 6 cats and multiple litter boxes in the garage. It instantly removed the odors from the litter boxes. I put in it in my office for a few hours to eliminate a urine odor (one of my cats has a toileting problem). Whew! Fresh air again. Once the odors have been eliminated, they are gone for good, unless new odors are introduced by additional urine, smoking, etc.

Use an odor sanitizer as a back end product to augment your services. You can even use it if you're just doing a consultation and only going to be in the home for a couple of hours or so. A simple search on the internet for odor eliminators should provide you with good sources. Since they come in many different sizes and price ranges, I'm not recommending any particular one. But you should be able to do the research and pick the one that is right for you.

Advanced Redesign

Chapter 4
Marketing Techniques

Developing Lasting Business Relationships

Don't sell your clients on a re-design and then just let them disappear from your thoughts. Keep them coming back with a follow-up program that is strategic and repetitive.

Just like you, I own a home-based decorating business. One of my constant challenges is how to help my clients and trainees while improving my own business. What is a challenge for me will also be a challenge for you. What are some cost-effective ways to follow up with clients so they keep coming back to do business with you over and over again?

Follow-up is extremely important to growing your business. Like anything worthwhile, consistent follow-up requires a lot of effort, but over time you'll reap the benefits of a steady stream of repeat business and referrals. After all, as I've already discussed, it takes far less time and money to sell to an existing client than a cold prospect (someone who doesn't know you yet). So here are 9 follow-up tools sure to motivate your clients to keep doing business with you.

9 Tools for Building Customer Loyalty and On-going Business

1. **Thank-you notes:** This is a no-brainer, but you'd be surprised at how many entrepreneurs neglect to write thank-you notes--especially when they get really busy. Take the time to show your clients that you genuinely appreciate their business. They'll remember your thoughtfulness because most of your competition won't send out thank-you notes.
2. **Postcards:** Since you are targeting homeowners, send out monthly mailings that make good refrigerator fodder, such as "Quote of the Month," "Recipe of the Month" or useful tips on such topics as time-management, gardening or anything else that interests the bulk of your customers. Avoid being too promotional here. Just provide the kind of information that clients will want to hang on their frig. The added benefit to you is that whenever guests visit your customers' homes, they'll see your name, potentially leading to conversations about your business. Make sure your card is attractive too. Remember to check out our custom postcards.
3. **E-mail updates:** Think of your e-mail update as a press release that you send to your customers. Providing them with regular product, service and client updates via e-mail at least once per month will convey a sense of positive momentum. This keeps clients in the loop and, over time, gets them excited to be involved with you and motivates them to pass on referrals. You have to be remembered favorably to get referrals.
4. **Getting together over coffee or lunch:** Try to spend face time in a non-sales environment with your clients if you can. Ask about their family, hobbies, personal goals and so forth. When you show clients that you really care about them on a personal level, they're yours for life. Become their friend.
5. **Birthdays, anniversaries, weddings, graduations and other special occasions:** These occasions are very important to your clients and their families and friends. Be among the few who actually remember a client's special days, and that client will never forget you!

6. **Follow up on well-being:** For example, if you find that a client's spouse has been sick, call periodically just to find out how he's recovering.
7. **Pass referrals:** One of the most powerful ways to encourage loyalty in clients is to pass them referrals, which can be related to decorating or not. When you get a chance, scroll through your client database and select people you know who might add value to your clients' lives or homes.
8. **Entertaining at your home:** Throw a party for your best clients. You'll be amazed at how much rapport and goodwill you can build with people when you get them in your home environment. Your guests will also find value in your party as a networking opportunity for them.
9. **Post-sale feedback:** Demonstrate that you care about the quality of your service. Call clients and ask them questions like:
    o Are you pleased with the service you received?
    o What did you like most about working with me?
    o What would you like to see improved?

Without this invaluable information, you'll have a hard time improving your products and services. Besides, when you ask clients for feedback and implement their comments, they feel a sense of ownership in what you're doing and thus become more loyal to your products and services.

I may have mentioned this already, but I publish two newsletters to my clients and subscribers who haven't even become clients yet, but who have signed up for the newsletter. These newsletters so far have been free, though they might not always remain so. In any event, this is the primary way that I stay in touch with my clients and prospects.

My newsletters are delivered by email which costs me very little to send. Since my time is extremely valuable, the most expensive part of publishing the newsletter is the value of my time, energy and expertise. But I recognize the importance of "spaced repetition", in education-based selling, and in giving back to my clients and prospects. Most times I am remembered favorably and I do see an increase in sales following the issuing of a newsletter. Subscribers can opt out of receiving a newsletter any time they wish. While it is all very low key, it is an important facet of my business -- and so it should be an important facet of yours.

Since most people have email these days, be sure to collect their email addresses. Depending on the size of your mailing list, you can send out a few emails at a time by hand or purchase some low cost software that will do it for you.

Finding material to share in your newsletter isn't difficult. You can research your chosen topic at the library or over the internet. Just be sure that any tips you use which you received from others is written in your own words. Don't plagiarize. Tie your material into the season of the year to make it timely and more applicable. It doesn't have to be long. Remember, you're sharing something free and in exchange you remind the clients and prospects that you are "still out there".

Exhibiting at Trade Shows

Perfect timing is critical for trade show planning. Here's an exhibiting task schedule to help you stay ahead of the deadlines. When you're planning for a show of any size, the logistical details can seem overwhelming. One method of control is to develop a time line to help you stay on top of each detail. Think of it as your "to-do" list. The following outline provides you with a basic list of details you need to track when planning for a show. (Feel free to add your own items.) Keep in mind that the suggested time frame (three months out, two months out, etc.) is just that - a suggestion. Your timetable may differ slightly depending on the complexity of the project. Use this as a guideline to develop your own ideal show planning time line.

12 months out - Determine purpose for participating in show. Select space. Study floor plans, traffic patterns, services, audience makeup. Read contracts carefully. Understand terms, show rules, payment schedule, space assignment method (by product category, seniority, membership, etc.). Send in space application and first payment. Prepare budget.

6 months out - Determine exhibit objectives. Select primary vendors you will use (exhibit house, transportation company, installation/dismantle supplier). Decide if new exhibit is needed. If so, begin design process. (If using a portable, the design process may not require this much lead time.) Plan your show advertising.

4 months out - Select staff. Make airline, hotel and car reservations. Determine exhibit needs (if using existing properties): refurbishments, additions, changes. Select display products. Plan inquiry processing procedures. Communicate with primary vendors (exhibit house, shipping, installation/dismantle) regarding services needed and dates. Develop floor plan for exhibit. Finalize new exhibit design. Execute show-related advertising.

3 months out - Carefully read and review exhibitor manual. Select portable exhibit supplier. Review exhibit floor plan and note target dates and restrictions. Plan any in-booth presentations/demonstrations. Create list of required services, noting deadlines for "early-bird" discounts. Distribute show plan to staff. Reserve any additional meeting rooms (hospitality events, press conferences, etc.) Select catering menus (for hospitality events, press events, etc.) Meet deadlines for free publicity in the exhibitor guide/preview. Submit authorization form if you are using an exhibitor-appointed contractor. Plan pre-show meeting.

2 months out - Preview new custom exhibit. Finalize graphics art/copy. Order staff badges. Send information to other departments exhibiting in booth. Create and order lead forms. Finalize inquiry processing procedures. Prepare orders for: electrical, cleaning, floral, etc. Take advantage of any pre-pay discounts. Follow up on all promotions, making sure everything is ready to ship by target date. Prepare press kits. Check with staff on airline and hotel reservations and travel dates. Make needed changes. Develop briefing packet for booth staff. Schedule training for booth staff at show. Send reminder to upper management about briefing meetings (in office and at show); include agenda.

1 month out - Follow up on shipping orders. Follow up on installation/dismantle schedule; get an estimate on costs. Call to reconfirm airline, hotel and car reservations. Make needed changes. Follow up on target dates with all vendors. Confirm availability of display products/literature. Preview new portable display. Send all needed materials by target shipping date to avoid express mail shipments. Distribute briefing packet, including training materials, to all booth staffers. Set up and hold pre-show briefing meeting in office. Set up in-booth conference room schedule for pre-arranged meetings at show. Send follow-up reminder to upper management about briefing meeting, include agenda. Determine date and time for briefing staff at the exhibit. Review agenda, purpose of show, demonstrations, rehearsals, show specials, etc. Ensure that you have the following items before leaving for the show: traveler's checks, credit cards, copies of all orders and checks for services paid in advance, phone numbers and addresses of all vendors, engineering certificate for exhibit, shipping manifest, return shipping labels, and additional badge forms.

Upon Arrival - Check on freight arrival. Check with hotel about reservations for staff, as well as any meeting rooms and catering orders. Find service area. Meet electrician and confirm date and time for electrical installation. Supervise booth setup. Hold pre-show briefing and training for staff the day before the show.

During the Show - Reserve next year's space. Conduct daily meetings with staff. Make arrangements for booth dismantle and shipping. Arrange for lead forms to be shipped back to office daily for processing.

After the Show - Supervise booth dismantle. Handle leads. Debrief staff. Send thank-you notes. Use the system I've already talked about to send out all of your cards for you. It will save you an immense amount of time and effort – and time is money. So work effectively and stay in touch with the people you met.

More Trade Show Tips

The internet has made an impact on the tradeshow market, but there are still instances where setting up a booth at a tradeshow is a great way to make contacts, sell merchandise or find people.

Finding the right show is still a challenge. If you sell handmade accessories in addition to re-design, you might get lost in a craft show but be a standout at a home improvement show. Find out where the people who buy your products and services go to meet regularly, and set up shop there.

Exhibiting requires some advanced planning and focus. Here are a few hints:

- Create an exhibit that stands out from traditional booth displays. Use large graphics and skip the show-supplied signs. And don't hide behind a table; lose it and get out front to meet the people who walk by.
- Place your booth where show traffic is heavy (such as on a prominent corner, near a large exhibitor, or along major thoroughfares. Avoid setting up a back corner, or directly next to bathrooms or food concessions (the smell and trash ruins your image).
- Avoid the pitfalls that plague exhibitors such as wasting money on gimmicky giveaways while skimping on lighting or backdrops, or rushing to put a booth together at the last minute.
- If you have a big booth, you'll need "show labor" to set it up. Prices vary depending on location. Booth space is similarly priced.
- Look your best (you and the booth!) Make sure displays are neatly organized and literature is not scattered around. Booth staff should be attentive and listen to customers--not aggressively "hook" them into the booth. Of course, you shouldn't smoke, drink, eat, joke loudly or act rudely while in your booth.
- Take a break occasionally and walk around to see what "the competition" is doing. You'll get new ideas. Emulate the booths where people are stacked three deep waiting to see the presentation.
- Finally, remember to follow up on leads immediately after the show -- no more than a day or two after your leads return home.

Advanced Redesign

Chapter 5
Products Clients Fail to Have

Not Enough Floral Arrangements

You don't have to be in very many homes to recognize quickly there are not enough floral arrangements. Flowers, even if they are artificial, add so much to a room. They soften the hard edged features of the architecture and the furniture. They bring the feeling of "life" into the space. They add splashes of color. They help bridge all of the colors in the room. They give a room a freshness and vitality that few other accessories can claim.

Astonishingly enough, most homeowners don't do a very good job of bringing floral arrangements into their decorating efforts. And when they do, they are usually pretty basic and way too small for the area where they are placed. If they are too small, they feel dwarfed and unimportant. If they are too basic, they lose the dramatic impact they could make and are hardly even noticed.

This is where the re-designer can shine. Being able to provide a beautiful floral arrangement that is custom designed for the room; this, when artistically done and of the appropriate size and shape, can make all the difference. The best part about it for you is that you can either learn to make them yourself or you can buy them at a wholesale showroom already made or have them custom made to your specifications. In any event, offering this as a service or product to your client is such an easy thing for you to do. Just imagine how easy it would be to sell a beautiful floral arrangement to your client at the re-design consultation if you just "happened" to have one with you and set it on her coffee table? If it's beautiful and reasonably priced, do you honestly think she will let you get out the door with it? Chapter 6 will discuss this in detail.

Not Enough Plants

I'm equally astonished at how few people incorporate plants of any kind into their decorating efforts. Plants are so wonderful. Just like floral arrangements, plants soften the hard features in the room. If live plants, they bring oxygen into the space. They serve as great filler when you need it and they can cover over a multitude of problems, like plugs and switches, mars, scratches, unsightly cords and on and on.

Again, the few people who have plants usually have very small ones that go virtually un-noticed, or they are half dead and spindly. Rarely do you find enough and rarely are they even of good quality and size. So for years I have always, always taken plants with me on my appointments.

It doesn't matter if they are live plants or artificial ones, I know without asking that most people don't have them and don't even know how important they are to a well-planned and professionally arranged room. So I take some along (artificial, of course) to give them an idea of the impact they will have.

Think of how powerful it is to bring in a couple of trees to place in a room, or one tree and a couple of table plants, and then at some point mention to the homeowner that they can purchase them if they want. The "puppy dog" close is so powerful. See Chapter 7 for more information on this.

Not Enough Art

This is another category where most people just don't get it. Granted, art is very personal and can be quite expensive, depending on the caliber of the art work and its size. But art is a very important ingredient in a well designed room. Here again, people who have art usually have small images scattered here and there with no rhyme or reason. Often the art looks dwarfed on the wall because it is not in good proportion. The scale is usually way off when it is incorporated around the furniture and they know something isn't right but they don't know how to fix it.

So imagine if you, the re-designer, had some fine art catalogs with you and you got your client to browse through some of them while you're rearranging the furnishings they already have? So you think you might have a chance to work with them to acquire one new work of art while you're there, particularly if in the new arrangement you can demonstrate the need for one, its size and format and where it would be placed?

When your client recognizes that art will express their personality and lifestyle like no other accessory on earth, and they see they have a need for something, and you've got the solution to their problem sitting right on the table in front of them, most will actively strive to resolve the issue right then, given they have the resources to do so. More on this in Chapter 8.

Not Enough Throw Pillows

Throw pillows aren't quite as neglected as other types of accessories, but they are an easy product to acquire or make, and you will run across people who have a need for them. Many people have purchased their sofa and chairs at furniture outlets and just use the pillows that came with the furniture. Few go beyond that to incorporate other pillows into the mix and often don't understand the impact the right number and types of fabric and styles can make. For very little money, a client can add a few pillows and perk up a room instantly. More on this in Chapter 9.

Not Enough Area Rugs

The major mistake homeowners make when it comes to their sofa is that they back it up against one wall in the room. Usually the sofa has no correlation to the room's focal point and is too far away from it even if it does. Often the floor in front of the sofa is soiled or stained. Many people put furniture in a room and never move it around at all, so the carpet or floor in front of the sofa becomes an eye sore.

Other people try to mix furniture together that might not really look good in the same room. Perhaps the colors are quite different. Something is needed to serve as a "bridge" between them so that they "settle down" and act as a united arrangement.

Here is where the area rug comes into play. Area rugs are great for anchoring a seating arrangement and for acting as a bridge to coordinate and unify the arrangement. They are also functional to protect the floor in front of the sofa and chairs and to hide soiled or worn carpet that cannot be corrected any other way.

Having the ability to offer your clients reasonably priced area rugs, or to have custom rugs made with the perfect colors in the perfect format and size is a very valuable service you can provide to them. It's not too difficult to find resources and even catalogs. I don't suggest hauling an area rug around with the goal of selling it in the same manner you would a plant or floral arrangement, but you should stick a 4x6 in your car just to help demonstrate the value of having one. More on this in Chapter 10.

Not Enough Candles

Scented candles are all the rage now. I've covered my home with them. I don't light them, just place them around in strategic places for the fragrance and atmosphere. Love it.

This is another accessory that few clients have invested in and it is such an easy product to carry with you. Whether you make them yourself or buy them wholesale or even at retail, candles are a "must have" accessory. It goes without saying that offering the appropriate candle holder will help sizzle the candles. An excellent accessory item you can offer a client at the re-design that is relatively inexpensive and one that will give their home that "decorator touch".

There you have it. Here are the six most often neglected accessories in the many, many homes I have re-designed. They are so commonly ignored I am suggesting that any one of them, when featured correctly and presented in the course of your consultations, would open excellent opportunities for a smart re-designer to up-sell and back-end-sell to clients, not only to make more profit, but to truly provide clients with affordable, quality accessories they don't even have to leave home to acquire. What could be better than that? It's a win/win for client and designer.

I once included a chapter in this book on how to make your own candles, but for liability reasons and because candles are so prevalent now everywhere, it's much easier to shop for unique and beautiful candles than it is to make them yourself. When you factor in the time it takes to make them, it hardly pays for your labor unless you own a retail candle store.

Designer Wholesale Showrooms in the USA

If you're looking for the finest home furnishings, many which are custom made products, here are the top interior design showrooms around the country. You cannot buy from these showrooms unless you are officially in the trade and can prove that. Before ever taking a client with you to a design showroom, be sure you have gone ahead and registered your company and set up an account. You will have to prove you are in the business with letterhead, business cards, resale licenses, and a business license.

California (Southern)

Laguna Design Center
23811 Aliso Creek Rd, Suite 200
Laguna Niguel, CA 92677

L.A. Mart
1933 S. Broadway
Los Angeles, CA 90007

Pacific Design Center
8687 Melrose Ave
Los Angeles, CA 90069

California (Northern)

Contract Design Center
600 Townsend Street
San Francisco, CA 94103

Design Pavilion at 200 Kansas
200 Kansas Street
San Francisco, CA 94103

Design Pavilion At 251 Rhode Island
251 Rhode Island Street
San Francisco, CA 94103

Manor House Pavilion
297 Kansas Street
San Francisco, CA 94103

San Francisco Design Center
Two Henry Adams Street
San Francisco, CA 94103

Showplace Square East
111 Rhode Island Street
San Francisco, CA 94103

Showplace Square West
550 Fifteenth Street
San Francisco, CA 94103

The San Francisco Mart
1355 Market Street, Suite 460
San Francisco, CA 94103

Colorado

Denver Design Center
595 South Broadway
Denver, CO 80209

Denver Merchandise Mart
451 E. 58th Avenue, #470
Denver, CO 80216

Florida

Carl's Furniture Showrooms, Inc.
5051 N. University Dr.
Lauderhill, FL 33321

Design Center of the Americas
1855 Griffin Road, Suite A-282 Dania, FL 33004

E.J. Schrader Bedding 6601 Norton Ave.
West Palm Beach, FL 33405

Jack Walsh Showroom
501 Ardmore Rd.
West Palm Beach, FL 33401

Mark Biller & Associates Inc.
Florida Design Center
North Palm Beach, FL 33408

Miami Design Dist.(Dacra)
180 NE 40th St.
Miami, FL 33137

Miami International Merchandise Mart
777 NW 72nd Avenue
Miami, FL 33126

Miami International Design Centre I
4100 NE 2nd Avenue
Miami, FL 33137

Miami International Design Centre II
4141 NE 2nd Avenue
Miami, FL 33137

Canada

Building & Design Resource Center
168 Bedford Road
Toronto, ON M5R

ProSource Floorcoverings
4390 Westroads Drive
West Palm Beach, FL 33407

Georgia

Atlanta Decorative Arts Center
351 Peachtree Hills Ave, Suite 244
Atlanta, GA 30305

Americas Mart
240 Peachtree Street, NW, Suite 2200
Atlanta, GA 30303

Illinois

The Merchandise Mart
200 World Trade Center Chicago
Chicago, IL 60054

Massachusetts

Boston Design Center
One Design Center Place, Suite 337
Boston, MA 02210

Michigan

Michigan Design Center
1700 Stutz Drive, #2S
Troy, MI 48084

Minnesota

International Market Square
275 Market Street
Minneapolis, MN 55405

New York

225 Fifth Avenue
225 Fifth Avenue
New York, NY 10010

Architects & Designers Building
150 E. 58th Street
New York, NY 10155

Decoration & Design Building
979 Third Avenue
New York, NY 10022

Decorative Arts Center
305 E. 63rd Street
New York, NY 10021

Interior Design Building
306 E. 61st Street
New York, NY 10021

Manhattan Art & Antiques Center
1050 Second Ave. at 56th Street
New York, NY 10022

New York Design Center
200 Lexington Avenue
New York, NY 10016

Carole Dixon
New York Merchandise Mart
41 Madison Ave.
New York, NY 10010

The Fine Arts Building
232 E. 59th Street
New York, NY 10022

The MarketCenter at 230 Fifth Ave.
230 Fifth Avenue
New York, NY 10001

The Art & Design Building
1059 Third Avenue
New York, NY 10021

Pendleton Square Design Complex
444 Reading Road
Cincinnati, OH 45202

Pennsylvania

Marketplace Design Center
2400 Market Street
Philadelphia, PA 19103

Texas

Dallas Market Center
2100 Stemmons Freeway
Dallas, TX 75207

Decorative Center of Houston
5120 Woodway Drive
Houston, TX 77056

Forty-One Madison -The New York
41 Madison Avenue
New York, NY 10010

Gary Buxbaum Co.(Workroom)
315 Hudson St.
New York, NY 10013

North Carolina

Hickory Furniture Mart
2220 Highway 70 SE
Hickory, NC 28602

International Home Furnishings Center
210 E. Commerce Avenue
High Point, NC 27260

Lynn Courtade
305 West High Ave.(B-47)
High Point, NC 27260

Market Square
305 W. High Street
High Point, NC 27260

Ohio

Longworth Hall Design Center
700 W. Pete Rose Way
Cincinnati, OH 45203

Ohio Design Center
2S533 Mercantile Road
Beachwood, OH 44122

Dallas Design District
1400 Turtle Creek Blvd, Suite 209
Dallas, TX 75207

The Resource Center

7026 Old Katy Road, Suite 301
Houston, TX 77024

Utah

Showplace Square
1025 East 3300 South
Salt Lake City, UT 84106

Washington D.C.

The Washington Design Center
300 D Street SW
Washington, D.C. 20024

Washington

Lenora Square Professional Design
1000 Lenora Street, Suite 117
Seattle, WA 98121

Seattle Design Center
5701 Sixth Avenue South
Seattle, WA 98108

Seattle Gift Center
6100 4th Avenue South
Seattle, WA 98108

Advanced Redesign

Chapter 6
Offering Floral Arrangements

Color Schemes for Floral Arrangements

A MONOCHROMATIC COLOR SCHEME - If you want to take advantage of the many tints and shades of just one color in a room, you will repeat them over and over again in the same arrangement. A monochromatic floral arrangement (except for the green leaves), concentrates on just one hue, let's say yellow, and all of the flowers are a tint or shade of yellow. Monochromatic arrangements will give the most punch, because the colors in the arrangement are so few. So for the most dramatic effect and power, select one hue in the room, and focus simply on that one color.

ANALOGOUS COLOR SCHEME - Hues that are found next to each other on the color wheel are referred to as analogous colors. An example would be purple and red-purple and red, or purple and blue-purple and blue. As you can see, the middle color in the trio of each example has some of both colors on opposite sides to it in the color. Because they are next to each other, they will always blend perfectly together. In a floral arrangement of analogous colors, one should always have at least 3 colors represented. You can use tints and shades of each hue you select, but you should not use more than one primary color in an arrangement, otherwise it can look too "gaudy".

COMPLEMENTARY COLOR SCHEME - Complementary colors are those that are opposite (or nearly opposite) each other on the color wheel. An example would be green and red (so loved at Christmas time). These two hues are opposite each other on the color wheel. You can refine this further by what we call a **split complementary color scheme** where you incorporate three colors together and where all three colors are equally separated from each other on the color wheel. An example of a split complementary design would be putting red, yellow and blue together in an arrangement.

CONTRASTING COLOR SCHEME - This color scheme focuses on contrast and high drama, such as creating an arrangement of black and white. You can also create high contrast by using a bright color and a soft color together, such as a bright yellow and a soft blue. Other ways to incorporate contrast in an arrangement are to use a combination of large flowers and small flowers, shiny and dull textures, large and small leaves. You get the picture.

Design Concepts for Arrangements

SIZE AND MASS - One of the most important decisions you will make is the overall size of the arrangement. This is important because you want the arrangement to look and feel comfortable where it will be placed. If it is too small, it will feel overwhelmed in the space. If too large, it will feel crowded and overdone. Therefore, when determining the final size of an arrangement for a particular place, you need to decide the sizes of the flowers within the arrangement.

The flowers you choose should be in good scale to the size of the arrangement and the container. For instance, you don't want to put a large flower in a tiny vase. On the other hand, you don't want to put a small, delicate flower in an enormous container or arrangement. The scale would be all wrong.

Then there is the matter of *density*. Some flowers are very dense and compact while others are open and airy. A carnation, for instance, is dense and compact. It has greater mass than an irregularly shaped flower. Look at the furniture in the room? Is it all fully upholstered and dense and compact? Or are the arms open and thin and visually lighter? Will the arrangement sit on a wooden table (condensed) or a glass table top (airy)? Think about these factors as you make your selections.

TEXTURE - There are rough textures and smooth ones. There are soft and hard textures; there are glossy and dull surfaces. To make something look larger, choose a smooth texture over a rough one. Color can also be affected by texture. A rough surface will make a color look more dull than a smooth surface. A mirrored surface will command a lot more attention than a non-mirrored surface.

SHAPE - There are only four categories of shape with a few variations off of them. Those basic shapes are: circle, rectangle, square and triangle. The variations (more on this later) can be altered into the shape of a "C" or "S". Arrangements can also be vertical or horizontal in format.

Positive Space is the space within an arrangement that is filled by the elements of the arrangement: flowers and leaves and other decorative elements. The Negative Space is the space that is between the flowers and the space immediately around the arrangement. Negative space is just as important as positive space. Good arrangements make appropriate use of the positive *and* negative space.

FORM - Form is very similar to shape in that it deals with the 3-dimensional end product. The arrangement could be loose, airy and spreading out, which is an open arrangement, or it may be compact and solid, a closed arrangement. Visually, a closed arrangement will "feel" heavier than an open one. Form doesn't just refer to the overall arrangement but to the individual elements as well. A serrated leaf forms an irregular shape. A round container forms a regular shape as would a carnation. The more tightly the elements are packed in the container, the more depth it usually looks like it has.

LINE - When you create an arrangement, you want the eye of the viewer to travel in a certain direction. The line you choose will dictate the basic structure of the arrangement. The line can be curved, diagonal, vertical or horizontal. Within that structure, the elements within the arrangement can be thin or thick, short or long or a combination of all. For a formal look, choose straight lines. For an informal look, consider curved lines.

There can be actual lines created by the elements themselves, or there can be invisible lines (or imagined lines) that are created by the placement and repetition of the elements within the arrangement.

Universal Principles of Design

Whether you're talking about 3-dimensional design of furniture, how furniture is arranged in a room or a floral arrangement, the design principles are the same. Each arrangement will need to be created with all of these elements to achieve an arrangement that's visually appealing. It should have a focal point, be in good scale and proportion, be balanced, have rhythm and achieve harmony.

SCALE AND PROPORTION – Essentially we can break this subject down into three specific components devised by ancient Greeks: The Golden Mean, The Golden Rectangle and the Golden Section. The **Golden Mean Theory** uses a ratio of 1 to 1.6. You get roughly the same thing in 2 to 3 or 2/3rds ratio. If you have a six foot sofa, a coffee table about four feet long is more harmonious than one that is shorter or longer. If you were deciding the placement of a tie-back on draperies, placing the tip back point half way down the drape would not be as pleasing as placing it higher or lower than the half way point. Notice in the arrangement below, the crossing point of the lower flowers I not at the half way point. The flowers are lower. Notice how the whole arrangement is divided into 3 parts but that the main focal point of the arrangement is in the bottom portion of the whole arrangement, not at the half way point.

The Golden Rectangle and The Golden Section determine the best ratios when comparing width to length. This holds for room length, picture length, table length and a host of other comparisons. Area rugs often come in these ratios: 3x5, 4x6, 9x12. Picture frames come: 3x5, 4x6, 5x7, 8x10, 9x12. A 4 foot work of art would look great over a 6 foot sofa. A 6 foot entertainment center would feel good against a 9 foot wall.

Scale refers to the size of one element in the arrangement compared to another element. In a wall grouping, one picture is compared to other pictures in the grouping to determine the proper scale. In a floral arrangement, if one flower is one inch across, the ideal scale for the next flower is 1.6 inches across. In reverse, if one flower is 3 inches across, the other flower would be 2 inches across (2/3rd the width of the first one). It's not a do or die rule, but if you come close to adhering to it, you can't go wrong.

The visual weight of each element can affect the actual measurement that looks best, as well as the size and type of container and other materials used in the arrangement. Furniture that is created for children is made in a scaled-down version of furniture made for adults because the bodies of children are smaller scale when compared to the bodies of adults. Scale can also refer to the size of furniture within a room. The space in the room is called its mass. So naturally you would want to see larger, bulkier furniture is a great room and smaller, scaled down furniture in a very small room.

BALANCE - There are essentially two kinds of balance: *symmetrical* and *asymmetrical*. When one discusses balance it is important to note that we are talking about **visual balance**, not necessarily actual balance. The eye is most pleased with the visual weight of an object when it is placed at the bottom, where it "supports" what is above, not the other way around. Since solid, darker objects visually carry more weight than their lighter, airier counterparts, they should be placed at or near the bottom of the arrangement.

In a *symmetrical* arrangement, if you divided the arrangement in half from top to bottom, both sides would look and feel equal. They would be mirror images of each other. The same principle holds true for furniture in a room. When placing furniture, you want to spread the furniture throughout the room to achieve balance in the room. The floral arrangement here is not symmetrical. In an *asymmetrical* arrangement, one side will have more mass, but because of the style of the arrangement, both sides will "feel" balanced against each other, in-spite of the fact that they are not mirror images of one another.

FOCAL POINT - Choose where your most visually dominant area will be for the arrangement. This will be the focal point and every arrangement needs one. This is typically where you want the viewer to look first. All other lines in the arrangement should extend to or away from the focal point. Select a large flower or a bright color and a strong interesting element to include in the focal point to anchor it.

RHYTHM - You can almost exchange the word rhythm for **motion or direction**. Rhythm or motion is most often created in an arrangement by the use of repetition which causes the eye to move in a specific direction. You can repeat the same colors, the same shapes over and over again leading the eye in a specific direction. Two matching chairs create rhythm in a room. Three pictures the same size hung side by side can also create rhythm in a room. You can also use *gradation* to create rhythm by gradually reducing or enlarging the size of similar elements in the arrangement. Here is where you would use the 1:1.6 ratio or the 3:2 ratio of scale to enlarge or reduce sizes. Changing sizes in gradual increments (say 1/3rd size reductions) help to make elements in a room or an arrangement form a "rolling hills" effect. Extreme height changes create the effect of "steep cliffs" in a room or an arrangement, which usually doesn't feel peaceful and harmonious. Rhythm will create excitement and make your arrangements come to life when used properly.

CONTRAST - You don't want too much repetition or the arrangement will start to look boring. Create contrast by putting elements next to each other that are opposite in size or texture or color. Just make sure that the part of the element that is in contrast with another element relates: smooth contrasting with rough, light contrasting with dark, large contrasting with small.

HARMONY - When you have successfully combined all of the principles of design into one arrangement, you will have achieved harmony. You'll know it because it will look and feel "right" or "finished". This will be a successful arrangement and one you can be proud to present to a client.

Eleven Ways to Design Great Arrangements

Flower arranging is generally considered a personal style, however there are guidelines that have been developed by professionals that govern some basic Western mass arrangements, as well as the more complex Oriental line compositions. I borrowed parts of this chapter from my ebook called **Great Parties! Great Homes** because, whether you learn to create arrangements yourself or not, you need to know what style and size would be most appropriate for your client so that you can custom order an arrangement, or simply give them advice on what to get on their own.

Following are eleven diagrams that show you how to construct some of the basic shapes. Once you have learned how to create these basic shapes, you'll feel comfortable designing your own variations. Place the flowers in the pot according to the numerical sequence shown, beginning with the number 1. The colors pink, blue and black are used simply to differentiate between the major stages in constructing the arrangement. However, when the actual floral is created, you can use any color of flower you choose.

One thing to remember: when working with live flowers and greenery, which tilt and bend in different ways, you will wind up creating arrangements that "interpret" the basic design but will not match it exactly. As you get more skilled, you will vary any basic outline with airy or linear materials that will add different textures, movement and drama. Remember too, that while the arrangements are shown in a specific manner, they work equally well if curved or shaped in the opposite direction. You can also turn a crescent shape into an "L" shape by using straight rather than curved stems.

Most of these arrangements are designed to be viewed from one side. To make them attractive from the back, duplicate the design on the other side of the container. Use outline flowers that face both directions.

Many garden flowers can be used in all styles of arrangements. You can also use them in artificial arrangements equally well. If using dried flowers, simply use more of them to compensate for their shrunken size and subdued coloring. Remember, that a successful design includes color, rhythm, balance and scale.

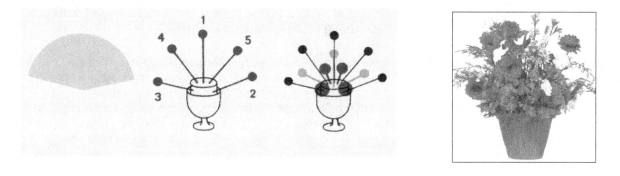

FAN ARRANGEMENT

The basic outline for a fan arrangement consists of five spoke-like stems of equal length. Place the first stem (1) upright in the center, with supporting spokes (2 and 3) angling upward on each side. Add another pair (4 and 5), then fill in with shorter flowers. In the photo, juniper and freesiz form the main spokes of the fan. Anemone and dahlia complete the outline and lead the eye to a brilliant dahlia left of center.

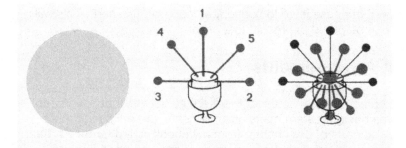

CIRCULAR ARRANGEMENT

The basic outline for a circular arrangement is the same as for a fan, except that here spokes 2 and 3 project horizontally from the raised flower holder. Fill in the outline with round flowers, some projecting downward to mask the rim of the container. This arrangement should be completed on all sides. In the photo, French marigolds and Queen Anne's lace round the outline of the floral. A bold pink cosmos draws attention at the lower left, balance by pink ranunculuses in the upper right.

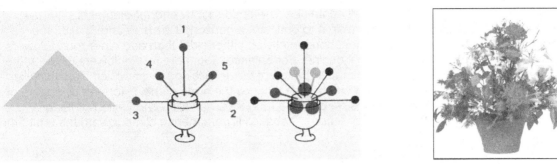

TRIANGULAR ARRANGEMENT

Start with placing the No. 1 flower, following the numerical sequence, but making sure that number 4 and 5 are shorter than the other ones. Use round flowers in the center. In the photo, you'll notice alba lilies and narcissuses, splashes of red nerine and freesiz move the eye from the outline to the core. Asparagus fern and gray-green euphorbia overhang the rim and soften the formal shape.

VERTICAL ARRANGEMENT

Choose a single spike-shaped flower, bud or leaf as your first addition to this arrangement (1). Flank it with three progressively shorter spikes (2 thru 4) to form a tapering outline. Then plump the center section with as many round flowers as you want. Balance the soaring vertical line with a large round shape at the base of the arrangement. If you use a tall vase with a narrow mouth, you may not need a flower holder. In the photo, there is a pale pink rosebud with an upturned leaf used as a starting point. It is supported by half-opened yellow roses. Acacia, brodiaea and Peruvian lilies fill the center of the shape. At the base, two fat rosettes of pink nerine repeat, in a deeper hue, the color of the top rose.

INVERTED T ARRANGEMENT

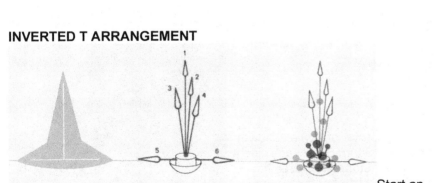

Start an inverted T arrangement with the flower holder raised above the container rim. Position a spike-shaped flower or piece of foliage (1) in the center of the flower holder, cutting the stem to a length that is more than twice the diameter of a low container or more than one and one half times the height of a tall container. Then add slightly shorter elements (2 thru 4). Use either round or spike shapes cut shorter than 4 to outline the horizontal arms (5 and 6). Add four round flowers shorter than these arms to project horizontally on either side, then add other round flowers of increasing lengths (blue) to fill in the vertical outline. For balance, add more round flowers (pink) at the base. In the photo, a star-of-Bethlehem spire marks the top of the T, followed by speckled Peruvian lilies and a half-open orange calendula. Full-blown calendulas balance the arms of the T, formed by spears of star-of-Bethlehem and spiky euphorbia leaves. Asparagus fern, Peruvian lilies and white bordiaea stabilize the center while larger blossoms of anemone, Tabasco lily and nerine climb toward the top of the arrangement.

CRESCENT ARRANGEMENT
To start a crescent arrangement, begin with a stem (1) that has a strong curve, fixing it securely in the flower holder slightly to the left of center. Using spike-shaped foliage or flowers to emphasize the outline, cut stems 2 through 6 progressively shorter and shape them to follow the curve of the first, inserting them alternately on either side. The top view shows front-to-back placement. In the lower half of the crescent, stem 7 continues the line of stem 1, with shorter pieces (8 thru 11) branching off on either side. Use round flowers (blue) to add fullness to the outline; place larger flowers (pink) near the top of the container for stability. In the photo, spikes of star-of-Bethlehem trace the sweep of the crescent from tip to tip. Delicate blooms and foliage of acacia and Queen Anne's lace support the curve, with two half-opened amaryllises to balance and embellish the design.

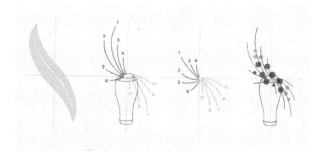

S-CURVE ARRANGEMENT
Position the primary curved stem (1) in the center of a raised flower holder, placing progressively shorter stems (2 thru 6) on each side to form the top half of the S. In the bottom half, stem 7 reverses the curve begun above by stem 1. Stems 8 thru 11 fill out the bottom curve on each side. The tips of the S curve (1 and 7) should be approximately the same distance from an imaginary vertical line

bisecting the arrangement. Use small flowers (blue) to make transitions within the principal lines and fill the center of the design with larger round flowers (pink). In the photo, two pliant branches of small-flowered euphorbia form the dominant line of the S, supported by rosettes of red nerine and white brodiaea at the top and sprigs of freesia and juniper at the bottom. A large red dahlia provides a pivot for the arrangement at the center, balanced by smaller dahlias on either side.

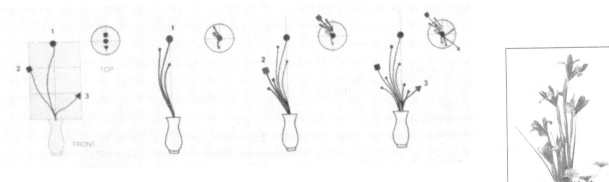

HORIZONTAL ARRANGEMENT

Start with a low bowl. In the middle, position a short flower (1), then add longer horizontal spikes (2 and 3) on each side. Complete the outline with shorter pairs of spike-shaped flowers or foliage (4 thru 7) to form an oval shape (top view). Group small round flowers (blue) toward the outer edge, facing them in all directions so the design is pleasing from any angle. Fill the central area with larger blossoms (pink). In the photo, spikes of snapdragon and star-of-Bethlehem extend gracefully from this low arrangement, framing a cluster of calendula, ranunculus and Queen Anne's lace.

Ikebana: A Natural Unity of Three

Japanese flower arranging tends to distill universal elements into basic trinities. In 17th Century Japan, three elements were used to signify the relationship between man and nature. The longest branch symbolizes heaven and the shortest symbolizes the earth. Man is represented by the middle branch. This symbolism remains to this day.

SHOKA STYLE ARRANGEMENT

In a Shoka arrangement, three curved branches rise in a front-to-back row (front views). The heaven line is half again as tall as the vase; the earth line is two thirds as tall as the man line one third as tall as the heaven line. In a tall vase, place the heaven line (1) so its tip aligns with the vase's center, adding similarly curving supplementary material. Then place the man and earth lines (2 and 3) so they extend equally in opposite directions (top views). Add supplementary material if desired. In this photo, golden marguerites aspire toward purple irises, seeming to mirror their vibrant accent color. The Japanese desire to reflect nature can also be seen in the orientation of flowers. In Ikebana, leaves and blossoms are placed so the flower is upright or slightly inclined as if growing toward the sun. You will notice in the small circles of the diagram here, a circle represents the heaven line, a square represents the mankind line, and the triangle represents the earth. The length of the stems reflect a plant's stage of development. The longest stem of an iris, for example, having had the most time to grow, has the most fully developed flowers.

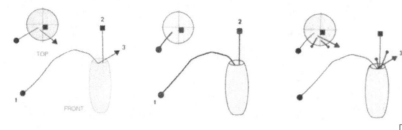

NAGEIRE STYLE ARRANGEMENT

Prune a distinctively curved branch to create a horizontal heaven line (1), fixing it with a wooden support. Position the man line (2) upright and slightly toward the opposite side (top view, center). The short earth line (3) needs a large, dramatic blossom to offset the pull of the heaven line, and is often assisted by one or two similar flowers (front view, right). In the photo, a red chokeberry branch, bent to accentuate its natural curve, slants outward to form the heaven line and upward to form the man line. Red anemones, the higher one representing earth, counterbalance the branch.

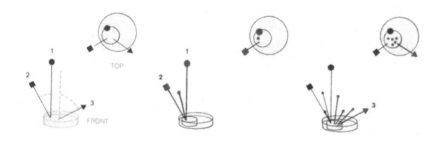

MORIBANA STYLE ARRANGEMENT

Using a pin holder, fix the heaven line (1) near the back or one side of a low container. Then position the man line (2) at a 45 degree angle to one side. Fill the spaces between these two and in the center of the container with some supplementary flowers before anchoring the earth line (3) at a 60 degree angle in the front. In the photo, orange lilies, their leaves overhanging the container edge, represent the three basic Ikebana elements, but they frame a Western-style mass of daisies.

Using Artificial Flowers Outside

Of COURSE you can! Make sure if you're using artificial flowers outdoors, to use ONLY polyester blend fabric flowers. Do not use naturals. And be sure to select flowers and greenery that have plastic stems. Don't use the hand-wrapped (paper wrapped stems)or latex coated flowers. Paper wrapped stems will deteriorate very fast in outdoor conditions, even if they're protected from the rain. The paper used to wrap those stems will absorb moisture over time and eventually fall apart. Latex flowers will dry out very quickly in the heat and cold and soon look dry and brittle. Plastic stems flowers won't fall apart in poor weather. Don't use natural eucalyptus and like products, they too will deteriorate and stain your exterior because of the dyes used in processing. Use the poly/silk blend fabric flowers. And one last thing...protect the poly/silk flowers by spraying them liberally with a fabric protectorant such as ScotchGard. After all, it's a fabric. Treat it, protect it and it'll last a LONG while and look beautiful.

How to Keep Silk Arrangements Dust Free

It's a lot easier than you might thing. If you'll use a feather duster made of Ostrich Feathers, you'll find that the static electricity created by lightly dusting with just the tip of the feathers will make the dust cling to the duster instead of your flowers. Just do it once a week or whenever you normally dust. You can also use a hair dryer for fast 'in between' dusting sessions. Just be SURE to use the cold air setting and not the hot air. Hot air will bond the dust to the poly-silk fabric. And NEVER use hot air on latex blooms; they'll melt like a candle.

Tools of the Trade

Having the right tools on hand will make your creations much easier. Here are the most important ones.

A Sharp Knife - You'll need the knife to cut the floral foam to the right size, curling ribbons and cutting stems.

Secateurs - You want heavy duty ones that will cut heavy stems, even wire or slim branches. Good ones have a wire or metal "shock absorber". This makes cutting easier on the hands and the secateurs open again automatically after each cut.

Scissors - Your scissors will be used to cut fabric, ribbons, curling ribbons, and numerous other things. Keep a second pair of scissors with your ribbon so you don't have to hunt for one.

Wire Cutters - Inside the stems of most artificial flowers is wire which helps to keep the stem erect. These can be pretty difficult to cut with a knife or scissors but easy for wire cutters. You can also use wire to reinforce stems that you want to shape by wrapping the wire around the stem at the angle or curve you want and then wrapping tape around both to conceal the wire.

Other Handy Tools - Hammer, screwdrivers, pliers, stapler, staple gun, buckets, bowls, hot glue gun, sharp knives, secateurs, scissors, wire cutters.

Equipment and Supplies

- a wide assortment of artificial stemmed flowers
- artificial flowering plants or bushes
- a wide assortment of artificial green foliage
- assorted vases and containers (different shapes and sizes)
- assorted baskets
- floral foam blocks or even styrofoam
- florist tape
- plyable wire
- assorted ribbons

- spray paints (including glitter in gold, silver, copper, etc.)
- work table
- dried moss (to cover foam)
- tool belt (optional)

The Vase Arrangement

NECESSARY INGREDIENTS - A wide-necked vase, some long stemmed greenery, 9-12 stems of flowers, filler flowers, ribbon.

Cut the greenery to 1-1/2 times the height of the vase. When you insert the greenery into the vase, try to "weave" or interlace them together. If inserting 3 stems, try to form a triangle with them. For 5 stems, make a 5-pointed star. If inserting 7 stems, create the 5-pointed star and then place the last two vertically.

The longest floral stem should be no higher than 2-1/2 times the height of the vase. Put it in the center of the vase. Then place stems in descending order with each stem slightly shorter than the one before. Place them in a circle evenly spaced. Then move on to the next variety of flower. Place all the main flowers first, followed by the filler flowers. Keep the filler stems to a minimum.

Add ribbon and/or bow for the finishing touch.

The Container Arrangement

NECESSARY INGREDIENTS - A container, floral foam, greenery, flowers, tape, knife or scissors.

Cut the foam to fit the container. To create more surface area, trim any sharp edges. Cut off the corners on a square or rectangular block. Glue or tape the foam in place.

Place the greenery first. Start at the lowest place and insert them evenly spaced. If you're creating a round arrangement, start by placing the greenery at the north, south, east and west points of the arrangement and fill in from there evenly around the whole foam.

Place the largest flowers next. When you cut stems, cut them longer than needed. You can always cut more off, but if you get them too short, there's nothing you can do about it.

According to the design of the arrangement, finish by placing the rest of the flowers, going from the largest to the smallest. Filler flowers are good for closing up gaps or holes in the arrangement.

Making a Portfolio

Take photographs of every arrangement you create. To get the best contrast and not have anything distracting in the background, drape plain white or off-white fabric from the wall down and over a table, arranging the folds in a pleasing manner. If you have a roll of wide butcher block paper, this can be used instead of fabric. This way you'll have a seamless background for the photo.

Lights placed about 3 feet away shining on the arrangement will help illuminate it evenly. Make sure they don't appear in the picture.

Be sure to take more than one photograph and from different angles. Get a bird's eye view, a side view and a front view. Be sure not to crop off anything from the arrangement by accident.

I always use 400 ASA speed film because it is faster, especially if you do not have a tripod to set your camera on. I also use my digital camera to get quick pictures so I don't have to be quite as concerned about how perfectly the other ones turn out.

Mount your photos in a professional scrapbook or photo album, either assigning a code or name to each of them. Be sure to include the finished measurements of each. Enlarge the best ones for some variety in your album. For the most dramatic effect, put like colors together. This will give your album more unity and help you quickly find the appropriate samples to show a client based on color. However, be sure to let your client know that you can create any arrangement they see in just about any color they choose.

Do NOT put the prices next to each arrangement. Keep that information somewhere else. You want your clients to fall in love with an arrangement first, then find out the price later.

Resources

If you live in a metropolitan area, most have convenient wholesale sources for the tools and supplies you will need. Check your local business to business yellow pages. You can even search for sources over the internet. You will have to prove with a business card and business license that you are in the trade, but once you do, you can purchase your products wholesale and get a net-30 credit account. Many distributors will require a minimum purchase, particularly on your first order. Get their credit application and open an account to make future purchases easier.

If you don't want to be involved with the actual creation of arrangements, it's good to know all of the elements that make an outstanding floral so that you can describe to someone else exactly what you want. Many cities will have wholesalers or distributors who also offer design services and you can order what you want over the phone and even have it delivered to you. Many of these companies have catalogs you can get or even online catalogs with special prices on their most popular items.

Pricing Tips

While it's important to do some price comparisons for your part of the country, this is really difficult in the flower arranging business because of the huge variety of plants and containers. So bear in mind that any figures presented here are just estimates and should be considered just a general guide.

I recommend you take your wholesale cost for all the ingredients and mark up your costs on the goods themselves for an artificial floral arrangement by 300-400% on the average to reach a fair retail price. For plants only, the percentage should be in the same (300-400%). If a plant cost you $20, you would resell it for $80-100 ($20 cost + $60 markup or $80 markup). You must factor in labor costs and other business costs to the equation. I have set the markup percentages high enough to account for the "hidden" costs that go into creating an arrangement: labor, gas, time, business overhead.

To help you with some additional guidelines based loosely on descriptions relating to size and overall involvement of an arrangement, think about some of these descriptions and price accordingly:

- Cute, modest, delicate, small, dainty
- Standard, popular, pleasing
- Lovely, beautiful, nice
- Showy, substantial, impressive
- Stunning, fantastic, gorgeous

- Spectacular, breathtaking, outstanding

Obviously the lower you go on the list, the more expensive the arrangement becomes.

Repeat Business and Generating Referrals

Expert marketers say that 60% of your advertising resources should be spent on your existing and former clients. These people have purchased a product or service from you in the past and assuming all went well and they were pleased, they are far more apt to purchase from you again because they trust you. They may even have already recommended you to someone else.

So it just makes good sense to concentrate a significant amount of your time and energy staying in touch with people who already know you, like you and trust you. This is just good business.

I've already given you some ideas on how to back-end sell to these people in a previous chapter. You can offer them **rewards** (more flowers or discounts), a special price on another product or service, a gift certificate, you name it.

Take the time to talk to your clients and find out specifically what they like, what they don't like, about their family, about their work - anything that helps bond you to them and them to you. These are the little aspects of doing business that build long term loyalty between you and your client so that they are not easily drawn away by some other sales pitch or bargain.

Create a quality floral arrangement and offer it for a fair price and you should have little to no problem having plenty of people who fall in love with it and place it in their home.

Some of your clients might even be willing to host a floral arrangement party or mini-seminar. You can take in several samples and your portfolio and teach them a little about how floral arrangements are made. This is a great natural leader into booking re-design presentations. Give a small floral arrangement to anyone willing to host a mini-redesign seminar or another floral seminar. Use your ability to teach and educate your clients and that in turn is going to make you an expert in their eyes and generate more referrals to sustain your business.

Whenever you can, build up the "perceived value" of each arrangement and then tell them their price will be X% off or that you're having a special *thank you* sale. I don't know a single woman who doesn't like a good bargain. Sometimes you have to create the "feeling" of a bargain. It's all about perceived value and perhaps contrasting your arrangements with the higher price a competitor would be sure to charge.

At the floral arrangement seminar, hand everyone a card with several notches to be specially punched or marked in some way by you. Every time they give you a referral, they get one step closer to a free floral arrangement. Every time they purchase an arrangement, or any other product or service you offer, they get another step closer to a free arrangement - or something else of value that doesn't cost you any thing to give away.

The point is that if you give away lots of tips and ideas and you are a generous person that has a quality product at a fair price and you help people feel they got a great bargain and value for their money, they will stay faithful to you and become an advertising ally bringing you even more business.

Advanced Redesign

Chapter 7
Offering Plants and Trees

Whether I was going on a re-design appointment or as a corporate art consultant, I always recognized the need for plants in the home or office and was prepared to offer a plant design service. You don't have to own a nursery or even know all that much about plants in order to add this product line to your list of services.

The reason is that you're not going to offer every kind of plant or variety to your clients. You just need to know which ones are the most popular, do the best job, and are attractive and easy to care for.

Offering Artificial Plants

If you're offering artificial plants, you want to have a good, quality source for your plants and you want to be able to buy them wholesale. I had a great gal about 30 minutes away from my office who had a beautiful showroom just for designers. The plants were affordable and of the highest quality. While the pricing on the plants was retail, I always knew that my price was half the listed price.

I could either go in person and pick out what I wanted or I could order custom plants and sizes in person or over the phone.

I always got my best pricing for large orders and ones that were repetitive. You'll not likely find much repetition in the residential market, but that is possible in the corporate market.

Only once did I have a client complain about a custom floral and my plant vendor was easy to deal with on getting the correction made. So choose a quality vendor who stands behind their product and you will fair very well.

My advice on artificial plants is that you try to stick to varieties that have small leaves, such as the ficus or maple. The larger the leaf, the more likelihood it will not look as real as you want. So take this advice for what you feel it is worth.

I also stuck to leaves that were dark green (a cool green) rather than warmer varieties that were more yellow in hue. The darker cool greens blend with any decor and you can't say that about the warmer greens.

Artificial plants are very easy to stick in your car or van and transport anywhere. Clients can see the effectiveness of the plant and what it will do for their home and they can see the quality also of what you would get for them. It's much easier for them to say "yes" when the plants are already on site and looking fabulous.

Artificial trees are the chosen option for those who live in limited space, or have no ability to take care of live plants but still long for a touch of green to relieve the hard edges of tables or desks, or hard flooring.

Artificial trees are increasingly being used in offices and homes, particularly since they are increasingly improving the life-like quality as I've mentioned earlier. I used to advise clients to purchase only small-leafed plants because they looked more real. While I still prefer small leaves, the larger ones are getting better all the time.

Of course, it's not just trees that you can market to clients. There are floor plants and table plants as well. I've dealt with custom floral plants in another chapter so I won't include them here.

If you want to branch out into the commercial market as well, another huge demand for artificial trees can be found in entertainment complexes like theatres or restaurants. Real trees can present real problems, however, such as insects or fungus, something that is particularly unwanted where people gather to eat.

Artificial trees mostly have ornamental value, though they can get pretty pricey for the top quality varieties and sizes. They now come in a variety of species.

I'm writing this on the brink of Christmas, so I'm particularly mindful of the popularity of synthetic pine trees, for use during Christmas. Some families prefer artificial trees because they can be reused the next year, they will not shed pine needles and even come pre-decorated in many stores. While I can appreciate the value of not having to spend $40-150 or more for a tree, I'm still personally partial to real Christmas trees, if for no other reason than the fragrance. But to each his own.

Artificial Christmas trees are durable and will last over the years. They are often made of plastics such as polyvinyl chloride.

The leaves of many artificial trees are made of silk and the cheaper varieties are often made of polyester. Sometimes, real plant materials are also used. The trunk could be made of fibreglass, but a natural bark would cover it. A quality tree or plant will have color gradation in the leaves and will not be too bright or a gaudy green.

Marketing artificial trees and plants is ideal because they are lighter and easier to transport. While buying one, however, keep in mind factors like: are the leaves are supple and soft, what are the colour variations and flexibility (how well does the plant react to shaping). It is also important to check whether it is fire retardant, because artificial trees can also catch fire, giving off potentially dangerous fumes - not to mention the damage to one's home and the safety of the inhabitants.

It would be almost impossible to plant a date or coconut palm tree in your client's living room or office. But an artificial one is available in various sizes and you don't need to be concerned about whether it will grow too big for your client to manage.

A common installation is the preserved palm. Preserved palms are entirely natural on the outside. The truck is hollow, except for a rod of steel or plastic, but the surface is made of organic materials like real fronds, real bark and real fragrance extracts, so that it looks completely life like. Naturally the prices are higher.

Most artificial trees are assembled products and come with a bucket or a pot that is filled with gravel to add to the aesthetic appeal. You'll want to add some dried moss on top and you can buy moss by the bag and it stores easily.

Maintenance for Artificial Plants

Artificial palm trees are increasingly becoming popular thanks to an almost natural look, easy maintenance and durability. Best of all, there is no need to water it, trim it, fertilize it or use sprays. Take them outside once a year and hose them down or use special sprays that promise to dissolve dust. One such spay is called **Artificial Flower Kleaner**. Be sure to test it first before using. If the color is not affected, use it on silk plants. You just spray. No need for wiping and it dries in seconds. It contains no fluorocarbons and is non-flammable, according to the label. The sprays do have a pretty strong odor, however, so be sure to use it outside or in a highly ventilated area. You can get some from *Klean Flower (714) 987-4994*. It is manufactured by SSG Can Corp, 1761 W. Hillsboro Blvd, Deerfield Beach, FL 33442.

Other Tips People Have Offered That You Can Try for Cleaning

- Try rice. Take a paper bag and place in it a cup or two of white rice (uncooked of course). Place the plant inside and shake. Give it a few good shakes and the rice will dust the plant off. This works great with wreaths and dried flower arrangements too. For the tree this may be harder, maybe you could do a section at a time.
- Take your silk plants outside, where you have an electrical outlet available (or use an extension cord) and take your blow dryer with you. Put the blow dryer on "low" speed and simply blow the dust away! If any dust remains, use one of the new 'Pledge' or 'Swiffer' cloths to gently wipe off the flowers and leaves.
- An older method is to again take your items outside and sprinkle them all over with cornmeal. Place a plastic bag over the item and turn them upside down, shaking them. The cornmeal works with a "scrubbing" effect to remove the dust from the flowers/leaves. When you turn the item upside down and shake, it is supposed to remove the dust by the scrubbing and also remove the cornmeal from the item.
- Fill your sink about 1/2 full with warm water and 2-3 tsp. of Dawn dish detergent. Take your silk flowers/plants and swish them in the sudsy water several times. Lay on a dishtowel to dry. This method will allow you to use the same silk flowers for years. They still look great so when you tire of one arrangement, just save the flowers to use later. They still look new even when they have been used in 2-4 arrangements over a period of about 8 years.
- Use a mild solution of dish washing soap (1/2 teaspoon or less) mixed with water in a 16 oz. spray bottle, and your garden hose with a showering nozzle. Pick a warm or hot day with a mild wind and move the silk plants and trees to the back patio or shaded area of the back yard. Clean them one at a time. Gently mist the plant or tree with the soap solution and then gently shower it with the garden hose until the dirt and soapy solution are removed. Most fragile silk plants come out looking like new. Don't expose them to sunlight. The warm breeze will dry the plants, trees, baskets or other containers in an hour or so.
- Put them in a plastic bag with a few tablespoons of salt and give them a shake. The dried arrangements do better if they have been gently sprayed with an acrylic coating previously (before they begin accumulating dust) so that they are more durable during this cleaning method. A little bit of salt does often stay even after shaking them out later but it shows up a lot less than the dust. Do be careful so as not to shake them right out of the setting!

- Your shower is the great source for cleaning silk plants and trees about once a month or so. There is no need for soap or any other household products. Just turn on your shower with a warm gentle spray and let it do the work. All the dirt and dust just rinses away and the "plants" look like new.

Wholesale Artificial Sources

I recommend you locate one or two good quality manufacturers and deal with them. Many have online catalogs and some also offer a printed catalog that you can order.

You'll find a beautiful 256 page offline catalog ($20) from http://www.autographfoliages.com. They even offer a 77 page Christmas catalog with very nice ideas for that season. These are great because there are no prices in the catalog at all. A separate price list is included so your client will not know your costs unless you choose to divulge that information.

Discounts are determined by the quantity you purchase (25% off for unit purchases, 35% off by the tray, 40% off by the case). They will even drop ship directly to your client for you. There is a $100 minimum order (after you take your discount). If you fall below the minimum, there is a $20 service charge, so try to always group your orders so you never fall below the minimum. Check out the rest of their terms yourself regarding returns, restocking charges, time limits and so forth.

You should pre-order your catalogs, including a credit application. Set up a 30-day net account. Place a test order for samples so you can test out their quality and speed of delivery. These can be samples that you take on appointments. It's your choice whether you want to sell your samples at appointments or not.

Their catalog is so nicely done and very professional it would be very difficult for any client who needs plants to refuse to get them from you - unless, of course, they have no budget.

A specific search on the internet will bring you lots of suppliers, but many are retailers only and might be some distance away from you. Then there's the issue of quality and service which you will need to investigate.

Here's another wholesaler you might check into using:
http://www.kinkadestudios.com/

With one good offline catalog, you can easily show your clients many different varieties. You can leave the catalog as is, with no prices showing, or you can place small stick-on labels right next to the item number and put your price on the label. Be sure to inform your client that all shipping/handling charges that you incur must be paid by them as well so there are no hidden charges.

Have your invoices made up or simply purchase some generic ones from your office supply store. When the client makes a selection, write in the Item Number, quantity, size, price and any other pertinent information.

Have the client sign your invoice as an approval, collect at least a 50% deposit if you are planning to ship to yourself and deliver later. If you are drop shipping the product, require the client to prepay the entire amount. You do not want to get stuck having product delivered without getting the full amount in advance.

Offering Live Plants

About 15 minutes from my office I was fortunate to have a company that wholesaled live plants and pottery and large containers. They sold their goods at the retail level too, but by going in and opening an account, I purchased all the plants I wanted at 50% off the retail.

Live plants are a little trickier and you need to know more about their hardiness and need for water and light, obviously. I found that varieties in the rubber plant family were very hardy, requiring little light and little water. A little more expensive, the Janet Craigii, a dark green leafed plant was one of the hardiest. Other good trees are the Dracaena Marginata, Warneckii, assorted Palms, the Dracaena, Corn Plant, the Spathiphyllum and the Schefflera. Bird of Paradise (left) is a very dramatic and colorful plant, say for on a table.

Unlike the artificial plants, I steered clear of ficus trees because they are very temperamental to light and heat. So my choice for plants that were alive consisted of dark green leaves exclusively. I found they could survive even with just florescent light and sporadic watering habits.

Questions to Ask Your Client

The ability of your client and their personal knowledge of plant care should serve as a good guide. You must ask the right kinds of questions so that your recommendations will survive. Here are a few suggestions:

- What experience have they had caring for live plants?
- Who will care for the plants?
- Will they hire a plant service?
- How often will they tend to the plants?
- What plants have they had success with in the past?
- What plants have they found difficult for them to care for?
- Where will the plants be placed?
- What are the light conditions for each?
- What kind of watering tools do they own?
- Are there small children or animals that will be near the area for extended periods of time?
- Do the plants need to provide camouflage?
- Does the client need slow growing plants?
- What heights are needed?
- What widths are needed?
- What kind of containers are preferable?
- Do they need any protective plastic containers?
- Do they like full trees or topiary?

With some smart questions, you should be able to find out sufficient information to go shopping on behalf of your client and bring them the best plants for their budget and ones that fulfill your design needs as well.

Recognize that you need to shop for interior plants, not exterior plants, unless you are working on their front or back exterior. Interior plants need less sun. So if you're having to purchase plants at an outdoor nursery, concentrate on the plants that are in the shaded area of the nursery, not the ones out getting full sun all day.

Examples of Some Excellent Choices

Plants do a world of wonders for any interior and most people do not have enough, if any at all. Often the ones they have are extremely small or totally unhealthy. You will do them a great service by adding a smart, affordable plant service to your list of resources.

Of course, you're free to choose whatever type of plant or tree you want, especially if an artificial one. But different parts of the country will have different plants that are preferred, in part because of weather, but also because of style. These are just a few of my "stand bys", the ones I can always count on, whether live or artificial.

Some are excellent for richness, color and texture. Some are great for their fullness; others for their light and airy qualities. Some are great because of the ability to spread them for utilitarian purposes. Whatever the case may be, plants add a wonderful, magical flair to decorating. No home or office should be without them.

Left: Palm
Right: Fern

Ficus (far left) – Schefflera (middle)

Marginata

Left: Spathiphyllum

Right: Corn Plant

Advanced Redesign

Chapter 8
Offering a Custom Art and Framing Service

Since most people do not have art, or it is usually pretty small and not very impressive, you could be a valuable resource for the perfect custom framed art images. You are already in their home for the re-design. What more perfect opportunity can you have?

Decisions for art for a room are best made right there in the room. By merely taking a few art catalogs with you to the appointment, you stand an excellent chance of adding a valuable service and product to enhance the interior and increase your profit margin.

First, let's discuss the art image itself. I'm not talking about originals. I am talking about fine art posters which are carried by wholesale publishers and displayed in their offline catalogs. These are images published and distributed by quality decorative distributors.

I'm not talking about the Aaron Brothers scenic posters that retail for $6.00 or the Walmart specials on extremely flimsy paper (Don't get me wrong. I shop at Walmart too, but not for art). Fine art posters are printed on a heavy-weight paper by the best printing houses in this country and abroad.

Good fine art images retail usually between $35-80+ each unframed, depending on size. While there are small images represented, the majority of these images are usually quite large, often 24x36 and larger. There are many beautiful images to choose from, with a great variety of topics, color palettes, styles and media.

Many of them come with a companion piece by the same artist. I recommend cropping the graphics off when having them framed. To the non-professional eye, these images can look as exquisite as originals, especially if they receive a quality framing treatment.

Typical Sizes of Fine Art Prints

Depending on size and framing choices, you can get a nicely framed poster/reproduction for around $200-250 framed. Oversized images (requiring mats that exceed 32x40) are more expensive due to needing an oversized mat and oversized glass, and the additional cost of the image itself. On really large images (double the size of standard images), you'll often need oversized plexi glass to keep the weight down and because a sheet of glass only comes as large as 40x60.

In a residence, a proper proportion to consider is 2:3 ratio. This means that the art on the horizontal measurement would cover about 2/3rds of the wall. A two thirds ratio feels good. The art is not too big for the wall nor too small. However, in a commercial setting, covering 2/3rds of the wall is not necessary and would be too much, unless the wall is a narrow panel. It can feel like too much, depending on how strong the image is in color and contrast.

The bottom line is, you want the art to feel comfortable: not crowding the wall; not feeling lost on the wall. If you just must have a certain image on a specific wall and it is going to be too small, then dramatically increase the mats and put a wider molding on it when framing it, and you might be able to increase it's outer dimension sufficiently to use it anyway. Conversely, if the image is a bit too large, have the framer crop some of the image off before it is framed. (Of course, you need to have an image which still looks beautiful even if a portion has been cropped so you need to be careful and not destroy the composition in the process.)

I divided images generally into 3 size categories.

- STANDARD SIZE = 32x40 or smaller (glass size)
- OVERSIZED SIZE = 40x60 (glass size) (over 40" on one side, automatically requires oversized glass even if the other side is under 40")
- DOUBLE SIZE = Anything over 40" on both sides, may require plexi glass, not only because of restrictions on glass sizes, but because of weight

---

These sizes and ranges are primarily based on the sizes of mat boards. The largest standard mat board comes 32x40 and has the broadest color selection. It is also the least expensive.

If the image requires a mat that exceeds 40 inches on one of its lengths, it will require an oversized mat board (at least for the top mat). An oversized mat board measures 40x60, therefore this is the largest size one can frame with a paper mat (without splicing the mat).

Fabric mats, or rather mats that are covered by fabric, can be just about any size but they increase the cost dramatically and you never want to use fabric mats on posters or reproductions as the quality of the art doesn't justify it. It makes no sense. If the image requires that the mat be larger in one direction than 60 inches, you would have to splice the mat or go to fabric.

As the sizes increase, the choice of glass becomes important due to the weight problem of extremely large images and the fact that glass does not come larger than 40x60 anyway. Standard glass sizes are also limited and images exceeding the 32x40 measurements require larger glass.

Plexi-glass is recommended for all images in the upper half of the Oversize Category, nearing the double size measurements. Not only does plexi glass weigh significantly less than regular glass, there are safety issues one should consider, especially in areas of the country that are earthquake prone like Southern California.

Making Art Recommendations for a Room

The wall is the negative space. What you place on the wall becomes the positive space. The negative space provides the eye with a place to rest, so to speak. Because of this, the negative space becomes almost as important as the positive space and the two need to work together to create the right feeling. This picture is a dramatic use of negative space. Notice how the shelf unit is placed below the center point of the wall vertically. Even with the art sitting on the shelf, the entire grouping is placed below the center point of the wall (vertically) which is a very pleasing placement and nicely done. Rhythm has been established with the repetition of art in a straight row. The grouping is asymmetrical with a strong center of interest on the left (two dark framed images), which sends the eye there first before moving elsewhere in either direction. Notice too that the focal point is not in the center of the grouping but left of center.

You should also note that dark and/or bright colors in an image can make it seem larger and more powerful. Strong colors or values in an image will create a lot of drama and contrast with the wall, therefore they can be smaller than pastel images and still carry the wall visually.

Most untrained buyers tend to underestimate the number of images necessary to make a room feel complete. I've found that homeowners seem to fall into two categories: people who have very sparse furniture and accessories; people who have way too much and who's homes look chaotic and messy.

They also tend to put images up that are too small for the wall and put them randomly everywhere, with no rhyme or reason.

Fear and doubt usually make people very conservative in their decorating. So in most cases, when you have made your decision on locations that need art, you will probably recommend more than your client thinks they need.

Generally speaking, all graphics should be cropped off by the framer when you are using fine art posters. Unless the graphics are an integral part of the image (where an artist places the title and/or signature well into the print), it is a good idea to eliminate the graphics during framing so that the picture looks more like original art. Some of the current posters are so beautifully printed it is next to impossible to tell a difference, even for the trained eye.

To sum up this section, design your client's room with plenty of size and a variety of sizes and formats. Hanging two or more together in a grouping is an excellent way of keeping good proportions between the negative space and the positive space and making the wall and placement design more interesting. In the end, if the art feels too heavy for the wall or lost on the wall, it should be moved to a different location where it will feel more appropriate.

Walls that have no furniture backed up to them will require larger images than those that have furniture, i.e. desks, chairs and tables, sofas, beds, chests, bureaus and so forth.

When hanging an image or two over furniture, you should return to the 2:3rds ratio. The width of the art should always be a shorter measurement than the width of the furniture, so that the furniture below the art feels supportive of what is above - like an anchor. (For instance, a piece of art over a sofa should be approximately 2/3rds the width of the sofa, as mentioned in an earlier chapter.)

If the width measurement of the framed art extends beyond the furniture, it will usually feel top heavy and this is not pleasing to the eye.

If there are several chairs placed side by side, with perhaps a table between, creating a very long horizontal line, the art should be a long horizontal image (or two verticals placed together giving the illusion of a horizontal format) to have the most pleasing effect.

Each wall being considered for decoration must be judged individually and a pre-determined decision made with regard to format, size and color. This plan will probably be altered some when the images are actually chosen, but you must constantly be aware of what the most appropriate size and format should be for any given wall.

I always make that decision for the client in advance. Then I say something like this when I show them in a catalog: "Mary, you need an image that is approximately 18x24 and it should be a vertical format to go over that chest. Look for something you like that has some red and gold in it." Naturally the size and colors would vary in your instructions according to what you have determined would be the right purchase for them.

I never discuss actual prices until after the images have been selected. You always want the client to be free of financial concerns. Let them fall in love with something in your catalog. Then you can look up the price of the print and add some kind of ball-park framing cost to it, including your mark-up, and give them a general idea of what to expect.

They won't be too likely to let it go once they have fallen in love with it and can begin to visualize how it will look in their home. You can sell it to them flat and your client can handle the framing of the print themselves with their own sources, or you can handle the framing for them.

Approximating the Finished Framed Size

To get to the appropriate framing size for any print, do the following.

When looking at the measurements of the image (not including any borders), add 10-12 inches each way, both horizontally and vertically, to the size of the image and then add twice the width of the frame molding to both measurements to get an approximate finished size for the framed art.

For example, if you choose an image measuring 22x30, and you design the two mats to be 3-1/2" wide, add 7 inches to the 22" measurement and 7 inches to the 30" measurement. The new measurement is now 29x37. To this add twice the width of your frame. Let's say the frame is 2" wide. Add 4" to the 29" side and 4" to the 37" side to get the outer dimensions. Your new measurement is 33" x 41". The glass and mat size will be approximately 29x37, but the outer dimensions including the frame will be 33x41 This is a standard sized image because the mat size on the longest side does not exceed 40" (standard mat size is 32x40).

By adding 3 ½" to each side (totaling 7") you will have approximately a 3" top mat showing and a ¼" under mat showing (if double matted). The under mat is the mat on the bottom next to the image and is called a filet. Usually the filet is ¼" in width for a 3" mat, but this varies with taste and budget. Most standard size images should have a 3" mat while oversized images feel good with 4-5" mats and larger, with wider frame profiles (molding) to visually support the image.

Framing costs for posters and reproductions are based on the size of the glass and the frame (molding) chosen, the number of mats and any fancy framing treatments. Smaller moldings tend to be less expensive, although there is a wide range of prices based on size, quality, color, stain, decorative elements, width and depth and types of wood or metal. Other factors that affect price are quantities, manufacturer, discontinued runs, over-runs and so forth.

All of these factors will need to be considered when formulating a budget that will give your client the most coverage and quality for the money. Remember, if you shave the size to save the cost, you will most likely be unhappy with the final result, because you may find the art simply looks and feels too small for the wall. I repeat, the tendency for the inexperienced consultant is to underestimate the needs of a room and underestimate the size needed to carry each wall. Great care needs to be taken to ensure the proper size is selected for each location.

Other Tips for Framing Art

Never make your top mat the same width as the frame. This will not feel right. I would advise making the mat a full inch wider, at least, than the width of the frame for the optimum feeling.

Some easy mat/frame ratios are:

1. 1/4 inch bottom mat, 3-1/4 inches for top mat, 2 inches for frame.
2. 1/2 inch bottom mat, 4-1/2 inches for top mat, 2-1/2 inches for frame.
3. 1 inch bottom mat, 1/2 inch middle mat, 5 inches top mat, 3 inch frame (triple mats).
4. And so forth.

Pick mats that compliment the image and that don't overpower it. You want the attention to go to the artist's image, not to what you put around it. The mats and frame are supposed to be "supportive" of the image and not detract from it. So choose carefully.

Bright mat colors are dangerous. So are very dark colors and very bright pastels. Unless the art proposal is a high-tech, very modern style, you are safest with soft, muted colors, especially for the top mat. A soft white is generally better than a bright white, which can be too glaring. I always look for some soft color in the background of the image to key into for my top mat choice. Then I look for some other darker colors in the image to guide me in my choice of filets. Then I usually look to the room for guidance in my frame choice. If the room has all dark wood furniture throughout, I'll look for a frame that repeats that dark wood.

If the image is a traditional image, pick a traditional frame or a transitional one for a more contemporary treatment. Traditional frames are usually more ornate and made of wood. They could be a warm wood, a gold leaf or gold paint, but they are typically wood with a design of some sort. It could be a moderate design or extremely fancy.

If the image is contemporary, consider a contemporary frame. Contemporary frames are more sleek and plain, wood or metal. They will rarely have any design at all. If they do have an element of design, it will tend to be straight lines and simply done.

If the image is very modern, high tech, consider a minimalist frame or no frame. A minimalist frame would be very narrow - sleek and hardly there - or perhaps the image will be wrapped around a stretcher bar or dry mounted to a flat surface and no frame is attached at all. Whatever the style of the frame, make sure that the color is appropriate to the colors in the image, the mats and the room. You don't want any part of the framed elements to clash.

Tips on Hanging Art

Art should be hung at eye level. But eye level is different for everyone. So the generally accepted median height is considered 5'6". People, whose heights are at either extreme, will need to look up at the art or down on it. Hang it at a height that is appropriate for a 5'6" person's eye level. But beware. While the image pictured is hung at eye level, there could be a huge gap between the base of the art and the top of a chest, for instance. If so the eye is drawn to the gap more than to the artwork. Correct this by placing tall books and a plant or two on the chest. For the most complete training on hanging art, get a copy of my ebook, **The Secret Art of Hanging Art** unless you already bought **Rearrange It** (where it comes as a free bonus). See last chapter for details.

Men generally have a higher eye level than women. And there is a wide range within each gender as well. So you need to place the art at the eye level for the majority of viewers.

Most walls are 8' high typically (unless you have a cathedral wall or newer construction). That means the eye level for someone 6'4" is above the typical focal point on an image, whether horizontally or vertically formatted. The focal point of an image (that point where your eye is drawn to first) can affect the placement of the image. If the focal point is in the bottom half of the image, it will be placed below eye level. If it is in the upper half of the image, it will probably be at or near eye level. A horizontally formatted image will generally be hung higher than a vertically formatted image. This is assuming the art is not hung over furniture, in which case the base of the art should be about a hand span above the top on the furniture.

Walls that have no furniture are called "walk by walls". They usually require larger images to carry the wall or more than one image. The distance from the ceiling or floor is going to depend on the size of the framed image. There is no specific rule to follow because art comes in all different sizes and two different formats. And the width of the wall might have an impact on placement.

But for purposes of some general guideline, a fairly large vertical image would probably be placed with the bottom edge approximately 3 feet from the floor. If the image is 36-40" high, the top of the piece would be about 1-1/2 feet from the ceiling of an 8' wall. Naturally, if the image exceeds 40" in height, the bottom would fall lower than 36" from the floor. In general, there will always be more space at the bottom below the picture than at the top. The art then will hang mostly in the upper half of the wall, not the lower half.

The mistake novices most often make is hanging the art too high, however. The closer the art gets to the ceiling, the more it draws your attention to the ceiling and, therefore, out of the room. This is not where you want to draw the eye. Extremely tall people naturally want to hang the art higher, but this is inappropriate. Again, we are somewhat dealing with a 2:3 ratio. Two feet of wall above the picture and three feet of wall below it. Not a bad place for a picture measuring 3 feet high.

Again, the artist's placement of the focal point might necessitate some sort of adjustments. Sometimes you can hang several pictures of the same size at the same height and one might not feel as good as the others. This phenomenon happens when the focal point of one image is extremely low or high, causing you to feel you need to compensate by adjusting the height up or down.

Dark or bright pictures might need to be placed a little higher. The reason for this is because they feel "weightier". The heavier a picture "feels", the more it will seem to be pulling downward. Therefore they might feel better an inch or two higher on the wall.

This is especially an important consideration when hanging art over furniture, in particularly over a sofa or chairs. Whenever there is an object of any kind situated below the art, the art will need to be hung close to it. Usually this means it will need to be hung lower on the wall than you would if it was a "walk-by" wall. Generally speaking, you need a hand span of distance between the base of the art and the furniture or object below it. It is important that the art be viewed as a part of the "grouping" that is formed by the furniture and art together. Too much distance between the various elements of the grouping will cause it to look disjointed. It needs to be seen as a "unit".

If there is too much space between, the art will have a tendency to draw your attention, once again, to the ceiling. You will psychologically feel uneasy and your eye will be drawn to the space between them, rather than to the art or the furniture. So be sure to keep them fairly close together. But remember, dark art or very bright, colorful art needs to be hung further from the furniture than softer tones and values. If you hang dark or bright art too close to the furniture, it will feel as if it is starting to fall down behind the furniture when you stand away from it. Give it a little more "breathing room".

For art in general, a general rule of thumb for distance above the furniture would be about 4-6" of space. However, there are people who are concerned about hanging art over seating arrangements. When the art is hung within 4-6" of the top of the seating, depending on the depth of the back of the chair or sofa, a person might bump the art with the back of their head.

Therefore, before hanging the art, sit in the chair or on the sofa. Move about freely. Get a feel for how close your head comes to the wall. If your client is concerned, cheat a little bit and hang the art higher than normal to eliminate concern. But know that most seating, plus the natural posture of people when seated, will prevent anyone from bumping their heads on the art. When people see there is art, they are generally more apt to sit forward in the seat. It's a natural, unconscious reaction. Remember, the depth of the back of most sofas and chairs is sufficient for this so it is rarely a problem.

Chair rails are handy in an office or home to keep the chairs away from the wall. If there is a chair rail, the art should be hung 4-6" above the chair rail rather than the chair or sofa. Most chair rails seem to be placed above the backs of furniture and are more decorative than functional at this point in time, but they are common and might be in any given space you run across.

To sum it up, make sure when you stand back and gaze at the art, that it is hung in such a way where it will not pull your eye up to the ceiling.

Ordering From Publishers and Galleries

Once you and your client have arrived at the final selections of art, your next task is to finalize the sources you will use to order the art. Always have your client's second choice for art noted just in case the first choice is out of print. If you have not already set up a credit account with the major publishing distributors, you will have to pay by company check or credit card at the time you place the order. This is fine if you have collected a deposit for 50%. I'm going to give you a list of the top art publishing companies that you should definitely have accounts with, but then I'm also going to tell you about an alternate way of getting your images, which I recommend on very small orders, or orders that need multiple sources or have a high volume of images involved.

First of all, let me explain how the distributing publishers normally process an order. Each of them publishes a catalog and price list that covers their inventory. Each art image in the catalog is assigned a code number. Most will indicate the artist's last name, the title of the print, the paper size and the image size. Some have started putting a letter code near the other code. The letter code stands for a specific retail price. This gives the publisher the ability to change the pricing for a particular code without having to change the catalog. They just change the price code sheet.

Other publishers print out an official price list, which could be a few pages stapled together or a small booklet. The catalogs come either as a hard bound book, as loose leaf pages with 3-hole punching so you can put in a binder that they supply, or as stapled tear sheets (with or without hole punching). Most are 8-1/2x11 but some are larger and odd sizes. There's no consistency at all.

Regardless of how they package their catalog and price lists, they usually have a minimum purchase requirement. A few do not; most do. If you place an order that falls below their minimum, they will tack on a penalty charge, which usually is somewhere between $5-7.50. Minimums are usually $50 and over. Some base it on a minimum retail total; others on a minimum wholesale total.

To the price of the art you order, they will add the shipping and handling charges. Some have a shipping charge already printed in their price list which is based on the number of images they can reasonably fit into a shipping tube. So whether you order one image or 16, you may pay the same shipping charge if it is a flat rate. This can be good at times and bad at other times, depending on the quantity you are ordering. For others, you will have to ask the salesperson, at the time you place the order, for the actual shipping charges.

ORDERING DIRECT VS USING A MIDDLEMAN VOLUME PURCHASER
There are several advantages to ordering direct from each publisher who has images you have selected for your project. For one thing, you find out immediately if a particular image is out of stock or discontinued. Then you can, hopefully, make a substitution right over the phone.

Another benefit is that you will get your images shipped either the same day or the next day and there is no faster way to get them than buying direct. The other benefit is that you can take advantage of any special pricing that might be available and many publishers will send you free supplements to their catalogs as long as you remain an active client. Additionally, if the publisher is offering you a credit on your first order equal to the price of the catalog, this will be the time to ask for your credit. You have to ask for it because they don't have a system in place to give it to you automatically.

The only disadvantage, really, in buying direct is the penalties for ordering under the minimum, and the increased shipping costs incurred from several publishers. However, when there is a way to avoid some of those costs. How do you do that? Well, there are a few companies that specialize in volume ordering. This is helpful if you are a corporate art consultant or doing several re-designs at one time and in need of several images.

Rather than making 4 calls to 4 different publishers, you make one call to a volume purchaser (contact information later). You tell them the name of the various publishers from which you need art and the appropriate code numbers. They take your order and add it to other orders they are processing. This way, if you only needed one or two images from a particular publisher and the total is below their minimum, you would not be charged a penalty because your order, coupled with their other orders, would exceed the minimum purchase.

Another advantage to ordering this way is that you get one shipping charge from the volume purchaser which is always going to be less than the sum of 4 separate shipping charges you would incur if you were ordering directly from each publisher. And another terrific benefit is that if your order is a pretty substantial one, you'll get additional volume discounts on the whole order you would not get if you were ordering directly from each publisher in smaller quantities.

But the disadvantage of this method is that it will take <u>longer</u> for all of the images to come in. Let's say you are located on the West Coast as I am. Let's say your volume purchaser (a middleman) is located on the East Coast, where one of the best publishers is located. Now let's say that two of the publishers you need art from are located on the West Coast as well. Placing your volume order through the East Coast middleman means that the art will be shipped from the West Coast suppliers to the East Coast, whereupon it will be gathered up and resent to you on the West Coast from that middleman.

In order to avoid excessive freight charges and "under-the-minimum" penalties, your images will have traveled from one side of the US to the other side and back again before getting to you. There is twice the risk of them getting damaged in the process. And, instead of getting the art from your West Coast publishers in a couple of days, it takes anywhere from 10-14 days for your order to come in. Well, if you've got plenty of time to get it then the savings on freight, discounts and penalties on large orders is well worth the wait and the extra risk. So you have to weigh the advantages against the disadvantages and decide the best course for each order.

A few other disadvantages of using a middleman are these. You won't know instantly if your publisher has all of the images you are ordering. The middleman company is supposed to notify you of shortages, but forget it. They just aren't very good about doing that. To their credit, however, they will try multiple sources to fill your order if your top choice doesn't have a particular image. They just aren't very good about letting you know if they can't get something at all. Then it's really aggravating to discover something is permanently unavailable after waiting 2 weeks for the whole order to arrive. In addition to that, sometimes 90% of the images will come in, with stragglers on back order. You waited all that time, and still don't have everything you need. The larger the order, the greater chance a few of the images will be on back order.

So be careful what you choose. Some clients get really annoyed if you take too long to deliver their product and the last thing you want is an annoyed client. Generally speaking, once they make the choice, they want it NOW!

So unless the order is really huge and you can get additional discounts, you might be better off with a volume purchaser acting as a middleman on your behalf. If I encounter fees ordering directly from the publisher, I pass the shipping and penalty charges along to my client, so it's not like I'm paying those charges myself. If the publisher is local to me (by that I mean within my own state), I order the images to be sent by UPS ground. However, if the publisher resides in a different state, I order the images to be sent Blue Label (which means I'll get the order in two business days).

Take note of the day of the week you are placing the order. If it is Thursday, you might as well have the order sent by ground and take advantage of the two day weekend. But if I'm ordering on a Monday or Tuesday, I'm going to request Blue Label every time. Don't order overnight. It's a complete waste of additional money for your client to pay.

No matter which method you choose to use, once you know the exact images you need, decide which publisher you will order from and make a list of all the images you need from that publisher. If you have multiple projects at the same time, try to group them and piggyback the smaller orders to the larger ones. This might help you get some volume discounts you wouldn't get if you placed the orders separately and it will definitely help you avoid "under-the-minimum" penalties.

Then call your orders in using the free 800 numbers most publishers offer. At the time you place the order, have the order taker read to you the title of the image so that you are sure there is no mistake and that you are getting the one you want. At the conclusion, before you hang up, have the person read back all of the code numbers to make sure they entered the right ones into their system. Then be sure to ask if all of the images are currently available.

Tell them how you want the images sent, whether by UPS ground or Blue Label. Then mark the date you placed the order on your paperwork and enter the Publisher's name on your Control Form. The order taker can give you the total of the artwork and the shipping charges right over the phone, so you can list that information on your Control Form. You'll want to check these figures against the actual invoice when it arrives in a few days. When placing a volume order, it's best to FAX over an official copy of the code numbers you want so that you eliminate errors. Just make sure you have typed it correctly.

The Top Decorative Art Publishers

Here are the top decorative art publishers that I use. These are the best, in my opinion, in terms of quantity and quality. There are, of course, many, many others you can explore. While popularity of images will differ depending on your country and your part of the country, in California the typical image at this writing that is popular is contemporary and impressionistic. Residentially, popular subject matters include: floral, country prints, landscapes, boating, seascapes, garden scenes, architectural scenes, sports (mainly golf), inspirational, scenic photographs, Asian, animals.

Here are some of the major publishers I favor; you may of course choose your own for your locale. I'm providing you with just their name and phone number and city because email addresses and websites change or are not available. But their toll free phone numbers and location rarely change and hopefully all of these will still be current for a long time to come.

- Winn Devon (800) 875-4150 Seattle, WA
- Bruce McGaw Graphics (800) 221-4813 W Nyack, NY
- Canadian Art Prints (800) 663-1166 Richmond, BC, Canada
- Editions Limited (800) 228-0928 San Francisco, CA
- Image Conscious (800) 532-2333 San Francisco, CA
- New York Graphic Society (800) 677-6947 New York, NY
- Top Art (858) 554-0102 San Diego, CA
- Gango Editions (800) 852-3662, Portland, OR
- Graphique de France (800) 444-1464 Woburn, MA
- Haddad's Fine Arts (800) 942-3323 Anaheim, CA
- Aaron Ashley, (888) 727-4539, New York, NY
- Wild Apple Graphics, (800) 756-8359 Woodstock, VT
- Bentley House, 800 227-1666, Walnut Creek, CA
- Image Source International, (800) 877-8510 Pembroke, MA
- Modern Art Editions, (800) 331-3749 New York, NY
- Joan Cawley (Southwest Art), (800) 835-0075
- Leslie Levy Fine Art, (800) 527-7502 Scottsdale, AZ
- Poems, (888) 447-6367 Salt Lake City, UT
- Galaxy of Graphics, (888) 464-7500 New York, NY
- Romm Art Creations, (800) 553-8466 Bridgehampton, NY
- Sagebrush Fine Art, (800) 643-7243 Salt Lake City, UT

- Mitchell Beja, (800) 847-4061 Manalapan, NJ
- Dina Art Company, (800) 635-3523 Hollywood, CA
- Schiftan, Inc., (800) 255-5004 Morrisville, PA
- Things Graphics (Afro-American), (800) 753-1990 Washington, DC

For volume purchases and to combine your purchases into just **one shipping charge (avoiding all minimum requirements)**, I recommend:

- Lieberman's Gallery (800) 221-1032 - Email: lieberman@liebermans.net Their website is http://www.liebermans.net. You can search their listings online for free and have them send you a free catalog that lists the various top publishers and what they carry. It takes longer to get your prints from Lieberman's, but you can get everything from one source with one shipping charge and you avoid the minimum purchase requirements that most publishers tack on. So if your clients are NOT in a mad rush, combine all your orders into one and save the extra shipping costs (and penalties) from multiple sources by getting your prints from one place.

There are many other publishers as well, some large and some small, but the above list will give you plenty of choices to fulfill most projects. To see an excellent summary of available catalogs from the widest selection of publishers, call Lieberman's Gallery at the number above and ask them to send you their booklet of catalog publishers. It's free. You can then order all of the catalogs you want directly through Lieberman's or call the companies directly and order the catalogs you want that way. I advise the latter approach because then you'll get any discount coupons available coming directly to you and you'll get the catalogs sooner. You can ask them to send you a credit application at the same time so that you can get your accounts established and order your images in the future on a 30-day net account.

Trade Discounts

Trade discounts are typically 50% off the suggested retail price. You can get additional discounts of between 10-25% off of the wholesale price for volume orders. These discounts vary from one publisher to another, but the initial 50% off discount is standard. Don't accept less. Some publishers like Image Conscious will also give an additional discount on all images they personally publish.

Presentation Sleeves

Presentation sleeves, sometimes called print protectors, are large plastic sleeves that usually are placed in art bins. These are important to have for when you are transporting flat images of any kind from one place to another. They come in various sizes for small, medium and very large art work. The more expensive ones have acid free heavy stock inside them for durability and stiffness. The acid free stock will not cause fine art paper, which is also acid free, to yellow. It is important to store original art in an acid free location. But I wouldn't worry about whether my protectors were acid free if I'm just placing a poster or reproduction in one.

It's a good idea to have a small supply of print protectors that will accept images up to 30x40 inches and some really large ones that will handle 40x60 sheets. If you don't put your images in some kind of protection, they are likely to get dog-eared, torn, dented or ruined in some manner and then you can't sell them to any client. So it's a good investment to purchase some sleeves.

You can do a search on the internet for presentation sleeves or print protectors. There are many companies that make them and you'll want to order from one close to you.

Art Bins

Art bins are also very useful to place your presentation sleeves in while you have art stored in them. You won't need an art bin unless you really get into the business of providing art to clients and you have a supply of art in your office or home for any length of time.

You don't want the sleeves to bend over and get damaged and you want to keep them together for optimum protection and order. Art bins are those V-shaped metal or wooden stands that you see in every art gallery. Again, check online for bin manufacturers that are close to you to cut down on shipping charges. You can always find ads in Decor Magazine for both print protectors and bins and you can get them from the same companies that offer sleeves.

Measuring an Image

Lay the image on a flat surface. Take a metal measuring tape and place the mark at "0" at the edge of one side of the image. Measure across the image to the other side and then add to that double the measurement of the width of the top mat and double the width of any under mats that will be showing. Mark down the measurement. Let's say you've just measured the longest side of a horizontally formatted landscape and the image is 36" wide and you wish to add 3-1/4" of top mat and 1/4" of bottom mat. The width of the mats totals 3-1/2" on each side, or 7" altogether. You add 7" to the 36" measurement to get the glass measurement. So 36" + 7" = 43" (you will need an oversized top mat) as you have exceeded the 40" limit.

Next you measure the height of the landscape, which let's say is 24". You will end up with 24" + 7" = 31" for the glass measurement. So now you mark on your paperwork that the finished framed image should be 31"x43" (the glass size) and you have chosen an oversized mat for on top (at least). However, always bear in mind that the glass measurement does not account for the width of the frame. You never use the width of the frame in your measurements for the framer, but it is a consideration you must always think of as a re-designer, particularly on narrow wall panels or over furniture.

I realize I may be repeating myself, but I want to make sure I have thoroughly covered this portion to ensure you don't make miscalculations that cost you extra money. If you have chosen a 2" frame for your subject, 1/4" of the frame width will overlap the mats. However, 1-3/4" on each side (top, bottom and both sides) will increase the overall size of the finished piece. So that 31x43 measurement above would now increase by 3.5" each way. The outside dimensions of the framed piece would actually be 34-1/2" x 46-1/2". If you have an absolute maximum size the finished piece can be, you need to always remember to account for the width of the frame you plan to use when designing and specifying any image. But you'll find out that this only becomes an issue on very narrow walls or for images that will be hung over furniture where you do not want the frame to be wider than the furniture beneath it.

Principles of Choosing Mats for Artwork

It used to be that a 3" top mat was the standard width for framing an image, but at this writing the trend is to make the mats wider, more generous. It is a good trend. It really makes the artwork feel more important and enhances it all the way around - that is, assuming the color for the mats are appropriate for the image. The last thing a designer of art should do is select mat colors based solely on the room and not on the colors in the image. I have often seen interior designers and consumers choose a garishly bright or dark mat for a work of art that so overpowers the image all of the attention goes to what is around the image rather than to the image itself. The mats and frame selections should be subdued and merely supportive to the art image. They should not compete with the image for attention.

As stated earlier, my mat selections are always soft, muted colors pulled generally from the background colors in the image. When no one color stands out as being appropriate, or my mat colors just don't blend appropriately with colors in the image, then I select a soft white or soft silver/gray, a neutral color for the top mat. The under mats (filets) can be stronger colors, pulled from colors in the foreground of the image, but the top mat (which is the most important one because it shows the most) should be subdued in color and value and intensity. It should never, never dominate the image.

Having said that, a re-designer's job is to select the appropriate mats on behalf of the client. In most cases, all of my framed images are double matted, some triple matted. I rarely use only one mat and almost never do a straight fit. A straight fit is where you only frame the image and use no mats whatsoever. Try to always create and agree on a budget that is sufficient enough to allow you to double mat every image in the art proposal.

Selecting Mat Colors and Using Fan Decks

Color Key I is the cool side of the spectrum, going from bright white to cool black. All of the colors in this key have blue undertones. Look at the image on the left.

Color Key II is the warm side of the spectrum. All of the colors have yellow undertones, so the whites are warm whites (off white) and even the blacks are warmer. Look at the image on the right. You should be able to tell that the colors in the right image are warmer than those in the left image below.

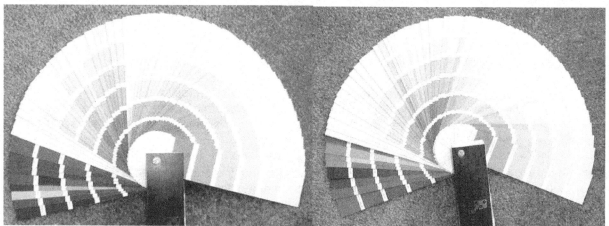

I've already discussed mat colors to some degree but let me just say this one thing here. Mat colors are, just like paint, divided into two Color Keys as already discussed at some length in **Rearrange It**. Attention to which Color Key is dominate in the room and the art image is important. Colors are definitely affected by the colors next to them and will literally "change" before your eyes based on the surrounding colors.

Lighting also makes a huge difference in the way colors appear. They will appear to be one color in incandescent or natural light, found in your client's home, but will look altogether different under fluorescent lighting found in many kitchens, offices or stores. or So when you are selecting the mat colors for your images, be sure to check them under incandescent or natural light rather than fluorescent lights. The work will be ultimately hung in an home with incandescent lighting (most likely) and you want the colors to blend perfectly with the art (kitchens excepted).

Whenever I selected mats at home, I always double check them against the florescent or incandescent lighting in my kitchen or other room before I write the numbers on my paperwork, making sure that the lighting I use to choose mats is the same lighting in my client's room where the art will hang. Some colors are affected more than others. But the last thing you want to have to do is bring an image back to framing and have it redone because the mat colors didn't look right in the client's home. This is not only time consuming and costly, but it definitely tells the client that you don't know what you're doing. So be careful. And when in doubt, choose colors that are safe. Whites are always safe. Maybe it's a little boring, but certainly safe.

Selecting the Molding

While the art images and the colors within the images will vary from one piece to the next, there needs to be one element in the whole program that is constant. Something must unify the whole program. Unity is gained by having repetition in an area that is subliminally noticed. The perfect unifying factor to your design is the molding or frame choice. So whenever possible, use the same frame on all pieces.

I don't necessarily mean the exact same frame, but use the same color. It can be the same frame, just a wider version, for the images in the more important locations. Or it can be a different profile that has the same coloring. But the importance is to use the frame as the unifying factor. Not only does this enhance the "flow" and continuity of the home, but it makes it easy in the future for the client to move images about to other locations in the home or to be very flexible in future homes they might have.

Using the same frame (or similar frames) for all or most of the pieces in the room also streamlines your paperwork and reduces the chances of framing errors.

Getting Molding Samples

It's a good idea to get your framer to give you samples of frame corners that you feel you will most likely use on a regular basis. My framer built me a framed board lined with velcro, with a handle at the top, and we chose about 50 contemporary frames with good price points for my samples. Velcro was added to the back of the frame pieces and I hung them on this board.

When I would make my presentation, I would take a few frame samples with me, just in case the client wanted to know how I was going to frame the images. I generally **never** let my client choose any mats or frames. And they generally never even asked to be involved other than to ask general questions. When you exude confidence as a re-designer, there is pretty much a silent acknowledgment that you are the expert and you will bring them a quality finished product without their involvement. Believe me, you don't want them involved in designing the art if you can help it.

In California I generally used contemporary frame profiles, but you'll have to judge the trends and tastes in your part of the country and choose your samples accordingly. Try to keep the choices on the lower end of the scale. I would never consider putting $1000 worth of framing on a poster or reproduction. The frames I choose generally price out between $150-200 each for standard sized images (including the art poster), between $200-325 for oversized images, and between $300-550 for double sized images. Currently the retail prices for the unframed images at this writing is around $40 for standard, $50-60 for oversized and about $80 for double sized images. So you can see that most of the value for this type of framed image is in the framing. That reverses as you move into limited editions, giclees (digital prints) and one of a kind original art.

Specifying the Design of Each Image

Most images have straight edges and in most cases you will design the mats to overlap the image a bit all the way around. But occasionally you'll run across an image that is printed with a deckled edge. The term "deckled edge" comes from handmade paper that has a ragged (deckled) edge. Deckling was and still is a natural part of handmade paper and is considered part of the art form. So there are times when the publishers allow the deckled edge from the original to be printed on the poster. Whenever I run across a deckled edge on the image, I never cover it with the mats. I always design my mats so that the ragged edge, still shows. Here the image is floated on top of the mat to preserve the deckled edge.

Sometimes I'll decide, based on the nature of an image, to create a deckled edge myself and float the image on a background mat for a different effect. The way you create a deckled image is to lay the image on a flat surface like a table, with the edge of the image just barely hanging over. Pull the border of the image down and away, gently and carefully tearing the border off. In the process of tearing you will created a small deckled edge on the remaining portion. Then have framing "float" the torn image on the under mat. Bring a top mat in just far enough to allow the torn, ragged edges of the print to show or simply frame the "deckled" edge image you created on the background mat and leave it at that. It's a great look, particularly for contemporary works.

Adding Fancy Treatments

The framer I use offers me v-grooves and French Cuts at no additional charge. But many framers charge extra for any extra element you would specify. While I don't want to overly use these "gifts", I will add these kinds of fancy treatments as I feel necessary. It is never something I promise to do for a client. I just throw them in as a "bonus" using my own sense of design. My framer will also allow me to use triple mats at the same price as double mats, so I do so only on important locations to dress them up more than the rest of the body of art.

A v-groove is where a beveled cut is made in the top mat, exposing some of the inner core of the mat which is a different color. A V-groove can essentially add an additional border around the image. I'll use V-grooves mostly to cut down on the width of the top mat if I have had to really add an extra amount of width to "build out" the size of a particular image that would be too small for the location otherwise. I don't want to see 8-10" of mat on these types of pieces, so I'll break up that width by adding one or two v-grooves at different intervals. When you do this, be sure to leave at least 3" of width between the frame and the first v-groove, however, as you want to keep the look of a generous top mat.

V-grooves are a simple treatment and don't draw much attention and are very useful for dividing space and adding a little extra value without adding extra cost. The other fancy treatment I can give without increasing the cost is a French Cut. A French Cut is where you cut all the way through the top mat and expose 1/8" to 1/4" of the bottom mat color. French Cuts add an even stronger additional border if they run parallel to the sides of the art image because they are wider and a contrasting mat color shows through rather than the soft grey of the inner core of a v-groove. I especially like to use a French Cut perpendicular to the sides of the image, which I'll explain next.

French Cuts can also be used as a break point in a mat. For instance, let's say I'm matting an oversized image or a double sized image and the mat color I need for on top just isn't large enough and the budget is tight and won't allow me to use a fabric covered mat. Let's say my problem measurement is the image's height. I can measure 1/3rd the way down from the top of the glass and add a horizontal French Cut in the mat on each side. This way I can use parts of two different mats in the same color and sort of "splice" the top mat so that I can use the color I really want. The French Cut (or splicing cut) looks decorative because of the color from the bottom mat showing through. Here in this photo is an example of a French Cut used on all four sides to accommodate this oversized image with a mat color that was only available in a standard size.

Submitting the Order to Framing

Once all of the images are in-house, you have carefully measured each one, you have selected the mats and designated their widths, you have specified the frame, and you have noted any special instructions regarding how you want each framed, you're ready to fill out the Framer's Form. Just transfer the information the form asks you to give. Then keep a copy for your records. Roll up the images, placing the smaller ones on top before you roll them up. Either put the images in a large tube for protection (or place them flat in a sleeve) while transporting to the frame shop. Your framer might even give or loan you some sleeves for that purpose. Place the paperwork for the framer with each tube if there is more than one. Submit the images and the Framer's Form to your framer or your framing department.

Methods of Delivery

By the time you submit the images to framing, you should have decided how you will deliver the framed art to the client. If you have a van, consider delivering them yourself, for a fee of course. If you don't have a van, perhaps your framer does and might be willing to deliver the framed art for you for a fee. If your framer can't deliver them and you can't do it, then you'll have to hire a professional moving company to do it for you. Whatever you do, you want to make sure that whoever is transporting the body of art has appropriate liability insurance. Unless you or another party has auto insurance for a business, the artwork will not be covered in the event there is an accident and anything is damaged or destroyed. You must have coverage *for a business* if you want to be fully protected. Be sure to add a fee to the invoice to cover any delivery charges.

Starting a Picture Framing Business From Your Home

This business can be started and operated within the comforts of home surroundings. You can start on a sturdy table or solid work bench in a small storage area, such as your garage, shed or basement; even a small room can be devoted toward this purpose.

If you are handy with tools you could be on your way to a nice sideline business that will enhance your redesign business that could grow with time. Many wood moldings can be bought at reasonable cost from lumber yards and can be used as the basic product for manufacturing frames. Everyone has photos and prized possessions which need framing. Many people don't like the plastic frames found in stores today, thus creating a ready market for beautiful, natural wood frames.

Quite often you can find old, beautiful, rugged picture frames at rummage or garage sales. They can be repaired and cut down to today's standards. Good frames can add substantially to the value of art, paintings, posters, certificates, etc. The list is endless. No matter where you live you can start a picture framing business if you're really enterprising. To some it can be an exciting and fascinating trade. I always preferred to job the framing out and concentrate my time and talents on the creative end solely.

However, with just a little experience and proper tools you can also learn to cut your own mats and glass for the frames. I do have my own mat cutter, however, which is very handy for small pieces and making corrections or for personal use.

Your local library may be a great source of information on the subject as I am not going to get into any serious detail on this aspect here. Also, in the various mail order magazines you will find firms that offer free information on custom picture framing.

Check out your local variety stores and others that handle picture frames and get ideas from what they have to offer. There are many variations and you may be able to dream up different and better designs.

Necessary equipment and supplies will include (but not be limited to): a mat cutter, a glass cutter, an electrical saw, a large staple gun, double sided tape, a vacuum mounting machine, large table, good lights, foam core boards, mat boards of various colors, mat cutting blades, and large paper by the roll, tubes and boxes, wire and hardware for the frames, and a selection of molding choices - just for starters.

A Bit About Forms

THE CONTROL FORM
The Control Form is a very efficient and highly effective form that will stay with the project from beginning to end. I rely on this form to have all of the pertinent contact information for the client, any and all appointment dates and times. It will also be the form I use to track my sources for product and services that I will need on the job. This is very important.

Your vendors are very important to your business. Without them you are out of business. So you want to make sure you have listed every one of them on your control form. As soon as their invoice arrives for what you have ordered, you will enter the totals on your control form and track receipts of their invoice and payment of such.

The Control Form will also list the total amount you have charged your client and the breakdown so that you can easily enter it into your bookkeeping records for tax purposes. Whether you use a Control Form like mine or not, be sure to have one and use it religiously because it will eliminate a host of errors and confusion that you might encounter, particularly on extremely large projects that may include several and other products and, perhaps, a dozen or more vendors.

The Control Form has all the pertinent information on it such as the following:

- Client's Name
- Date
- Purchase Order Number (if any)
- Sidemark (name of the client who is your contact person)
- Client's Phone Number

96

- Client's Address (street, city, state, zip code)
- Client's Fax number
- Contact's Email Address
- Name of Supplier #1
- Supplier #1's Wholesale Charge
- Supplier #1's Shipping/Handling Charges/Under-the-Minimum Charges
- The same for Suppliers #2, #3, #4, #5 and so forth
- Date that I paid each supplier
- Check No. for each supplier
- Amount Paid to each supplier
- Balance owed to any supplier
- Total amount of my sale
- Total amount of sale which was retail sale
- Total amount of the sales tax I charged
- Total amount of the delivery and installation charges
- Total amount of freight/handling charges I assess my client
- Total amount for any portion that was for resale (if I sold to a designer or framer)
- My total profit from the project
- Date product was delivered
- Total amount of client's deposit
- Balance due by client
- Date deposit received
- Date balance received
- Date project was entered into my bookkeeping records
- Date and time of any appointments made with client
- Special notations

On the back of the form is where I write the directions of how to get to my client's home, their color palette, furniture style, and any other information I gleaned from prospect in the initial phases. This Control Form will stay with the project paperwork from start until finish, and by finish I mean until everything has been delivered to the client, the client has paid for everything, every vendor I hired has been paid in full, and all figures have been entered into my bookkeeping records and all money has been deposited into my bank account. It literally "controls" every step of the process so that nothing gets overlooked along the way. It has really served me well through the years.

THE PROJECT FORM

This double sized form (11x17) is where I enter all of the particulars necessary to control the acquisition, the source and the design of each and every individual work of art that I include in a project. I generally enter all of the various art selections in a sequence of planning, starting always with the art for the most important rooms first. I like to keep all of the work that will be "like kind" together as much as possible, but still have an orderly sequence to the images.

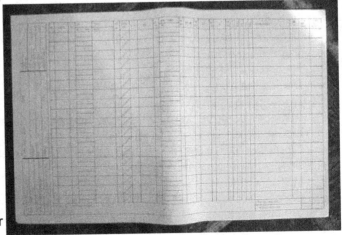

The Project Form is used to record all of the design instructions you will give to your framer or framing department. It will enable you to record your decisions for every image and keep you from omitting critical information, and will insure that you are charging the correct amount based on how you have framed an image. It will also help immeasurably when it comes time to install the body of work as it will be filled out in a manner that is consistent with the rooms in the home.

Here is a list of the categories that I have on my Project Form:

- Name of client
- Client's address
- Client's phone number
- Name of Contact Person
- Client's FAX number (if any)
- Order Date
- Anticipated Installation Date
- Name of Consultant (if you have more than one)
- Lead Source (if you pay out finder's fees for referrals)
- Boxes to check whether it is a new client or repeat order
- Number of pages in this order

The above information is entered along the left side of the form, perpendicular to the rest of the form. The design instructions for the artwork uses up the majority of the form. The categories for the design of the images are as follows:

- Quantity
- Location
- Source (name of publisher and their code number)
- Title of Image and Artist's Last Name
- Retail Amount of Art Image
- Size of Image
- Size of Framed Image (this will be larger after you add mats and is the actual size of the glass)
- United inches of the framed piece
- Manufacturer and code number of the frame to be used
- United inch price of that frame
- Top mat code number
- Top mat width
- First filet code number (under mat)
- First filet width
- Second filet code number (2nd under mat)
- Second filet width
- Museum mounting, if any (only use for original works of art)
- V-grooves, if any
- French cuts, if any
- Deckle the edge, if any
- Float image, if any
- Any special requests or instructions (like cropping, from where, special fancy treatment measurements)
- Wholesale cost breakdown (how much for art, framing, oversizes, fancy treatments, plexi etc.)
- Total wholesale cost of image and framing
- MSRP
- Corporate price
- Volume price

You will work from this form when you fill out the forms that your framer or framing department will use to actually build the frame and put everything together for you the way you have specified.

INVOICE FORM

In most cases you can use the same form for listing the art that you sell to a client as you use for your re-design project. It's important to state the quantity, the finished glass size, the title and name of the artist on the invoice. You really don't need to put any additional information on the invoice unless you choose to.

If you are delivering the art to the client's home, you might want to include that in the total price or make it an additional figure. I always included the delivery charge into the installation charge. I never trusted my clients to be sure to hang the art correctly. By offering a complete installation service along with the sale of the art, I made sure the finished room was according to my specifications and it added to my profit margin.

Besides that, you want to be in the home when the art has been hung because that's when you're going to want to take the "after" pictures for your portfolio and marketing purposes.

Becoming a Corporate Art Consultant

For complete training on how to become a professional Corporate Art Consultant and provide custom framed art to businesses where you can sell an immense amount of art all at one time, get a copy of **Pro Art Consulting**, my exclusive tutorial on the subject. This is not recommended if you live in a rural community. To be successful in this business, you need to live in a metropolitan area where you are near to plenty of medium and large size businesses. I not only discuss the design side of corporate art consulting, but how to acquire clients and develop a very lucrative business in this specialized area. For more details about this opportunity, please see Resources section at the end of this book.

Advanced Redesign

Chapter 9
Offering Custom Throw Pillows and More

We've been discussing many different ideas you could implement to add value to your re-design service, from offering additional services beyond rearranging furniture and accessories, to acquiring accessories that vendors sell you at wholesale or making products yourself. If you can sew, you'll love this one.

While many women are fortunate to be able to stay home and rear their children without holding an outside job, more and more women are having to work or choosing to work whether they have to or not. Regardless, this brings opportunity knocking at your door. These women don't have time to sew any more. They would rather purchase what they need. I know I put away my sewing machine many years ago even though I had enjoyed sewing and crafting (I made quilts).

Now I just buy what I like and need. It's a lot simpler.

You can add some nice profit for your business and work right there in the comfort of your own home. If you don't know how to sew or don't have a sewing machine, don't worry because it's easy to learn and you can be making custom throw pillows immediately. I've also listed a few other accessories you might like to add to your decorative arsenal.

Idea 1

DESIGN AND CREATE CUSTOM THROW PILLOWS Clients are always in need of throw pillows. Sure you can find pillows all over the place, but you will have some special clients who are in need of something really creative or unusual. Some people just like the idea of getting something no one else will ever have a chance to acquire. Some people just like to buy from "artists". You can become a pillow artist. If you have a supply of pillows that can only be purchased from you, and you have created a portfolio of samples and have a few with you, I can almost guarantee you that you will add more profit to your business by offering custom throw pillows as a back-end product.

Here are a list of fabrics you could use: prints, toiles, cotton duck, twill and brushed twill, poly-velveteen, denim, micro fibre, faux suede, chenilles, damask, bark cloth.

Create pillows that are prints, solids, stripes, mini prints, tone-on-tone, ticking, checks, plaids or tropicals. The combinations are endless. Just use your imagination. Let something in the client's home serve as your inspiration or find it elsewhere.

Choose from plain edges, square welt edges, ruffled, tasseled, fringed, round, neck rolls or bolsters. You can even make them in different shapes: triangles, round, oval, square, rectangular, tubular, diamond shaped, heart shaped or odd shaped.

You could also make a matching *throw* for over the sofa or lounge chair.

Idea 2

DESIGN AND CREATE CURTAINS AND DRAPES Not very many people go into the custom curtain and drapery business. It's a little more complicated. But think of how great to have little competition for a similar product. You'll need to keep your prices affordable, and you can do this by offering custom treatments for the same price as "in stock" prices that the stores carry. Getting the word out is quite easy too. Here is a sample ad.

> DRAPERIES AND CURTAINS made to order at reasonable
> prices - usually no more than stock items in stores. Best
> selections of material - all work guaranteed. Free estimates.
> (put your phone number here)

To get samples, contact a wholesale fabric distributor. Most will give them to you free in anticipation of getting business from you; others may charge a small deposit for them. Be sure to select a wide variety of samples, in all price ranges. Almost all drapery and drapery hardware manufacturers also sell or give away instruction booklets on how to measure material and hang draperies. This can be so easy; it's just a matter of doing it and learning what you need to know.

Your earnings can be unlimited. One lady started offering custom drapes, and worked about 5 hours each day at the beginning. Inside of two years her husband quit his job to become her installer - and stayed busy. Her policy was to obtain prices on standard drapes from several stores in the area, and then offer a better quality in custom drapes at the same price. It didn't take long for the word to get out and she was soon manufacturing all the drapes for several housing contractors in her area. This could be bonus income to your re-design business or you can build it into your major source. It's all up to you.

Idea 3

MANUFACTURE RUGS Any heavy material, such as canvas or burlap can be used as a backing for rugs. On this material you simply draw a pattern that you wish to create, or use transfer patterns which are available at most supply houses. You then wind your yarn around a guide and stitch the material. You will discover that with a little practice you can complete even the most delicate pattern on your rugs.

Each finished rug can be an original creation, and you will have a ready market for them from your re-design clients. Or they can be the catalyst that brings you re-design business. In addition to your redesign clients, your best bet is to offer them to consignment or gift shops, furniture stores and perhaps appliance stores in your area. A 30% commission is a fair amount to offer. Rugs of this type command a generous market price, and your mark-up will be excellent. The average small throw rug should sell for about $12.00 and even allowing a 30% commission this will still give you about 6 to 1 mark-up. Some parts of the country will handle larger mark-ups. Getting to at least 10 to 1 is ideal.

Also consider selling your rugs at the local flea markets and swap meets. You can hire teenagers to work these markets for you, handing out your re-design card or brochure at the same time. One gal in San Jose is averaging about $200.00 a week in sales at the flea market alone. A lot of her customers are back time and time again - they like the quality. Do good work. You will get repeat business if you have a quality product.

Idea 4

APRONS One of the most overlooked items to come off the sewing machine is the apron. Come up with a dozen designs and offer them "imprinted" with the personal name of your customer. Offer them to your re-design clients. Who wouldn't want an apron with their name on the front in the colors of their kitchen? Also consider "custom" pan holders, scarves and you name it. The material cost is very low and the time involved is very short. You can even place a few samples with gift shops and offer them at 30% commission. Staple your re-design card to each item. Let your imagination run wild with these products. It could blossom into a full time venture for you overnight and become your major source of income - who knows!

Idea 5

KITCHEN OR BATH TOWELS Never forget the advantage you have of being right in the client's home doing a re-design, hopefully. You'll be able to really hone in on the right products and services you can also offer because you'll not only **see** the need, you'll be able to offer a custom product they can't get anywhere else - in their colors and style. Stop and think about how easy it is to make towels and wash cloths. We all need them. They constantly wear out or get stiff or stained. How great to be able to make them for your clients.

In general your skills will be important, but your business will grow and be profitable because you develop a clientele that comes back to you because they are satisfied. When they are happy, they will be happy to give you referrals. Referrals are the life-blood of your re-design business.

Repeat business is always more valuable than new customers. New customers are harder to find and advertising is more expensive then "keeping in touch with people who already believe in you and love what you offer." You'll might find it easier to get repeat business for your accessories than for a re-design itself, you never know.

Items you will need for custom throw pillows:

- Hot Iron
- Scissor
- Fabric Needle
- Thread
- Sewing Machine
- Polyester filling

- Glue
- Paint
- Glitter
- Transfer tape and paper
- Heat and bond tape
- Lace

Directions for Making a Typical Pillow with a Design:

For the backing material, you will need to choose a heavy fabric for making throw pillows, available at any craft or fabric store. If you really build up your business to some significant volume, you can purchase fabric by the bolt, which should be cheaper than by the yard.

For the surface material, look for a lighter weight fabric with an intricate design or pattern that you would like to use. I do not recommend spending a lot of money on the lightweight material as you will be cutting the designs out to apply to heavier fabric for making pillow.

Be sure to pick up some lace, cording or tassels that will bring out the color of both the heavy fabric and the design of the lightweight fabric.

While at the craft store, you should be able to find some transfer tape and paper. This is paper that you will use to attach to the back of the lightweight fabric for cutting out your design and applying with a hot iron to the heavier fabric that you will be using.

Once you have all of your supplies, you will need to find a workspace.

The first thing that you will need to do is lay out your lightweight fabric and examine it. You are looking for whole designs or small individual designs that you can cut out. Once you have picked out the areas that are appropriate, apply transfer paper to the back of the fabric and follow directions on transfer paper for attaching with hot iron.

Once you have attached the transfer paper, then take your scissors and cut the design out. Be sure to cut out all areas and trim any edges that are not part of the design.

Now lay out your heavier fabric and cut it into equal proportions. (Optional: Some people prefer to use a pattern for cutting out their throw pillows.) Now place fabric front side down, with the wrong side showing upwards. Using your sewing machine, stitch around the edges of the fabric, attaching them together. Remember to leave one of the four sides of the pillow open in order to stuff it with filling.

If you do not have a sewing machine, you can use heat bonding tape.

Peel backing from one side of the tape and attach to the wrong side edge of fabric. Place the tape around all four edges.

Now peal the remaining back off of the tape and place the other piece of fabric (wrong side down) on top of the tape and fabric bottom.

Take a hot iron and press firmly along the edges of the fabric to seal together.

When using heat and bond tape, try to cut the fabric as evenly as possible. When laying the fabric over tape, try to position as accurately as possible. Once sealed with the iron it cannot be repositioned. If there are some strings hanging from the edges, trim if necessary. However, this area will be covered with lace, so a few imperfections are permissible.

Once the edges have been adhered, take your cut out designs and arrange over the fabric until you get an arrangement that makes you happy.

Once you know how to place your designs, peel backing off of the transfer paper and place the design in the appropriate place. Then take a hot iron and run it over the design until it has adhered to the fabric.

Do this with all of your designs. Do not forget to decorate the back side of the pillow also. Allow the designs to cool for one to two hours.

After the designs have cooled, take polyester filling and stuff the pillow as full as you can.

Once stuffed, if you have a sewing machine, sew the remaining edge together.

If you prefer, take a strip of heat and bond tape, attach it to the inside of the fabric edge and using hot iron, press firmly along the edge of the fabric until adhered.

Now that you have made your pillow, you just need to put on some finishing touches.

Apply heat and bond tape along the edges of pillow. Attach the lace to the tape and apply hot iron to adhere, if so desired.

For an iridescent effect, take clear glitter glue paint and brush it over the designs.

Use glue to apply the colored stones or other decorations you have pre-chosen.

Rejoice! You've created a custom, one-of-a-kind pillow.

How to Make a T-Shirt Pillow

To make pillows from t-shirts, turn the shirt inside out. Sew the neck and arm openings closed. Sew the bottom and leave about a 4 inch opening. Turn it right side out. Stuff with fiber fill. Stitch opening closed. What could be simpler?

How to Make a Pillow Cover

Change or enhance the look of a room simply by changing the covers on your client's throw pillows. The size they already have may be perfect but it's time for a change. You can give a good price if you don't have to replace the whole thing. Covers will also help protect your pillows from everyday wear and tear. I like covers because I can recycle older pillows, particularly ones that are just sitting in a spare room or closet. The instructions here are for a 24-inch pillow. **Easy Steps to Take:**

1. Choose 1-1/4 yards of 45-inch-wide home decorating fabric for your pillow cover. Choose a coordinating thread and 20-inch zipper as well.
2. Prewash the fabric and iron if necessary.
3. Use a fabric-cutting board, yardstick, fabric-marking pen and scissors to measure and cut out two 25-1/4-inch squares of fabric.
4. Add any fabric paint or appliqués to your pillow before you start to sew the cover. Refer to the above instructions for that.
5. Place your pillow pieces right sides together and pin one edge to another. Make sure that edges line up evenly.
6. Insert the zipper into the center of one of the seams. Open zipper and pin the other pillow edges together.
7. Stitch 5/8 of an inch from the pinned fabric edges and sew the remaining seams. When you reach a corner, lift the presser foot of your sewing machine and swivel fabric so that your stitching line remains straight. Keep the needle inserted into the fabric as you reposition it.
8. Turn the pillow right-side-out. Push out all the corners and insert the throw pillow. Close zipper. Quick! Easy! Simple! And it's good to recycle!

Additional Tips:

- Make your pillow cover any size. Just remember to adjust the yardage amount and zipper length accordingly.
- Taper the seam allowances at the corners so that seam allowance is less than 5/8 of an inch.
- Use tassels and cording to decorate your pillow covers. These items should be applied to the seams and corners of your cover before you sew.
- Make sure that the zipper for your pillow cover is in the seam at the bottom of the design, not on the side or the top. If there is no designated top or bottom to the design, then place the zipper in any seam.

How to Decorate a Throw Pillow

Steps to Follow:

1. Decorate your pillow pieces after they are cut and before they are assembled.
2. Choose to decorate your pillow with motifs that reflect the room in which they will be used or the season. Use nursery rhyme or cute animal motifs on a pillow made for a child's room. Use holiday prints and trims for a pillow used as part of your client's Christmas decorations.
3. Appliqué fabric cutouts onto your pillow pieces. Apply a paper-backed fusible web to the appliqué fabric, cut out the design, and iron design onto the pillow piece (see above instructions for more detail). Satin stitch around the appliqué by hand or by machine for a more professional touch.
4. Use fabric paint to decorate your pillows. Paint can be applied with a brush, brush and stencil, sponge, or decorative rubber stamp. Make sure that the paint you choose is made especially for fabrics.
5. Use tassels and cording to decorate your pillows. These items can be applied to the seams and corners of your pillow before you sew everything together.

Things You'll Need:

- scissors
- stencils
- threads
- irons
- fabric paints
- ironing boards
- cording
- sewing needles
- paper-backed fusible webbing
- decorative rubber stamps
- applique motif
- tassels
- holiday trim
- sewing machine
- holiday fabrics
- zippers
- decorative craft sponges
- brushes
- sample throw pillows

One Last Tip:

- Make your own tassels to decorate your pillow. They are easy and fun to make and you can make them in any size or color you desire.

OK, there you have it in a nutshell. For those of you who love to sew, this is the perfect add-on, back-end, front-end all around product. It's easy to do and should be easy to sell. All you got to do is do it.

Advanced Redesign

Chapter 10
Offering Custom Area Rugs

To update, revitalize and beautify your client's home, suggest the inclusion of area rugs, custom or otherwise, if they do not already own any. A good area rug can add dramatic design, pattern and color to any room or bring an understated elegance and refinement. They can also help you create a focal point or define areas (like seating arrangements) by giving the appearance of an island in the middle of the room. Area rugs tend to be something your client will most likely not have, according to my experience. Area rugs are a re-designer's best friend, besides plants and art. Oh heck, they are all important ingredients.

They can also add warmth and softness to the look and feel of tiles, stone or concrete flooring because they will be pleasant to step on. They also serve as protection for hard floors or wall-to-wall carpeting and serve to reduce noise. Periodically replacing an area rug is much less expensive than replacing an entire floor. While some designers don't believe in putting area rugs on top of carpeting, I do it all the time. You'll probably need to add a rug pad to prevent it from migrating, however (more on this later).

Area rugs can also help tie elements of a room together - serving as a color bridge. Much less expensive than wall-to-wall carpeting, you can change rugs when the seasons change, if they get too soiled or you tire of them, and when you move you can take them with you. It is not surprising that home area rugs are of great interest to re-designers and their clients alike. So they make the perfect add-on service for a re-designer to offer.

Short Guide in Choosing Area Rugs

In addition to function, color and feeling are the most important elements in interior design and should be at the top of a re-designer's list of requirements when selecting rugs. If a room has a lot of bright colors and looks very busy, it's best to choose a neutral color or a subtle design for the rug - perhaps just a simple border rug. You don't want to overpower the room. When you consider how large an area rug can be, overpowering is a definite consideration you must guard against.

If, however, the colors of the room are soft and neutral, and the room really needs to be "punched" up, you can add a splash of color and interest with a bright rug or just with a dramatic design. Perhaps a Persian rug or Oriental rug, heavy on design, would work well.

To enhance the color scheme that already exists in a room, select a rug that repeats the dominant or accent colors. The rug should definitely bear correlation with the other colors in the room already. For those rooms that have yet to have a color scheme chosen, or where your client is planning to discard all or most of the furniture anyway, acquire an exceptionally beautiful rug and decorate the room around it.

The pattern on the rug must not clash with patterns on the wallpaper, window coverings, pillows, cushions or other fabrics in the room. You definitely do not want to overdo on pattern. Dark colors add warmth, however they will make the room "feel" smaller. On the other hand, light colors will make the room appear more spacious, but they have their downside too - showing dirt and stains more easily.

The amount of traffic your client will have in the room is also a consideration for both re-designer and client to think about. If there are children or pets, or the rug will get steady use, darker colors and intricate patterns will not show dirt or wear as much or as quickly as light colors. However, darker colors will show lint more easily, so I tend to recommend colors in the medium value range. With a medium value range rug, you will still get good contrast with light furnishings as well as dark ones.

If you buy a rug for the bathroom and you already have a bath mat, make sure the colors are compatible. Since there is a lot of moisture in a bathroom, it's wise to avoid rugs that are not compatible with moisture. Rugs that can be thrown in the washer are ideal.

Maintenance is an important aspect to consider whenever you choose rugs for high traffic areas, such as a bathrooms, kitchens, stairs or halls. Your emphasis should be on rugs with designs and colors don't show the dirt, are stain resistant and are easy to clean.

One client of mine had her husband lay a parquet floor in the kitchen, dining room and hall. As a senior citizen, she found she could not walk on the floor in bare feet because it makes little cuts in the skin on the bottom of her feet. Wearing socks only leads to the early demise of the socks caused by the edges of the parquet blocks of wood. Area rugs strategically help eliminate this dilemma placed over the floor. (Although I suppose she could have worn slippers.) Anyway, you get the point.

Why You Should Recommend a Rug Pad

It is a good idea to add padding under a rug because it will not only keep the rug from moving, it will also extend its life, absorb sound and make vacuuming easier.

For rugs placed over carpeting, it's a good idea to choose a pad of thin polyester fabric coated with adhesive. This type of pad will prevent a dark rug color from bleeding through onto a light carpet underneath. It is also soft enough not to cause undue wear on the wall-to-wall carpeting underneath it. A pad made from slightly heavier polyester coated with PVC will hold a rug firmly on wood or other smooth-surfaced floors.

Types of Rugs

Persian, Traditional, Victorian, Country, Transitional, Tropical, Natural Fiber/Sisal, Oriental (synthetic), Oriental (wool), Tribal/Southwest, Plain & Simple, Border Rugs, Sheepskin/flokati, Animal Skins, Runners, Novelty, Children, Custom Designs.

Variety of Fibers Available

Originally, area rugs were made from wool or cotton, however, today happily you have a choice between several fibers: natural or synthetic. How does one recommend which one to get for a client? Evaluate these 3 areas: how much traffic the area will receive, rug maintenance and your client's budget.

Synthetic Fibers

- **Acrylic** — If you want something that is highly resistant to sunlight, stains and mildew, choose acrylic. You'll mostly find acrylic fibers in bath mats however.

- **Olefin/Polypropylene** — This is by far the most stain-resistant synthetic fiber on the market today. It will repel water and is impervious to most stains. It is also usually less expensive than other fibers, which is always a plus.

- **Nylon** — Nylon is versatile, easy to maintain, durable and clean. It's good for high traffic areas because it withstands heavy foot traffic.

Natural Fibers

- **Wool** — Wool is wonderful because of its dye-ability, durability, softness and clean-ability. This makes it the superior fiber. Wool has been the standard by which all other carpet fibers are measured. However many people suffer from allergies, so wool would definitely NOT be a good choice for them. Be sure to discuss allergens with your client before choosing wool (or even down pillows and comforters).

- **Cotton** — While it is softer than wool it is also less durable. Happily it comes in a wide variety of colors.

- **Jute** — The softest of all natural fibers, jute cannot be exposed to direct sunlight, or it may fade or darken in color. Another problem is that if exposed to prolonged moisture, the fiber disintegrates. It is extremely hard to clean as well.

- **Sisal (Hemp)** — On the other hand, sisal is stronger and more durable than any other natural rug fiber. And since sisal is static-free and colorfast, it makes it perfect for just about any area. However, it is also hard to clean.

Fiber Blends — Blends are where two or more fibers have been combined into one rug.

Weaving Methods

The following definitions of common weaving terms will give you a better grasp of how rugs get from the weaver's hand or loom to your client's floors.

Hand Hooked — This is where the weaver pushes a hooking tool through the foundation cloth to the front of the rug, then pulls the yarn to the back, leaving a loop of yarn on the surface.

Hand Knotted — Each knot is individually tied by hand. These knots are single strands of yarn that have been looped around two adjacent warp threads.

Hand Tufted — An inked-on foundation cloth is stretched over a loom. Then a manually operated hand-tufting gun pushes the yarn through the back of the cloth. When the rug is taken off the loom, a layer of latex and scrim is placed on the back. A back-cloth is then sewed on to the latex and scrim to protect your floors.

Jacquard — A mechanized loom that has an endless belt of punched cards. The holes in the card are arranged to produce the weave of the rug.

Wilton Loom — These rugs bear a close resemblance to hand-knotted rugs, but are machine made. The pile is woven between two backings and then split down the middle — so you get two separate rugs. Machine rugs are generally less expensive than handmade rugs.

Rug Making Terms

Here is some terminology every re-designer should know. Not only will you feel confident about your rug recommendations; you'll really impress your client and the salesperson where you buy.

- **Hand Carved** — Using hand shears, the weaver cuts a design into the rug. The carving gives the rug a sculptured look which makes it look distinctive and unique.

- **Heat Set** — When the yarn is set with heat, it will have a wool-like appearance. A twist is put in the yarn using a polypropylene process.

- **Line Count** — One indicator of rug quality is the number of knots or stitches per square inch (just like thread count in sheets and towels). The count in rugs may be calculated differently depending on where the rug was made, so you cannot easily make comparisons from one rug to another.

- **Pile** — Pile refers to the surface yarn that makes up the face (or top) of the rug. When I refer to "low cut pile", I mean the yarn on the face of the rug is very short.

- **Stitches/Needle Count** — The higher the stitch or needle count in a specific area of a rug, the denser the rug. Higher density rugs will last longer and wear better than more loosely woven constructions, but they are more expensive as well.

- **Warp and Wefts** — The warp yarn is the stationary thread on the loom. These fibers are the strongest part of the rug. They are intersected with wefts — the filling yarn that is woven though the warps.

- **Border** — The border is composed of decorative designs repeated in one direction around the circumference of the rug. Some rugs, such as border rugs, may have 2-3 borders, either plain or patterned.

- **Field** — The field is the larger background of the rug inside the border, usually accounting for 2/3-3/4 of the surface of the rug. It may be a solid color or patterned.

- **Medallion** — The medallion is a round or oval design in the center of the rug, if any.

Checking Sizes Needed

If you want an area rug to cover most of the floor in a room, an even amount of bare floor should be exposed on all sides of the rug, even if the room is an irregular shape or there is a closet or fireplace extending into it. Think of it as if you are "centering" the rug on the floor. If this is not possible, make two parallel sides of the room uncovered in equal amounts.

When choosing an area rug that will encompass a seating arrangement, leave at least 6 inches, but no more than two feet of empty rug extending out from behind the furniture on all sides. A rug used in this fashion will unify the items placed on it as well as those surrounding it. You do not want the furnishings on the rug nor the furnishings surrounding the rug to feel cramped.

If you are going to place a large rug in the bedroom, it need not be centered but the same amount of floor should be visible on two or three sides of it.

In the dining room, the rug should extend somewhere around 18-24 inches beyond the table. An 8'x10' or 9'x12' rug will work well in most living rooms and dining rooms.

In a living room or family room, a 4'x6' or 6'x9' rug will be fine if it is for a small area, such as under a coffee table. Be sure the entire coffee table sits on the rug and all other furniture set back from it at an equal distance. You will see pictures in magazines and books where the front feet of the chair or sofa are on the rug and the back end is off the rug. This is often done to make the photograph look better. While some professionals arrange rugs and furniture in this manner, it is not recommended, especially if you're a novice decorator.

If your client has trouble visualizing what a rug will look like in a room and can't decide what size would be best, use masking tape to define the space. If that doesn't help, cut pieces from a paper roll (or lay out bed sheets) to cover the area to help them decide what size they feel comfortable buying. If you're not sure yourself, always test - you don't want any miscalculations.

Summary for under the coffee table:

- Typically 4'x6' and 6'x9' area rugs will work well under coffee tables. The size you should recommend depends on the size of your client's coffee table and surrounding furnishings. Typically you want a rectangular or oval rug under a rectangular or oval table. Put a round or square rug under a round on square table.
- The area rug should be large enough to accommodate all four legs of the table. If it is not, it will feel like part of the table is falling off of the surface of the rug.
- The area rug should be approximately the same length and width of the space in front of the seating arrangement or at least 2/3rds the length, say of the sofa.

- To accent the furnishings most effectively, leave some flooring exposed between the area rug and the furniture.

Summary for under a dining room table:

- Most dining room tables will need an 8-foot wide area rug.
- The chair legs should NOT be off the rug when people are seated at the table or pulling the chairs away from the table to get in or out.
- To be safe when determining what size the rug should be, measure the length and width of the table and add at least 4-5 feet to each measurement.

Special Effects

If a rug is to be the focal point of a room, consider purchasing one with a central medallion (see definition of medallion above), which is a popular design for an oriental rug. If the medallion will be hidden for the most part by a piece of furniture such as the dining room table, large coffee table or a bed, forget the medallion and select a rug that has an all-over design or one with detail on its borders.

Oriental rugs, very popular in modern and traditional homes, are a term which refers to rugs from any Asian country. You can expect to pay more for an imported Persian rug because it is considered by many to be superior to all other oriental rugs. Tibetan rugs are also beautiful and popular - and not as expensive. You can also choose a rug from Afghanistan, Egypt, Pakistan, or China, as well as other countries. Any product from Japan will probably be quite expensive.
For Early American themes (country), a round braided rug, popular since the early settlement of North America, will probably be very suitable and colorful too.

Using a Navajo rug, with its geometric designs and flat weave, can sharpen a southern or desert theme. If your client's taste runs more to the comfort and appeal of animal fur or wool, look for a flokati rug - a hand-woven Greek woolen rug with a thick, shaggy pile - it may create just the look they want.

Contemporary rugs come in every variety of color, design, texture, size and price. Don't overlook them when you are searching for the perfect home rugs, even if your house is decorated in a traditional style. Just as a traditional rug can look great in a modern home, a contemporary rug can add to the appeal and charm of a traditional home, so long as there is a good mixture of furnishings in the room from both styles. Let your creative spirit soar and make sure the rug can be returned or exchanged in case your client discovers your creative spirit soared slightly in the wrong direction.

Considering Costs

The cost of a home area rug is closely related to the fiber from which it is made and the source you get it from. The most expensive natural fiber will be found in a wool rug; other less expensive natural fibers are cotton, jute, silk and sisal. As stated above, popular synthetics favored for quality rugs are acrylic, polypropylene and nylon. If your client is on a tight budget, look for discount and bargain outlets, but be sure the dealer is reputable. You should find a wide selection. Again, check the return policy and warranty before you buy.

Expanding on the Recommendation Guidelines

When you begin decorating a client's home, there are some important factors to consider as you don't want to make any mistakes. Their floors will usually be the foundation for your design but not always. The placement of furniture will also be a determining factor. An authentic handmade area rug can visually integrate or harmonize diverse elements in any decor or can re-energize a room.

1. Size of the Rug - Area to be covered

- The coffee table should sit all the way on the rug, not half off as pictured.
- Below is the correct way a rug should be sized under a coffee table.
- Size up the room and the area you want to cover.

- The most common area rug sizes are 4-by-6 and 6-by-9 feet. They work well under a coffee table and in front of most sofas.
- An 8-by-10-foot area rug or larger can cover an entire room. When you want the seating to sit fully on the rug, this size and larger are ideal.
- Smaller area and scatter rugs can be ideal for adorning smaller spaces — in front of a hearth, beside a bed, the area in front of a kitchen sink, in the bathroom, down a hall, in the entry.

2. In the Home

Living Room

- In a living room the area rug would most likely be placed in front of the sofa and under the coffee table
- Measure the open space up to the sofa and chairs making sure that the individual seated will have both feet on the area rug.
- To place a room-sized area rug on a hardwood floor, choose an area rug which allows eight inches of wood to be exposed around the rug's perimeter.
- More than one area rug is acceptable but they should be compatible, both in design and color.

Dining Room

- There should be room to pull the chairs out from the table with the back legs of the chairs remaining on the area rug. Important!

Stairs

- Recommend busier or darker patterns to diminish the appearance of soil and stains.

Hallways & Entrances

- Dense Patterns - use short pile for high traffic;
- Wool pile is ideal (most durable). Use a cotton foundation (strong and does not loose shape).

- Do not recommend a room size Persian/Oriental area rug for the bedroom. Most of the pattern will be hidden under the bed in the dark making the rug prone to moth damage. Instead, use multiple small area rugs: one at the foot of the bed and one on each side.

3. Furnishings

- It's always a good idea to lay out on paper what your ultimate design will look like. Do a paper layout to scale. What type of style does your client prefer: uncluttered and spacious; cozy and filled?
- Large area rugs are very strong in a room, particularly if the colors are bold or the pattern is busy. If there are no furnishings yet, choose the rug first. Then pick the fabrics that will blend with the rug. Let the rug be the dominant visual and plan everything else to be visually supportive of it.
- Next comes window treatment and walls; neutral, muted or soft shades are recommended. Remember, these areas are **background**. Don't over design them. Don't make the windows more important than they are. Flashy window treatments can easily compete for attention. Be careful. Painting the doors, window sills and other elements in a contrasting color may draw unnecessary attention to elements better left un-noticed.
- To repeat design elements taken from the rug, such as a floral, add framed prints or flowers in similar colors.
- Conversely, if the furniture is the focal point, subdue the colors and designs in the area rug. It then takes a supportive role, not a dominant one.
- Don't get discouraged if you are having problems finding an area rug to blend in with your client's decor. We suggest you surf the internet for sources of rugs or check your local business to business yellow page directory for distributors. You can always buy from retail stores, but you'll make more money if you can purchase at wholesale prices.

4. When Using Multiple Area Rugs

- Clients often ask, "Should I use one rug or two?"
  ~ The general rule is only one rug. It coordinates the room as well as anchoring the main part of the room.
  ~ However, in a very large room, more than one rug can be used to separate the room into two parts - in other words, creating two "rooms" within the room. The designs of the rugs should be different enough to create a separation (not unlike two rooms divided by walls), but similar in color and quality to maintain the flow of the room because they will most likely be seen at the same time.
- Two or more rugs should be compatible in color and feeling:
  ~ however, one needs to be dominant in size and visual strength
  ~ and they should be similar in at least one element for unity: design/color/size
  ~ be sure smaller rugs don't look like clones - something should be different. When in doubt, it's best to make it a different pattern, not a different color palette.

5. Color

- If redecorating an already furnished room, choose a rug to pick up the colors used in your client's furnishings, but probably a softer tone;
- Paint or paper the walls in colors found in the rug when color coordinating. Select from one of the softer background colors in the rug.
- To avoid changing the walls, look for a rug that has commonality with the existing color of the walls.
- If the room already has a chair and sofa in a solid color or soft patterns, feel free to recommend a rug that is stronger in color or overall design.
- Remember, if your client wants coziness, go dark. If your client wants spaciousness, go lighter.

6. Durability

- The preferred choice for durability is wool, as it resists daily wear better than synthetics, however it may be a problem for allergy sufferers.
- Silk rugs and tapestries are very suitable for living rooms. Silk rugs are better used for walls, throws etc.
- For a more consistent and durable color, recommend chromium dyes.
- For a more casual look, recommend vegetable dyes which give the rug a patina of color. This can be very attractive.

7. Shape

- Let your client's decorating style and the most appropriate placement of furniture determine the shape of the rug.
- If possible, think beyond the standard rectangular shape.
- A circular or octagonal-shaped floor covering can add flair and elegance because it is so unexpected and outside the norm.
- If the space in front of a seating arrangement forms a square (two sofas or loveseats the same length, placed perpendicular to each other), consider a circular rug instead of a square one. If one side of the arrangement is longer, however, forming a rectangular space in front of the seating, consider an oval rug instead of a rectangular one. Square = circular; Rectangular = oval.

8. Clarify the dealer return policy before you buy on behalf of your client.

- Insist on at least one week risk free trial period for your client to experience the rug. In that time your client can test the texture, dye quality and placement. To test the dye quality, take a moistened paper towel and run it along the edges & center. The dye should not bleed out.

Other design and miscellaneous considerations:

- Medallion, oval and round rugs should be centered in the room & directly under the chandelier, assuming there is one.
- Don't combine busy rugs with busy fabrics.
- Don't let rug corners extend into traffic lanes. This will prevent accidents.
- Advise your client to vacuum carefully if there is fringe. Make sure it is sewn on to the rug in a sturdy manner.

- You can tell by the back of a rug if it is handmade or machine made. It's a machine rug if the fibers are straight and stiff and if they run up and down the back of the rug.
- Do not purchase from a company going out of business. You will have no recourse if there is a problem down the road. Even if the product is discounted, you very well may be sorry in the end.
- Avoid letting a corner of the rug end in the middle of a door way or an archway. It just doesn't feel good and might be dangerous.
- Pick the pattern according to the size of the room. Smaller patterns are more suitable for small rooms and will help the room appear larger.
- Handmade rugs are not made with as much precision when it comes to being squared off. If you're really particular about evenness, buy machine made rugs only.
- To best absorb the impact of feet and noise, recommend a pad. It will reduce wear and tear on the rug and make vacuuming easier.
- Rotate rugs end for end on a yearly basis to equalize wear. Another reason to have the re-designer return and rotate the furniture as well? You better believe it!
- Oriental rugs fade, as does upholstery. Avoid direct sunlight. If unavoidable, suggest window treatments that reduce sunlight, such as sheers and ultra-violet tints to the windows themselves.
- Always recommend that rugs be cleaned professionally.
- Labels using the words Indo-, Sino- or Pak- indicate that a rug came from India, China or Pakistan respectively. This is to meet Federal Trade Commission requirements.
- Rugs woven by nomadic groups are referred to as being "tribal".
- Consider what you want the focal point of the room to be. If you want the rug to serve as a focal point, consider choosing one with a central medallion. However, if there is another obvious focal point of the room, such as a fireplace, you may want to use a rug with a more repetitive pattern but no medallion.
- Notice how much traffic the area receives. In high traffic areas, selecting a rug with a detailed pattern or low cut pile may be more practical. The more pattern and the lower the pile, the lower the maintenance.

- Keep in mind that texture is an important element in your décor also. Several different fibers within a rug or carved areas can add more pizzazz to an area rug's texture. Rugs made of sisal or jute add an interesting texture to smooth hardwood or tile floors.

Securing Sources

Again, finding outlets for area rugs should not be too difficult if you live in or near a major metropolitan area. Check your local business to business yellow pages for manufacturers and distributors. Perhaps you are near a design center where you can easily order custom rugs. Surf the internet for rug wholesalers. Send them email to enquire about drop-shipping capabilities. Most wholesalers won't drop-ship for you, but it's always worth asking. Once you find your sources, go in advance and register your business as a legitimate re-seller. Ask for catalogs. If you get two or more, you can cut them up and create your own catalog of examples to put in your portfolio. Be sure to get up-to-date price lists from your sources. Find out specifically what their terms are. You don't want to be caught having to pay penalty fees or shipping when you have not been expecting to do so.

Advanced Redesign

Chapter 11
Offering an Organizational or De-cluttering Service

The organization industry, it seems, is more relevant today than ever before. Take a look around you. Look in your own home. I know my closets are bursting with stored clothes. Are yours? Offices are overflowing in rivers of paper. Even my own business suffers from lack of storage space. Living rooms and kitchens everywhere have been swallowed up by stuff. Personally I just spent some time just last week thinning out some of the rooms in my own home - removing old framed photographs of the family and accessories that I am temporarily tired of seeing.

The demand for managing the piles of stuff all of us are accumulating in our daily lives is growing—and businesses have sprouted to meet every possible need. A friend of mine owns a company that puts the data of other companies on disc for them so that they can throw away the mounds of paperwork they have collected. Some smart re-designers are combining their redesign skills with their organizational skills and offering both as a unique service to homeowners. Others manufacture organizing products - like my original decorating organizer.

We have in Southern California a few companies that have developed some strong market share in creating custom closets for your bedroom, laundry and garage. I know someone who interviewed for a position with *Closet World* but it wasn't her cup of tea, however, it might be a consideration for some of you.

They send you out as a "closet designer" primarily, after you take their two week training program. You go into people's homes and discuss their organizational needs and literally design a custom closet for them, or an entertainment center or storage closets for the garage - whatever they need and can afford. The nice part about doing something like that is that the company provides you with all the leads and may even set your appointments for you.

Then it's up to you, once you've built rapport with the client, to let them know what other redesign services or back-end products you could offer them on an independent basis. Naturally it would probably be best to "clear" this with your closet employer first - but these two businesses are clearly related and could be successfully combined by the right person.

Barry Izsak is president of the National Association of Professional Organizers Board of Directors (NAPO). Their membership has doubled over the past two years—of both professional organizer members and associate members (like organization product manufacturers). Since public awareness is gaining, we've seen the introduction of retailers specializing in container products for every room in the home or office.

The increased production of home-improvement and home-makeover shows has helped raise the industry's profile as well. Even as I write, TV producers are dreaming up different reality shows that focus on various aspects of interior design and such involving pitting one designer against another. Organization is all the rage. Is this your passion? Do you have a knack for de-cluttering a space? Consider combining it with your redesign business for a winning combination.

Contain the Excitement

It was both an interest in and a knack for organizing that inspired one gal to forego the daily grind of an office job to start her professional organizing business. In 2000, this big city renter was looking for a napkin in one of the cabinets of a friend. The cabinet was stuffed full of all kinds of things and she said to herself, "I must organize this for her."

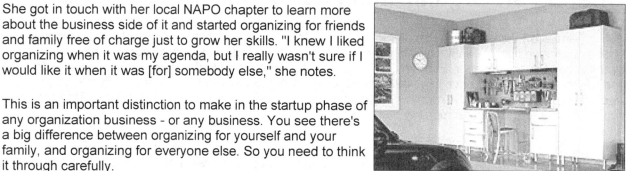

She got in touch with her local NAPO chapter to learn more about the business side of it and started organizing for friends and family free of charge just to grow her skills. "I knew I liked organizing when it was my agenda, but I really wasn't sure if I would like it when it was [for] somebody else," she notes.

This is an important distinction to make in the startup phase of any organization business - or any business. You see there's a big difference between organizing for yourself and your family, and organizing for everyone else. So you need to think it through carefully.

Professional organizing is such a customized business. You have to constantly seek the right solution for each customer. It's not a matter of an organizer coming in, cleaning up, and everything is just fine as is often portrayed on the TV shows. Professional organizers must work closely with clients to help them achieve their own ways of organizing just as they must work closely with the client to redesign a space.

People can really be sentimental about their things - even worthless junk. You're dealing with hoarders. They have psychological issues that are getting in the way of their ability to make a decision. Many things have memories attached to them that the owner can't let go of. That explains all the boxes in the corner—people hang onto things because they can't decide what to keep and what to let go of. A professional organizer needs a keen eye for detail and a good ear for listening to his or her client's specific needs.

Recently I went through my garage and tossed out a huge assortment of art catalogs thinking I would never need them again. Then I got interested in decoupage and, wouldn't you know it, now I wish I still had those art catalogs. I also threw away some notes and drawings and handouts from a seminar I used to do for the same reason. Now I wish I had it. So this is my personal dilemma.

I could easily throw many things away or give it away - but I always fear I'll need it again some day, or my two young adult children will want it when they finally move away from home. So I hang on to stuff by the truck load - old furniture, shelf units, pillows, equipment and the like.

Another thing to remember is that there's often a lot of shame about being disorganized that prospective clients will feel. But once they let you into their home, they're really grateful to talk about it to someone who's not judgmental and whose outlook will be a bit more objective than their own.

Be advised that disorganized people often have trouble keeping appointments, so you'll want to have a system where you confirm and then re-confirm your appointments with them.

Most professional organizers charge by the hour— although the amount varies per job. Fees vary widely, depending on an organizer's level of experience as well as the nature of the job, although many charge between $50 and $200 per hour. So the fees you can expect to charge for this service are pretty much aligned with the fees for a redesign business.

Getting Your Ducks in a Row

The organization industry is full of opportunities. But even though organization is in increasing demand, it takes more than just a keen interest in it to become a successful organizer. You'll have to perfect both your business and your organizing prowess. One way to train for the industry and learn about its ins and outs is to work for a larger professional organizing firm first if you're really nervous about it - or if you're like me, just jump in and use your common sense.

Residential organizing continues to be a hot area and organizers can specialize in a myriad of organizational areas like collections/memorabilia, photographs, garages and moves/relocations. You might even specialize in targeted groups like seniors or students. You can also contract out your services to be the on-call organizer for local businesses.

Like any business, do your research to find out how much people are charging in your area for similar organization services, and check out your local NAPO chapter. And if you do decide to start part time on evenings and weekends, realize that means you won't be able to target the office market.

Phase into working weekdays (like adding Mondays and Fridays to your schedule) until you can go full time. Just don't neglect staying organized yourself — especially when your schedule gets busy. Calculate the amount of time you'll spend with clients and factor in travel time. Set aside enough hours to accomplish your own "back-office tasks", like phone calls and bookkeeping, so you can be both an instructor and an example to your clients.

Be sure to take before and after pictures of your own organizational efforts at home and in your client's homes or offices. These can be very useful in your marketing and for establishing credibility.

The Container Store and Urban Outfitters offer many great organizational products. Go to your local one and arrange a business account with a discount. You'll probably have to purchase products for your client to accomplish their goals for them.

People are going to continue to struggle with the issue of personal organization and this need will continue to grow. I don't see the demands on people's time becoming fewer so professional organizers are here to stay!

Best Use of Closet Space

To boil it down to the basics: you need to weed out what your clients don't need, get their closets organized and leave them some room for new fashions. You'll have to make some decisions for them, however, and this is hard to do even for the best decision makers.

Before you discard anything, you need to look at the situation as a whole. So take the time to go through the entire closet. Take out what doesn't fit your client. Take out what doesn't belong. Bring to the pile anything they want to add in it that wasn't in it before.

Decide whether the contents should just be seasonal or whether they want everything in it all at once. In places like Southern California, there aren't many seasonal changes to one's wardrobe, so most people keep everything in the closet at one time. However, northern states where climate changes are really noticeable, are more likely to require "seasonal closets".

OK, now you're ready to decide whether your client needs a permanent or temporary organizer. If they're renting, the free standing, movable closet organizers will be best. If they're a homeowner, they might want something permanent. If they'll settle for permanent fixtures, you'll find them in wood, plastic, wire or wood composites. Visit your local Home Depot or other hardware store for ideas and products.

Now decide if their shelves should be moveable or permanent. Choose a "layout" for the shelves that will accommodate enough space for the different storage purposes they have: hanging clothes, folded clothes, shoes, hats, etc. It might be a good idea to count the number of items in each category first and then go from there.

According to what they have, you'll need rods, shelves, boxes, hangers. Draw out a simple plan and compare it with their budget. Allow 20% extra for surprises. Remember, they'll always buying new clothes, so plan plenty of space for them to "grow into".

How much vertical space should you allow for each segment in their closet? Well, that depends on their size and the amount of clothes you plan to accommodate, but here are some general guidelines:

Women's Clothing

- Dresses (50 inches)
- Suits (40 inches)
- Blouses (34 inches)
- Long dresses (68 inches)
- Coats (53 inches)
- Skirts (38 inches)
- Robes (53 inches)

Men's Clothing

- Suits (40 inches)
- Slacks (cuff-hung) (44 inches)
- Slacks (double hung) (30 inches)
- Shirts (36 inches)
- Topcoats (52 inches)

Don't cram them in so tight they become wrinkled. Give them space to breathe.

Lastly, you'll have to decide where best to put the shelves. You can put them below the hanging items, above them or beside them. Your client's height will determine that. Strive to make it as easy as possible for your client to store and retrieve items.

Place the shelves relatively close to each other. You don't want to have huge stacks of clothes in a pile on each shelf in order to utilize the vertical height more effectively. This is not only detrimental to the clothes, but it gives the appearance of a disorganized closet.

When you start placing their clothes in the closet, it helps to color coordinate the placement. I place all of my black shirts together, all of my red shirts together, all of the brown ones together and so on. That's because I usually select clothes by their color. When they are grouped by color, it makes it very easy to find what I'm looking for in a matter of a few seconds.

Since most people choose their clothes by color, it makes good sense to teach them this handy little trick which saves valuable time for them every day.

Speaking of Organizers . . .

Want to feel totally professional and organized whenever you're out shopping for home decorating products? Ever feel disorganized because you can't find your measurements, your swatches and samples, or the receipt for that sofa, wallpaper or paint? We've got the perfect Organizer/Tote for you. It's beautifully designed, with expert craftsmanship, and very well thought out. I wish I had created it myself. I love mine and use it often. More details at the end of the book in our Resources section.

Advanced Redesign

Chapter 12
Offering Accessory Exchange Program

How to Start and Operate an Accessory Exchange Service

(Decorator's Bartering Club)

This is not bartering, but rather you could think of it as a close cousin. The idea for this re-design service is to offer your clients a way to get rid of accessories that they either don't like or are tired of having and exchange them for something else of similar value, or if not of similar value, combine other accessories together so that overall the exchange has a similar value. This is a revolutionary way to provide an answer to tired and worn-out accessories that still have value, just cease to be of interest to their present owners without the owners having to purchase something new.

First, let's discuss briefly the whole concept of bartering and then apply it to the redesign field. Bartering is not negotiating! Bartering is "trading" for a service or for the goods you want. In essence, bartering is simply buying or paying for goods or services using something other than money (coins or government printed paper dollars). In re-design, it merely means that the homeowner gives up some accessories they own to the re-designer, and the re-designer brings in other accessories that are suitable to their taste and style which had belonged to someone else she had done a re-design consultation for in the past.

Typical bartering has been around much longer than money actually. Recent estimates indicate that at least 60 percent of companies on the New York Stock Exchange use the principles of bartering as a standard business practice. You only have to watch a few segments of the hit show "The Apprentice" to see bartering on the corporate level in action today. And congressmen barter daily to gain support for their pet projects. U.S. aircraft manufactures barter with foreign airlines in order to close sales on million dollar contracts. Even children make bargains with their toys though they don't know that's what they are doing.

The reason bartering enjoys renewed popularity in times of tight money or sluggish economy is simply that it is the "bottom line" method of survival with little or no cash. Even though right now we are not in a time of high interest rates, cash in your pocket is indeed a very precious commodity, and bartering is more popular than ever. A recent high point for bartering was when, in the early 1980's the country went into a serious recession and lots of businesses went out of business and many, many homeowners lost their homes. In a business, good cash flow is imperative. Bartering affords both the individual and established businesses a way to hold onto cash while continuing to get needed goods and services.

Benefits to Your Clients

Can you see how easily this whole concept can be brought over into redesign and made an integral part of a re-designer's arsenal of products and services that can be offered?

In addition to saving a homeowner from spending money on more furnishings, bartering can improve their cash flow and liquidity. For anyone trying to operate a successful business, this is vitally important, but for the purpose of our discussion here for individual families in these times, it makes possible the saving of cash funds for those purchases where cash is necessary. Making slight adjustments in one's accessories is not necessarily a place one must spend cash in order to improve.

But it does require some strategic pre-planning on the part of the re-designer to pull it off. Built into the program is a method whereby the re-designer gets paid for services rendered.

How to Get Started

To start and successfully operate an **Accessory Exchange Program**, *you must think as if you were a banker.* After all, that's precisely the reason for your business---to receive and keep track of people's deposits (accessories) while lending and bringing together other people wanting or needing these deposits (accessories) who may or may not have made deposits (accessories) of their own.

So your first task is to round up depositors (people willing to contribute accessories to your inventory). As a one-decorator operation, you can start from your own home with nothing more than your telephone and kitchen table. Initially your business will be very small but could become very busy (probably both).

You can run a small display ad in your local newspaper. A good ad would include the following ideas:

NEW DECORATOR'S EXCHANGE CLUB!
Trade your accessories, expertise and/or time for the merchandise or services you need. We have the traders ready---merchandise, specialized skills, buyers too! Expert redesign and decorating advice available by appointment. Call now and register. DECORATOR'S EXCHANGE CLUB (123) 555-1313.

When respondents to this ad call, you handle them just as a banker handles someone opening a new account. You explain how your club works. Everyone pays a membership fee of $100 to $300, and annual dues of $50 to $100. The depositor tells you what she wants to deposit, perhaps $150 worth of art, and what she's looking for in return---shelves for the family room. If you have a depositor who makes shelves and needs some art, you may have an independent transaction which is not part of your re-design service, but you'll profit from it anyway.

Offer your redesign services FREE to members. Set an appointment for a redesign consultation ($75 value) for the same time you give them the member's packet. This puts you right in their home to let you check over their need of your rearrangement services, as well as get a look at any accessories they might like to place in your inventory.

On your list of depositors you may have a homeowner who's offering $300 worth of lamps looking for carpeting for a child's bedroom. A woman with a quilted bedspread hoping to get some art for the living room. An unemployed painter is willing to paint houses in exchange for carpeting for his home, and a handyman is looking for plants for his yard in exchange for doing repairs around the house.

Remember, when a new member joins your club, she makes a deposit and states her wants or needs. In the above example, you have a typical decorating bartering club situation. Your service is to line up those deposits to match the wants or needs of the club members.

Now you can make this as broad as you want or keep it more narrowly defined and restricted just to your clients who make a deposit of accessories in exchange for other accessories of similar value. You as the re-designer must know what goods and services are available and be able to successfully match the wants and needs of one "redesign client" to another "redesign client". The first example has the potential of becoming a large and profitable business that could require additional help to service. Keeping the exchange service just between your redesign clients will be easy to manage all by yourself. But it may be much more difficult to find enough people willing to participate to make it truly viable.

What You Need

An affinity for people, a digital camera, a measuring tape and a good memory or computer database software for tracking purposes are vital to this kind of business, especially if you're running a "one-decorator show." Generally, when you have a "buyer" for one of your depositors, you notify him or her right away with a phone call. You simply tell her that Club Member A wants to have their home painted. She tells you fine, but she wants draperies. You simply tell her to hang on because you are currently in the process of contacting Club Member J, who'll supply the draperies she wants. And so it goes in the operation of an accessory or decorator's exchange club or service.

Some of the larger bartering clubs (with several thousands members), simply list the deposits and wants or needs on a computer or on their website, and then invite their members to come in and check out the availabilities for themselves. Others maintain merchandise stores where the members come in to first look at the current listing, and then shop, using credit against their deposits. The smaller clubs usually publish a weekly "exchange newsletter" sheet and let it go at that.

Some re-designers are hired by the client to do a complete redesign of a living room without even being present. They trust the re-designer explicitly to do everything for them without them even at the site. These types of homeowners are the most likely to have the re-designer pick out alternative products or services for them and simply bring them into the home for their final approval. This type of arrangement has it's advantages and disadvantages.

A Decorating Consignment Store (of sorts)

If the re-designer is really good and has some terrific accessories to pick from, the whole exchange can be handled quickly and efficiently during the rearrangement of the room. This type of service generally requires two appointments with the homeowner: one to discuss the rearrangement of a room and take measurements, note colors and style and collect items for the exchange service; the second one to bring in the new accessories and rearrange the room.

However, if the re-designer misjudges the taste of the client totally, it can involve quite a bit of extra time. But one must remember that the re-designer earns her money essentially from the membership fees and not by "selling" or "placing" the accessories. Remember to refer to all accessories as "previously owned accessories", not as "used accessories".

Obviously, if you're going to have a re-designer exchange, where you take and receive the accessories as part of an inventory, you must have a place that is clean and secure to store them. It might even turn into a home interior consignment store of sorts. Typical consignment stores are set up for the general public to come in and make a purchase from the inventory. All purchases in the exchange club, however, are done for club credits, not cash.

As for storage, I don't recommend your garage. When small, you could rent a storage unit in a facility near where you live. As your inventory grows, just rent more space. You can open your inventory up to the general public or keep it restricted to being available to clients only. As your expenses go up, your membership fees may need to be increased as well. Back yourself up with sufficient insurance on the goods while in your care.

As your products for "barter" grow, you'll want to categorize them by color and style. Don't rely on memory to ascertain the value. Value should be determined at the rate of 50% of what the original owner paid for the item (or less depending on age and condition). Everything should be adjusted up or down depending on the condition of the piece and it's rarity. Whenever possible, ask to see receipts for the purchase of the item before assigning value to anything.

Be sure your clients know that every attempt will be made to make all exchanges fair to all parties involved in putting together a successful exchange. Never pressure anyone to agree to an exchange. On the other hand, limit the time anyone can change their mind or undo a transaction.

All paperwork that is passed between parties should spell out clearly the terms of the exchange, deadlines, penalties and so forth should anyone have "buyer's remorse" after the fact.

Growing and Managing a Large Exchange Business

These methods all work, but you'll probably find that instead of leaving your clients to fend for themselves or make their own trades, the most profitable system is to hire commission sales people to solicit (recruit if you will) new members, specifically with deposits to match wants and needs of your present members. Without a fairly large number of accessories and services to trade with, it will be pretty hard to make your clients happy, much less get them to renew their membership each year. These sales people should get 20% of the membership fee from each new client they sign, plus 3 to 5 percent of the total value of each trade they arrange and close. This percentage, of course (to be paid in club credits) is "spend-able" merchandise or services offered by the club members.

You'll need a club charter, a board of directors or officers in many areas, a city or county license and all the typical business organization and set up one ordinarily does. Check with your city or county clerk for more information on these requirements. You should also have a membership contract, the original for your files and a duplicate for the member. In most cases you can write your own, using any organization membership contract as a guide, or you can have your attorney draw one up for you. You'll also need a membership booklet, or at least an addenda sheet to your contract, explaining the rules and bylaws of your club. It's also suggested that you supply your members with consecutively numbered "club membership identification cards" for their wallets or purses. Some clubs even give membership certificates suitable for framing. You can pick these up at a large stationary house or commercial print shop.

Two things are important to include in the membership package you exchange for membership fees:

1. It must be as impressive as you can make it - something of real, tangible value.
2. It must be legal, while serving your client's needs almost exclusively, as well as your own.

When to Launch It

Basically, you should have at least 100 members before you begin concentrating on arranging trades. As stated earlier in this chapter, the easiest way to recruit new members is to run an ad in your newspaper, and perhaps even on your local radio station as well.

Follow up one of these inquiries with a direct mail package, which would typically consist of a brochure explaining the beauty and benefits of being a member of your decorator's accessory club, a sales letter, and a return reply order form. After you've sent out the direct mail piece, be sure to follow up by phone, and if necessary, make a call in person as any other sales person would do.

Another way of recruiting new members who are not redesign clients is via a mini-seminar program that is held in the home of a client or other member. Allow a certain number of club credits for each party a club member arranges for you. Insist on at least 10 couples for each party, and then as the "Attraction of the Evening," you or one of your salespeople give a "benefits available" recruiting talk. Be sure you get the names, addresses, phone numbers and email addresses of everyone attending, and be sure that everyone leaves with your literature.

If all those in attendance at these seminars do not join, then follow up on them, first by phone and then with personal sales presentations. Once you've got them interested in your club, do not let go or give up on them until you have signed them as members. Make a list right now of people you feel would be interested in hosting a seminar to get the ball rolling.

Offer them an item of merchandise they might be particularly interested in, and club credits if they'll not only join, but also stage a party for you.

A bit more expensive, but just as certain of success are large free seminars. Rent a large meeting room, advertise in your local papers, and then put on a hard-sell recruiting show. Such a plan is very similar to the party idea, but on a larger scale. An inside tip: Whenever you stage a recruiting party or seminar, consider "peppering the audience" with current members, who can ask questions. No one likes to feel they are the only one interested, so make them feel comfortable and make sure all of their questions are properly addressed so they can make an informed decision.

As stated earlier, you can start operations out of your home, but working out of your home has a number of growing inhibiting factors. After a certain period of time, the growth of almost any kind of business is retarded when it's operated out of a home. So just as soon as you can possibly afford to, move into an office of some sort. Keep your eyes open and consider the feasibility of sharing an office with an insurance agent or real estate broker. Check your newspaper classifieds for businesses willing to share office space or rent desk space or other office amenities, especially including a conference room.

Crucial Marketing Strategies

This is the kind of business that demands an image of success. You just can't keep people from "dropping in" when you're operating strictly on a local basis. And when you attempt to hire sales people, a place of business to work out of is just as important to them as how much commission they're going to receive. Image is super important, so don't neglect it!

Ideally, you should have one salesperson for every 50,000 people in your area. Run an ad in your local newspaper, and also list your needs with your state's employment service. Hire ONLY commission salespeople. If they don't deliver paying clients, they don't get paid. Don't pay any benefits, at least not in the beginning.

If you want a large exchange program and you hire salespeople, assign each of your people specific territories, and insist that they call on potential homeowners during the early evening hours or on weekends. There's plenty of business available in every city or metro area in the country. Encourage your sales people to be creative and imaginative when calling on prospects. Then, be sure that you keep an open mind and listen to their wild trading proposals (some "wild proposals have been known to become "wildly successful)!

Managing and Growing Your Business

Schedule "open discussion" sales meetings periodically before salespeople "hit the phones". Have each of them report on their selling efforts from the day before, and present to you a written list of prospects they plan to call that day. Set up sales motivation workshops to be held at least once a month, and periodically schedule a motivational speaker or play one of the widely available success/inspirational tapes available to salespeople as a closing feature of your sales meeting. Have available an assortment of success books and encourage your people to borrow them, take them home and read them. Your sales people will make you rich, but only if you turn them on and keep them flying high with personal motivation.

Should you or should you not accept installment payments from new members? Yes, by all means! But only when you've got their signature on a contract drawn up for your benefit and deemed legally binding by your attorney. What about bank cards? Yes indeed! In fact, you'll find that your capability of handling bank cards will double or even triple your sales. I know this from my online business. Offering credit card purchasing of membership fees is critical to your success. It's not difficult to set yourself up with a credit card merchant account.

What Will It Cost in Time and Money?

Precisely how much are you going to need in actual start-up costs? We would estimate at least $500+ for your printing and legal fees, unless you can trade charter memberships in your club for these services or you know someone who will help you out. Time wise, you're going to be putting in 18-hour days, and 7-day weeks until you get those first 100 people signed. And there won't be any money for salary or long-deserved vacations from these first 100 members you sign. You'll need it all for advertising, membership packets and office set-up. However, if you can really work at it, you should be home free in eight weeks, maybe less, maybe more depending. Then you can set up your office, hire a couple of minimum wage employees to handle the paperwork, and take on a salesperson or two.

Reputation and success in matching offers to wants will be just as important as image, so give it your all. Don't give up; stand behind the implied promises as well as the "real" ones that you make to members.

What About a Guarantee?

A couple of final notes: Should you offer a guarantee of satisfaction? Only so long as it makes money for you, and you can back it up and you attach a time limit to it. There's not a person in business anywhere who enjoys refunding a customer's money. But don't forget that the existence of your business depends on service. The more you project an image of a "need meter" or "problem solver", the greater success you're going to achieve. This is definitely not a business for someone who doesn't enjoy "waiting on" people. You've got to like people, enjoy helping them, and want the inner satisfaction that comes from creative new ideas by which to solve their problems.

This is definitely a growth business no matter how you structure yours. Bartering Clubs in metropolitan population areas of 300,000 or more are reporting incomes of over a million dollars. The average in cities of 100,000 population is about $150,000 per year.

Actually, no experience or special training is required. The operation of a Bartering Club, or more specifically an Accessory Exchange Club, is equally suited to women or men. Both do equally well as salespeople. It's a business that fills a need, and a kind of membership program people will stand in line to be part of, once they've been introduced to the benefits.

This is the plan. It's going to take your time and effort to get organized, but after your initial work to establish this business, you stand every opportunity of becoming quite wealthy in a relatively short time compared to most businesses. Read over this plan again; determine if this is "the one" for you, and then go all out. It's up to you, and all it takes now is action on your part.

A Good Resource

One of the best of all the available sources of ongoing help and knowledge about bartering is a quarterly publication entitled BARTERING NEWS. Write and ask for a sample copy, then adapt it as necessary for your own unique twist on this age-old method of doing business. The address is:

Bartering News, PO Box 3024, Mission Viejo, CA 92690.

Advanced Redesign

Chapter 13
Offering a Furniture Refinishing Service or an Upholstering Service

In an attempt to give you the broadest base possible of add on products and services to take your redesign business to the next level, it only makes sense to zero in on other services that relate to furniture itself, since a re-designer works so closely all the time with furniture that the client already owns.

I can tell you for a certainty that there will be many clients who hire you to do a redesign for them whose furnishings are old and dinged and in need of a refurbishing treatment. Whether you do the labor yourself or not, you'll be able to perfectly dovetail it with the business of redesign.

If you have a garage or work shop and are willing to learn an additional craft or skill, the fields of upholstering, re-upholstering and/or furniture refinishing would make an excellent add-on to your redesign business. The additional investment is comparatively small compared to many businesses and there is always a market for these skills and the products that come forth.

If you do not already know how to upholster or refinish wood, obviously you'll have to take some training in those areas or set up a business relationship with other businesses to do the work for you. If you are experienced, you can begin with small projects and work your way up to the more complex and better paying ones in no time. Do you really care where your money comes from?

I don't care what source generates income for me so long as it is profitable and I enjoy the work. Obviously, reupholstering or refinishing furniture is more labor intensive and will involve the use of equipment, but the subject remains the same - furniture. So before you tell your clients that they need to get rid of some piece of furniture, analyze it to see if it just needs to be refinished or reupholstered. Remember, older furniture was generally better constructed than many newer pieces.

If you're married, you could have one spouse specialize in redesign and the other one specialize in upholstery and refinishing work! If you can't or don't wish to take a class, start by buying books on the subject and then practicing on furniture you already own. If possible work for a while in the field to learn directly from professionals already successful in the business. There's no excuse as there are many different resources available to teach you the skills you need to know.

While you're studying, decide on whether you want to specialize or not -- perhaps you'd like to concentrate just on modern furniture, just on antiques or just on chairs and sofas. Sometimes it's better to be really tight in your niche.

When you are ready to service clients, have a sign made (if you're in an area where you can have outdoor signage) and place an ad in your local papers that announces your services. Make the ad as benefit driven as you can. Add some signs on your car or truck too, so people can see them when you pick up or deliver furniture.

Naming Your Business Ventures

Look for a way to incorporate your redesign service and the furniture service together into the name of your business. A good business name is one that really tells people instantly what you do. When I first started my flagship website, http://www.decorate-redecorate.com, I was concentrating on making the name something that would be search engine friendly in a broad sense. And that was good.

However, the name is almost too broad and non-descript in many ways. So for a subsequent website I chose the name www.furniturearranging.com. That's far more specific and really identifies a tight niche market. The verdict is still out on this for me, but I do believe that when you only have a couple of seconds to interest someone and make your business stand out in the crowd, it's good to be as specific in your title as possible.

A classic example of someone that chose unwisely is the retailer "Tuesday Morning". Now while it's a clever title that might get remembered easily, it tells you absolutely nothing about what kind of business it is. I remember seeing the name for months as I drove by without ever darkening their door.

However, once I found out the nature of their product line, I've returned occasionally for merchandise, but pretty much only because I saw a TV ad. I asked a clerk if they got their new products in on Mondays or Tuesdays, hence the name, but she said they arrive all days of the week. So I continue to be at a loss for why the name *Tuesday Morning* was used.

So try to choose names for your business(es) that are pretty descriptive in and by themselves as to what you offer. In the long run your business will be much easier to grow and publicize.

Take Before and After Pictures

It is imperative whenever you work in a field where change is being made in a dramatic way that you preserve something that depicts the past and differentiates it from the present and future. When you bring in pieces of furniture which are badly in need of repair, take "before" pictures of them - to compare with "after" pictures after the service has been provided. You want these, not only for your portfolio and for examples to show quality workmanship, but to untangle any problems you might encounter after the fact. Never forget that clients have their own private expectations that may or may not be based on reality. Having photographic proof of every step from pick up to delivery could become valuable if a client becomes unhappy.

Place the best photos in an album to show prospective clients and to use in any advertisements or press releases. You'll need black and white photos for the newspaper but color for magazines. Caption each photo appropriately and try to show several examples for each type of service you offer. A photo album on the dining room table of your redesign client can be very useful while you are moving the very furniture that needs refurbishing.

You talk about credibility?? You will be seen as THE furniture person to talk to. You could provide your client with a brief list of do's and don'ts regarding furniture and the proper care of it. Make sure your pictures are very good and that they represent your workmanship very well, even if you have to hire a professional photographer to take them for you.

Planning Your Work Space

Refinishing tables and sofas, of course, will require more room. You'll also need some kind of stand or table to work on smaller items. If you're doing wood finishes, you'll need a dust free place. If you're doing upholstery work, you'll need a place that is free of mice and moths.

Making Recommendations

Clients are always going to ask you about your opinion on finishes, fabrics and methods. You, as the perceived professional, are often in a better position to answer these questions than your clients, but watch out for always recommending products and processes that make you the most money. People can spot that in a hot minute. Lots of people get multiple opinions and you could lose the project if your advice is perceived as self-serving. Always try to give the type of advice that you would want someone else to give to you.

A Bit About Pricing

Get used to the idea of giving a free estimate. It will be essential in a business like this. However, that's not to say it's difficult. You'll have to give estimates on most of your work. And since it's not an unforeseen fact that you may have to charge more than you estimated, build in a slight buffer. I always quote a range.

By quoting a range of prices (preferably in writing), the client only seems to remember the lowest figure (miraculously!), but at least your estimate was not a hard fast figure that is difficult to move off of in the event you really need to charge more. In any event, if you see the cost is going well over your estimate, give the customer a call before proceeding.

The golden rule here is "Never surprise a customer with bad news." You wouldn't like it if it were done to you. If the cost is slightly more than you estimated, absorb the loss as the price of a "lesson" in how to estimate more accurately in the future. Base your estimate on the cost of materials, labor and utilities plus your profit, and then add a little extra to form your "estimated range".

Note that labor and profit are two entirely different categories.

Labor is the amount you would have to pay someone to do the job; profit is your "override" on the labor plus your profit on the materials (usually 25-40%).

A fully qualified upholsterer or furniture refinisher should not earn less than $10 (gross) per hour -- and in some areas, $25+ per hour may not be out of line for top quality work.

When making your estimates, add a little "padding" (perhaps 5%) to cover unforeseen costs. Always figure your estimates and prices with good quality materials - when you use lower quality materials, usually to save money, give your client the option and let it be *their* decision if they want to save money. Clients always like to see the final bill come out slightly less than the quote.

Your First Projects

Practice on your own furniture before you ever "hang out your shingle". You want to be very sure of yourself and exhibit quality work before you attempt to do it for someone else for a fee.

Take a chair or table, set up a practice area and try your skill. Use BIX finish remover (available at most hardware stores) to remove paint (a second coat will also remove the stain), clean thoroughly, sand and apply the new finish.

The secret is not to get in a hurry! Let the wood dry between operations; take the extra few minutes for a first class sanding job; wait another day for the finish to dry enough for the next coat, and go over the surface with fine steel wool (if recommended) and wipe thoroughly between coats.

In a business, you will have several pieces in different stages of completion, so the temptation to rush will not be so great. Another way to help expedite your "education" is to hire an experienced helper, but this can get expensive - for both the assistance and "lessons."

Marketing Tips

In addition to your signs, have a good quality 3 or 4 line rubber stamp made to turn generic invoices and business cards into your own if you're really hard up and need to save. Make business cards on your computer or go to Staples, Office Depot or Office Max and have them printed up. The more you do at one time, the cheaper each card becomes.

If funds are scarce, get some duplicate ticket books at the local stationery store and stamp your name on each original ticket to get "custom printed" invoices. People don't expect professional invoices in this type of business so you can get away with generic forms if you have to. Better yet, take a look at all the forms at the end of this manual and see if you can make them work for your purposes.

As long as your business is not too professional, you can place 3 x 5 cards with your name and services on supermarket bulletin boards. Keep an ad in the local paper, but change it a little every so often (like a new special every month), to help stimulate interest. When you are ready for more business, put an ad in the yellow pages.

Unlike the redesign business, yellow page advertising for upholstery or furniture refinishing can be a profitable way to advertise. Consider ads in an internet yellow pages as well, as more and more people are searching online for everything these days rather than hauling out those huge phone books.

Whenever business lags, you can always contact rental agencies (both real estate and furniture) to either buy used (but good quality only) furniture that needs repair, or to do their repair work. The profits will be lower, but low profits are better than NO profits. Visit swap meets, garage sales, estate sales and second hand stores to get good buys on furniture that you can restore. Place ads in the paper or those weekly throw away advertisers saying you will "buy furniture".

The items you buy to refinish must bring at least double its cost PLUS a fair return for your labor and materials to restore it. For this reason, buy only high quality or antique furniture, so you will "have something of real and lasting value" when it is completed. If you want to resell them, join one of those antique malls where every booth is owned by a different seller of antiques. These stores are usually managed by other co-op vendors and you'll probably need to take your turn on the showroom floor to assist customers, but it's a relatively inexpensive way to place your refurbished furniture pieces where a target market will see them up close and personal.

Naturally you'll want to place advertising of your redesign services there too.

Pitfalls to Avoid

One possible pitfall in the refinishing and upholstery business is unpaid bills (well, actually it can happen in any business). People sometimes really want to have a sofa recovered and visualize how nice it would look with a nice, quality (expensive) fabric.

Trouble is, while the sofa is being re-covered, they spot a new one at half what they owe on the old sofa - and they go and buy the new item! This leaves the upholsterer with $100 worth of material cut and sewn onto a $50 sofa. Not good.

The warning here is to protect yourself. Get enough down payment to ensure the recovered sofa will be worth your investment should the customer "miraculously disappear". At the very least, make sure you have received enough up front to cover all of your materials costs. It's easier to "eat" your labor than to eat your labor plus the cost of materials too.

Stripping Furniture

Stripping furniture can be relaxing or frustrating.

It requires a good deal of patience. Try to do multiple pieces at one time, all in different stages, and this will help you be patient during the various processes.

Furniture Restoration Cleaning

The first step in furniture restoration is cleaning. This type of cleaning could be considered the same as spring cleaning your house. Although your furniture is clean, there is a residue left from typical average daily cleaning and generally the average supplies won't do the necessary job to remove the residue.

Furniture Restoration Cleaning Tools

There are several tools that are handy to keep around for the periodical job of buildup removal and general furniture restoration. Furniture cleaner #0000 Steel wool, toothbrush, pencil size dowel, sharpened, for corner and crevasse cleaning, soft cloth (cheesecloth works good), small paintbrush (1 inch), paper towels, and anything else that will work that won't damage your furniture.

Cleaner for Furniture Restoration

You will need something to dissolve old wax and polish so that it can be easily removed. Many concoctions have been mixed to work as a cleaner through the years. Some work and some don't. Lots of build up on antiques are due to home made cleaners that didn't quite do the job. Many people suggest paint thinner. It will dissolve wax and polish, but leaves a white residue of it's own which needs to be cleaned off.

The easiest way to do the job is with a good commercial furniture restoration product designed for the job. Prelude Cleaner is a good heavy duty, yet gentle product that is linseed oil based and will make short work of removing wax, polish and dust build-up.

#0000 Steel Wool - #0000 Steel wool is handy for removing those stubborn spots that don't dissolve too readily.

Generally when you use #0000 steel wool on a small area, you will need to use it equally over the whole connected surface, because when you rub a small spot it will be noticeable. If the finish is more of a sheen than a shine it won't be noticeable if you rub, for instance, a whole top, but not the vertical surfaces.

It isn't a good idea to use #0000 steel wool on a high gloss finish, because it will lessen the glossiness.

Be sure to always test any procedure that you do in an inconspicuous place.

Toothbrush For Furniture Restoration - A toothbrush is one of the handiest tools you can find for removing things you don't want from cracks and crevasses, carvings and embossments, or any other irregular surface.

A soft bristle toothbrush is better to use as a stiff bristle brush could scratch the finish.

Pencil Size Dowel - If a finish is fragile, rubbing with a toothbrush too much can make it even more fragile, so you can get out your trusty dowel sharpened with a pencil sharpener when you have indented areas to clean out. The sharp point of the dowel can gouge if it's dry so be very careful. With care the sharpened dowel can remove gook from even the most delicate carvings. The sharp point will soften as it gets soaked with cleaner, so keep your pencil sharpener handy.

Small Paint Brush - A small paintbrush, approximately 1 inch wide is real handy for daubing cleaner on raised or indented areas and on the narrow places on turnings and spindles.

Soft Cloth and Paper Towels - There's lots of wiping to do in furniture restoration cleaning and paper towels are the least expensive wipers. It's best to use the more absorbent and softer paper towels. After the initial heavier amount of residue is removed with paper towels and cleaner you can give a final cleaning with fresh cleaner and soft cloth. It's best to use soft clothes on fragile antiques.

Other Renovation Cleaning Tools - Anything you can find around the house that will be gentle on the finish and will work is fair game. Cotton swabs are real good helpers. String really simplifies cleaning the narrow areas on spindles.

Metal Container With a Metal Lid - The metal container with a lid is very, very important. Almost every kind of cleaner, polish and wax are volatile and if left in a pile can cause spontaneous combustion. Even a used polishing cloth stored in a plastic bag in a closet or cabinet is a potential candidate for spontaneous combustion.

Be sure to dispose of used paper towels, used cloths and any residue in a safe manner.

Paint Stripper

First, not all stripping products work the same way on all finishes. Some will work good on some finishes and others will work good on other finishes, but try the cheapest first, because the ones that are most expensive are the ones you see most in magazines and other ad media, so you pay a lot for their advertising and are not necessarily receiving a better product. You just may find your favorites are among the cheapest in this area.

There is an exception, however. There are environmentally safe strippers that you can use inside that won't drive you crazy with fumes.

Citristrip paint stripper is one of the very good ones which will cut the time factor of stripping paint and old finishes and has a very pleasant orange fragrance. With so many products having displeasing odors, it's refreshing to find one that is pleasant.

Used carefully, spray paint stripper can really be an advantage on spindles and carved areas. When you're stripping chairs or any other types of spindles, or something with lots of nooks and crevices, there is nothing like a spray, a piece of string or a toothbrush for scrubbing hard to reach places. However, you need to make sure that everything that could be damaged with over spray is covered, but the time saved by spraying is far greater than the time taken to cover other things.

Let the Paint Stripper Do the Work

If you're working hard and getting frustrated because the finish won't come off, it's probably because you aren't letting the remover do its work. Some times it is necessary to put several coats on before the old finish is ready to come off. If you try scraping the old finish off before it is ready, you waste paint stripper and energy. Use a scraper with rounded corners. If the remover laden finish dries before you get back to it, it can be reactivated with another application.

Gloves

Gloves can be a nuisance when you're stripping furniture, but they sure make things better for your flesh. Gauntlet gloves that can be turned up can save you some exercise, dancing around because stripper ran up to your elbow on to your more tender skin.

Furniture stripping and refinishing chemicals can be very hard on your skin, from drying your skin to causing a burning, stingy feeling to very severe chemical burns and blistering on sensitive skin. It is imperative that you carefully read the instructions on any product you purchase to provide the service.

Eye Protection

Eye protection is always a good idea when you're working with chemicals or anything foreign that may fly into your eyes. All it takes is just one little fleck of stripper laden paint in your eye to burn and sting and cause you immense agony.

Read a Good Book

It's always good to have another project going when you're stripping to keep you occupied, because stripping is boring rather than labor intensive. Furniture stripping is a good time to catch up on that good book you've been going to read or, better still, marketing your redesign business. Let the stripper sit and continue on with your other business strategies while waiting.

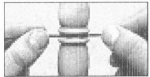

Stripping Spindles

Flat surfaces are quite easy to strip, but spindles can be kind of tricky. This is where you need to counter with some tricks of your own. First, strip the heavy stuff off, then on to the final stripping step. Pieces of burlap, or other coarse cloth, work good on spindles, worked around, back and forth on the softened finish. String or rough twine is also good for tight turnings. One of the most used tools as mentioned earlier is a piece of dowel about the size of a pencil, sharpened in a pencil sharpener. It's good for the grooves in turnings, cracks, gouges and lots of other uses.

Sanding cord is another great invention for working on spindles and for use as a removal tool. It's like sandpaper on a string. Stripping pads are very useful too. They're about equivalent to burlap and can be rinsed out and reused until they come apart.

If a spindle that you are working on is moveable, like chair rungs, and you are using liquid remover, support the spindle over a pan (a 9 x 14 cake pan from a thrift shop is good or an inexpensive aluminum baking pan) and using a brush, keep daubing stripper on the spindle. Use your sharpened dowel periodically to remove any softened finish from grooves, then go back to daubing. Eventually the finish will all come off. Even ten coats. In a situation where old paint just won't come off of a spindle, try an old screwdriver that has rounded corners. Don't sharpen the screwdriver or you may ruin the spindle.

Clean Up

Use a commercial after paint stripper wash, such as *Citristrip Wash* or denatured alcohol, and #0000 steel wool as a final wash. Let the piece dry thoroughly (overnight is best), then rub it all down with #0000 steel wool to remove flecks of wax and check to be sure that all of the old finish is gone. Almost all strippers have wax in them which forms a skim on top to slow down evaporation. The #0000 steel wool rub also prepares the surface for a new finish.

Always remember that the surface preparation is the most important part of a good finish. You can use the very finest of finishing procedures, but not have a nice appearing finish if the surface isn't prepared properly first. As a final touch, go over the whole piece with a tack cloth to remove any steel wool strands and dust.

Disposal Of Waste Products

Be very careful of disposal of your paint stripper waste products, residue, paper towels, rags, etc. A pile of rags with residue of flammable material can catch fire by spontaneous combustion. It's best to keep a bucket of water handy to throw used paper towels and rags in and another container to hold the gooey stripped residue or other finish until you're ready to dispose of them.

Check with your waste disposal facility (garbage dump, from years past) to see how to properly dispose of the remnants. If you have very old painted furniture, which may have lead paint, check with the hazardous waste people in your area to see how to dispose of the residue. **ALWAYS** wear gloves when stripping old paint. **NEVER** sand old painted finishes. The paint may contain lead and you could create a lead cloud, very detrimental to you and to others who might come in contact with it. Using a stripper will keep it moist and dust free.

Stain

Staining wood furniture is generally a necessity after you strip and prepare it. If you don't, the piece of furniture will quite often look uneven in color or kind of blotchy. An exception to this is a *clear finish* over light colored wood where you want to keep a natural appearance.

You can get products that are a combined pigment and finish that dry quickly (other than the pigmented oil finishes), but they will generally give a muddy opaque finish. There are vinyl or aniline stains, and many more that are quick to dry, but are usually very difficult to use or just plain frustrating, because they dry before you can get the effect that you want. It's just like most things in this life: If you want it fast, then you have to give up some quality.

There are pigmented oil finishes that generally give good color. Watco Danish Oil is a good example. Some refinishers like a good oil stain because they give you lots of control. Always pick a color no darker than you want the furniture to be. If the furniture is too light you can always apply more stain and let it penetrate longer, but it is a lot of work and sometimes the result isn't what you want. If the color you want is in between the colors available, you can mix oil stains to get your desired color. Make sure you mix enough the first time because you'll never get the exact same color in a second mixing.

Oil stain can be applied with a brush, cloth, roller, your bare hand or by any other means as long as you get it on evenly. After applying, wipe the excess off and let the furniture dry overnight. It is very important that the stain is completely dry before applying a clear finish.

Sanding Sealer

Somewhere along the way someone has come up with the erroneous idea that you should seal the wood before you stain. If you want to save yourself some disappointment, _don't_ seal before you stain. If you seal the wood before you stain, then there is nothing for the stain to soak into and you end up with a smeared appearance.

Sealing _after_ staining is a very good idea. Some stains will bleed through a finish giving an undesirable appearance and it is a good idea to seal them in. Besides using a sanding sealer, you can sand it with a very fine sandpaper to give a good, very smooth surface to apply the final finish to.

Be sure that you use a sanding sealer compatible with your stain and with the final finish product. Ask a fellow refinisher or your hardware store salesman if you have questions.

Different Finishes

You have gone through the difficult part, stripping and preparing your project - now it's time for the final step, applying a finish.

There are many products available for finishes, some very hard and some quite soft. Some will give more protection than others, but some pieces of furniture don't get much use, so will do fine with a less protective finish. Be sure to ask your client about the usage they expect to get from the furniture before you settle on a finish.

The Finish

Flexing - Your client's furniture will change continuously all day long. The only thing is that the change is so slow moving you can't see it happening. As temperatures change, the whole piece expands and contracts.

Exposed bare wood is very susceptible to moisture changes. If you have electric baseboard or forced air heating the atmosphere becomes very dry.

Every time someone takes a bath or shower, even with venting, or when you fix meals there is a terrific rise in humidity.

The exposed bare wood expands, then the air dries from the heating system, so there is constant expansion and contraction. The upside with a finish sealing it that it isn't as susceptible to the ups and downs of humidity all day.

The warp and wane of the bare wood puts stress on the finish and joints on furniture. Natural finishes, lacquer, shellac, oils, etc. are flexible and can withstand the constant stretching, shrinking, and twisting. That's part of the reason for joints loosening and why hard inflexible polyurethane will crack along a joint line.

Polyurethane - By now you probably have figured out that polyurethane is not one of the favorite finishes to use on furniture. Although there have been improvements in polyurethane, it still is a hard plastic coating that doesn't have much give. It may be good for decoupage, but not for refinishing furniture. If you are working on an antique and you use sandpaper and polyurethane, you no longer have a provable antique and the antique value will drop drastically.

Oil Finishes - There are many different kinds of oil finishes: some are easy to use and some are very time consuming.

Linseed Oil, Boiled - Linseed Oil was the choice of the old timers.

Using the word "boiled" after the linseed oil is to draw attention to it rather than to indicate that there will be other types covered. The other type is raw linseed oil; it will never dry, but will become gummy and sticky, so be sure to get BOILED linseed oil if you decide on that kind of finish.

Linseed oil gives a fantastic finish, but you need a year to apply it. The general rule of thumb for a linseed oil finish is once an hour for a day, once a day for a week, once a week for a month and once a month for a year. The finish was usually French polished once a year after that. That's a lot of work.

Other Oils - The other oils are much easier to use. Danish Oil and Tung Oil are two popular oil finishes. They are very easy to use and come in clear and in pigmented colors. Just follow the directions on the container, but double the number of coats they recommend. They aren't as durable as some other finishes, but are very easy to repair. If you get a light scratch in the finish, just grab a cloth and apply another coat of the finish and generally it's all taken care of.

Shellac - Shellac is a good durable finish, except that it is very susceptible to water and alcohol. Alcohol dissolves shellac.

Lacquer - Last, but not least, is a favorite, lacquer. Lacquer is a very durable finish, is flexible and is very easy to keep up.

Regular lacquer can only be applied with spray equipment, but it isn't necessary to have expensive spray equipment. You can get some reasonably priced airless spray equipment. You can use spray cans of lacquer and get a nice smooth even finish. There is a product called brushing lacquer, which is treated to extend it's drying time so it can be brushed. Lacquer is one thing that is fast, but is also good.

About the only mistake you can make using brushing lacquer is to apply it too thinly or to over-brush. If you apply a good liberal coat and let it dry properly, it will flow together so there are no brush marks or other imperfections. If you do have imperfections, dust or bugs, it is very easy to work them out with very fine sandpaper and #0000 steel wool.

Like with all products be sure to read the directions on the container and follow them explicitly for best results.

Wicker Cleaning Tools

Some real handy tools to use for cleaning wicker are a tooth brush, a paint brush with its bristles cut to about half the length, a medium bristle small brush, like a fingernail brush and a piece of dowel about the size of a pencil and sharpened in a pencil sharpener. The reason for cutting the paint brush bristles is to make them stiff enough to have some tension, yet soft enough to work into the weave of the wicker.

Let Water Run Off

The wicker furniture should be tilted when you're cleaning it, the same as when stripping, with the tighter weave to the top so that excess moisture will run down to the looser weave where it can be wiped up.

Keep the Weave Straight

It is very important to not disrupt the weave pattern or spacing of the weave on your wicker furniture when it is wet, because it will shrink its length to its original shape wherever it is, so if the strands have been separated, it will dry with a gap in it. If the strands are too far out of position, they will put stress on the joints of the wicker furniture and pull the piece askew.

Keep Water to a Minimum

Water should be dipped out of a pan or bowl during the cleaning part, to have a minimum of water at any particular place at a time. For a final rinse, a quick squirt with a garden hose and drying with paper towels or cloth works well. Be sure to let the wicker furniture or accessory dry for 24 to 48 hours before you do anything else to it.

Wicker, Rattan and Cane require no special stripper. A liquid stripper, any brand, is easiest to use and clean up.

The wicker will become supple and loose as it absorbs the stripper, but will tighten back up when it dries.

The job will be easier and quicker if you clean the wicker furniture first. You may even find that stripping the wicker won't be necessary.

If the wicker furniture has been painted you probably won't be able to get it back to a natural color since the wicker would have soaked up a lot of color initially and will soak up more pigment as it becomes moist from the stripper, so you would be better off to strip any large build up of paint that will come off easily, then after it dries, repaint with light coats of paint using a spray can.

Be sure to let the stripper work long enough so it will liquefy so you can push it off with your brush, because you won't be able to do any scraping, like you can when refinishing wood furniture. Remember, tilt the wicker furniture so that the tighter weave areas will be uphill so that liquefied residue will run toward the looser weave and not have a tight place to puddle up.

You will probably have to go back and re-strip some areas, because with a job like this it seems that the residue jumps back on when you aren't looking. Stripping wicker furniture and other wicker items is very tedious and will take a lot of patience, but it is all worth it in the end. Be sure to allow for this in your quotes.

After you are through with the stripping let your wicker piece dry thoroughly, at least 24 to 48 hours before finishing.

Paint is best applied with a spray can, because you can get into all the nooks and crannies and tight weave of the wicker.

Deft brushing lacquer is a good clear finish to use. It gives good protection inside and out. It is available at most paint stores or paint departments in other stores and is also available in spray cans.

Polyurethane is best avoided, as it dries to a plastic coating which is very hard and brittle and will probably crack with all the flexing of a piece of wicker furniture.

Furniture restoration is enjoyable and beneficial and should always be done in a safe manner.

Some Upholstery Business Resources

MINUTEMAN, INC., 115 N. Monroe, Waterloo, IA 19101. Sells furniture refinishing supplies, plus a "business kit".

BEDFORD LUMBAR CO.,Box 65, Shelbyville, TN 36710. sells unassembled cedar hardwood furniture.

DATHO MANUFACTURING, INC.,Box 12110, Lubbock, TX 79452. Manufactures of upholstery sewing machines.

MODERN UPHOLSTERY INSTITUTE, Field Building, Kansas City, MO 64111. Offers a course in upholstering; free booklet.

UPHOLSTERY TODAY, Box 2754, High Point, NC 27261. Trade journal for furniture upholsterers. Note: this is the journal of the Upholsterers International Union of North America, 25 N 4th St.,Philadelphia, PA 19106.

JIM DANDY SALES, Box 30377, Cincinnati, OH 42530. Upholstering instructions and supplies.

FREESTYLE, 17835 E Skypark, Irvine, CA 92714. sells "Sundura" furniture kits wholesale. Free info.

Advanced Redesign

Chapter 14
Redesign for Real Estate Investors

One neglected area a re-designer might consider is that of working on improving historical homes or "fixer-uppers" in general. Unlike the typical re-design of going in and rearranging someone's furniture, or working with a home owner to improve the interior and/or exterior of a home they wish to sell, there is a good source of income you could tap into in the real estate investment arena.

Many people are interested in becoming professional investors but lack the time or expertise to go in and fix up the properties they buy, whether on the open market or thru foreclosures. Often several people will go together and form an investment company and pool their money. They may do all of the fix-it solutions themselves, or just a part or none at all. An enterprising re-designer just might be able to position herself as the "go-to" person to make the investment property ready for sale.

Hooking up with professional investors can also provide the re-designer with a good source for trade references. As you become more involved in retro-fit redesign projects, you'll need the services of plumbers, electricians, drywall installers, tile layers, roofing contractors, and many, many other services. Very often the main aspects of a foreclosure property or "fixer" property is repair of the kitchen and baths. Psychologically these are the areas that most prospective buyers are highly concerned about.

The first time investor, especially, is always looking for a contractor, so you may be able to help the investor and the contractor at the same time by putting them together. Word to the wise, however. Much thought needs to be given before referring trades people. Your reputation is on the line and you want to protect it. Be sure to check if any contractor is licensed and insured and get references.

You might even be interested in becoming an investor yourself and "hiring yourself" to do all of the re-design, repairs and improvements. In that case, look for fixer-uppers with only cosmetic problems. This is one of the keys to picking a good property.

Exterior additions or major defect repairs can be costly, and the expense of correcting major structural defects may not add a penny to the market value of the house. This is not a concern if you are working for other investors. It is their job to pick the right properties. Just keep in mind that "fixers" that have only cosmetic problems, such as ancient shag carpeting or bad wallpaper, are ideal for first-time investors and re-designers. Cosmetic repairs can be relatively inexpensive (especially if you do them yourself), and some fixer-uppers will pay back double their cost. Always have a fixer-upper inspected before you buy.

Here are a few pointers:

- **Evaluate the floor plan carefully.**
  With a good basic layout even the most hideously decorated house is an ideal fixer-upper. Taking it from hideous to amazing can often just be a matter of pulling off wallpaper and a fresh coat of paint. On the other hand, a house that seems a maze of rooms may have a defective floor plan that can't be fixed - in that case no amount of paint or anything else will solve the problem.

  Estimate renovation/repair costs accurately before you buy. Chart out a budget and stick to it. Be thorough. If you miscalculate, your profit will be affected.

  Ask 3 contractors for a detailed bid. If you buy it in "as is" condition, have the property inspected as a condition of your purchase. One additional repair can wreak havoc on your bottom line. You don't want to have to fix unanticipated defects.

- **Be wise.**
  In planning your remodel, even if you plan to live there yourself for a while, always keep "resale" in mind. Kitchens, bathrooms and storage spaces are important to today's buyers, as mentioned previously. Curb appeal sells houses, so concentrate on improving the landscaping and front entry as they set the tone for the entire home. Keep your color schemes neutral. You want to appeal to the widest number of buying prospects.

Working with a Contractor

Picking a competent and reliable contractor is the most crucial decision you will make. Everything hinges on them doing a professional job for you. Here are a few other factors that are also important to consider.

- **Draw up a well-written contract.**
  I advise you to hire an attorney for this. Any ambiguities in the wording of a contract always go against the person who drew up the contract in a court of law. In addition to detailing the work to be completed, you'll want to specify the amount to be paid, and the responsibilities of each party, a fee assessed to the contractor should he/she fail to complete the contract on time. Your contract should include provisions to protect both you and the contractor if terms are not met. Most contractors have their own documents but you should realize that their goal is to protect themselves, not you. So it's good to draw up your own contract. If you wind up using theirs, don't hesitate to negotiate changes in a standard contract. Just because it's written down, doesn't mean you have to accept it. If you're unsure of any legal language, consult your attorney. Well-written contracts leave little to debate in a court of law.

- **Develop a work schedule that makes sense.**
  Contractors are notorious for starting projects, then leaving them mid-stream to start other projects. You should always try to include a completion deadline, backed by a completion bond. Give your contractor plenty of incentive to finish the job and to finish it on time. You'll need to discuss daily start and stop times. You'll want to define completion dates for each phase. Penalize the contractor monetarily if he does not complete the project on time. Clue in the neighbors in advance that work will be done. This is only polite. Make sure that start times are not abused causing neighbors to become angry because of noisy power tools.

- **Do not pay in advance. Set up a payment schedule.**
  Most of the time it works best to pay for projects as they are completed. As an example, on a $10,000 kitchen remodeling project, you might set up payments this way:

Project stage	Payment
Down payment (to be paid on signing contract)	$1,000
Demolition and clean up	$3,000
Install cupboards and fixtures	$4,000
Finish Project	$1,000
NOTE: 10 percent final payment (paid within 30 days of completion)*	$1,000

- *To ensure the contractor will return to fix problems, withhold around 10 percent of the project's cost until after completion.

- **Hold weekly meetings.**
  It's a good idea to hold weekly meetings with the contractor and project manager. Use this time to discuss details such as scheduling, work hours, cleanup issues, safety issues, etc. Any problems or other issues that arise can be easily discussed and resolved at these meetings.

- **Keep accurate files.**
  Set up a good file system to keep the plans, scheduling charts, order changes, insurance documents, all warranties for equipment, appliances, fixtures and such. All of the major players should have access to these files. As a precaution, make a duplicate set for your personal files.

- **Set up a system of communication.**
  Create a detailed log of contact information regarding everyone involved in the project. Use an Excel spreadsheet to record phone numbers, fax numbers, pagers, cell phone numbers, addresses. Make sure all parties have copies of this contact log. Post a copy at the job site. Insist on being kept in the loop regarding all details, especially if they involve changes in scheduling.

- **Pay attention to safety issues at the site.**
  It is not uncommon for construction workers to behave inappropriately while at the job site. Make sure no workers ever bring any alcohol onto the site. Require daily clean-up of building materials, junk, hazardous substances. Make sure your contractor carries worker's compensation insurance. Contractors who are diligent hold regular safety meetings with their workers. Lack of knowledge of safety rules and regulations is not an excuse. Make it your business to know.

- **Final clean up.**
  I hired a contractor once to put in a new drive-way. To my horror, the workmen washed off their cement covered tools over my plants and on the sidewalk, living residue to dry on the sidewalk. Many plants died. I was terribly unhappy and let him know. A post-construction mess will ruin an otherwise good relationship. Arranging for a professional clean-up service to come in at the end might be a very good idea. Be sure this is dealt with in the contract.

If you're doing re-design services for an investor, recouping the costs of the remodeling investment will definitely be the goal when the home is sold. But resale value can be tricky. Not all homes can be resold for the same profit margins. As a rule of thumb, kitchen remodeling projects and bathroom additions almost always pay back 90 percent or more of their costs. However, finishing a basement usually pays back less than 50 percent. Other improvements fall somewhere in between. For these reasons, it is important to control costs every step of the way and make wise decisions on what to fix up and what to let stay "as is". Consider these payback estimates* for the most typical home improvement projects:

Project	Cost	Average Payback
Add a new heating or air conditioning system	$2,000 to $4,500	100% for heating; 75% for air conditioning
Minor kitchen remodeling	$2,000 to $8,500	94% to 102%
Major kitchen remodeling	$9,000 to $25,000	90%
Add bathroom	$5,000 to $12,000	92%
Add a family room	$30,000	86%
Remodel bathroom	$8,500	77%
Add a fireplace	$1,500 to $3,000	75%
Build a deck	$6,000	73%
Remodel home office	$8,000	69%
Replace windows	$6,000	68% to 74%
Build a pool	$10,000 and up	44%
Install or upgrade landscaping	$1,500 to $15,000	30% to 60%
Finish basement	$3,000 to $7,000	15%

*Compiled from several published surveys - not to be taken as iron clad. These are estimates and will vary with time and location.

How Payback Value Works

Payback value depends heavily on the real estate market and prevailing property values at the time of a sale. If the market is slow, expect to see less payback than you would in a fast market because the buyer is more in control with more eager sellers than there are buyers. You also need to consider the neighborhood. Avoid remodeling a house that is twice the size of other houses in the neighborhood. You are very unlikely to get double the money upon sale.

Issues that can influence payback value include:

- **Type of Improvement**
  Kitchen and bathroom remodeling projects consistently return the most in resale value and almost always help sell a house. Why? Because the woman of the household is mostly concerned about having an up-to-date kitchen that is clean and functional; no one likes to clean or bathe in an old, run-down bathroom. However, converting a basement into a family room isn't considered high on the list, therefore it will bring the least amount of return.

- **Extent of Improvement or Repair**
  Projects can be large or small. Often times there is a cumulative larger payback from several smaller remodeling projects than from one single large one. Small projects tend to be cosmetic in nature, such as fresh paint, new doors, garden windows, upgraded appliances or ceiling fans. These can be easily pointed out to prospective buyers and used quite easily as selling points. Large improvements involve adding or upgrading living space and it is more difficult for buyers to relate to this.

- **Desirability**
  What was unusual years ago may have become a standard inclusion today. Such is the case with

144

- **Cost**
  The current economic conditions and the region of the country where the home exists will affect the pay back values. You may live in an area where remodeling costs are particularly high. Or your region or city may have low sale prices. Metropolitan areas that are bursting at the seam with very little room to expand will make homes sell at a premium price, whereas cities or towns surrounded by lots of open land for expansion will not enjoy that value. These and other factors can affect the profit margin one can expect to reasonably get for a home upon sale. One thing is sure: attractive homes way outsell unattractive homes and sell for a greater price, and sell faster.

So this is an excellent aspect of re-design the enterprising decorator should definitely explore. Hopefully you can see how great a "marriage" it is for a furniture arranger to also offer resale services. They are so complementary to each other.

Words to Heed

Avoid Mechanic's Liens
Whether you are the investor or you are doing re-design services for another party, you can easily avoid a mechanic's lien by paying all parties involved with the project on time and as agreed to. Be sure to ask for lien releases from the contractor, subcontractors, specialists, and suppliers before you make the final payment on the project, however. It's also a good idea to require the contractor to give you a payment and performance bond, which commits a bonding company to complete the project or pay damages up to the amount of the bond. I wrote about this earlier. Refuse to deal with any contractor that has a problem with this, no matter how good a price you are quoted. Reputable contractors recognize the need for these protective arrangements and won't have a problem with it.

Change of Orders
You're always going to run into the need for changes. Some will be last-minute and can't be helped. But too many changes can lead to delays, cost overruns, and a deteriorating relationship with the contractor and/or workmen. If you plan your projects well and have detailed, written orders, you'll go a long way to avoiding these types of problems. Always specify in your contract that you and the contractor must approve *all changes* and additional costs. You want to avoid having a contractor make changes without your knowledge or approval. Make all change orders in writing. File a copy with the records and have a duplicate copy for your personal files.

Want to Fix Up Historic Homes?

There is a difference between "restoration" and "renovation". So if you want to tear out the electricity and make it all appear to be just what it was when originally built, it's not a restoration. It's a renovation.

If your goal is to modernize it, that falls into the category "rehab". You should never ever rehab an historic home or building. A rehab will completely change the style and feeling of the historical space and ruin it forever. So briefly here are a few tips to help guide you.

Get a detailed inspection
First off, hire an experienced inspector who is fully qualified to make such an evaluation. Your real estate agent or local historical commission should be able to make recommendations.

Then it's important to have someone objectively evaluate the problems. This takes knowledge as to whether the wiring is up to code or not, if there are any problems with the foundation. You don't want to get involved with homes or buildings that have serious problems.

Don't settle for a one-page checklist of items that need to be done. Insist on a detailed, written report on the estimated cost of renovation. While a detailed inspection will no doubt cost more money, it can save you thousands of dollars in the long term. A detailed inspector's report can be used as well to pressure the seller to lower the selling price and you can save quite a bit there if that happens.

A good inspection will help you decide the most important issues that need to be done inside and whether or not you would need to "gut it" and start from scratch. In some communities, if the renovation involves more than 50 percent of the house, the entire house has to be brought up to code. In others, the simple act of taking out a building permit triggers that requirement. Make sure you are up on your codes before signing any documents.

Know your historical limits

If the house is located in an historic district or listed on the National Register of Historic Properties, you will be limited as to the kind of renovations you can do. They are particularly concerned with what might be done to the exterior. Save yourself time, frustration and money by getting a copy in advance of the preservation guidelines before you start. A visit to the closest historic commission should net you some detailed guidelines to follow.

They can also give you ideas which will be very valuable. Visit them early and take advantage of their advice and ideas. Some people have poured foundations for decks and had a contractor standing by only to learn that decks were inappropriate for the type of home they were working on.

You might be able to contact family members who lived in the home previously to get details such as the look of the windows, woodwork, doors or carvings. An historical commission may also be able to provide you with photos of the house when it was first built that will greatly aid you in the project. Help can be acquired from multiple sources if you just put in the time and energy to seek it out.

Following is a Q & A I recently did with one re-designer that works for a group of investors who are restoring historical homes in Tennessee. She has much to share and is really making a comfortable living combining her redesign business, her home staging business and her restoration business together.

Interview with Teresa Truitt Weidner

Teresa Truitt Weidner was the very first re-designer to purchase my ebook, **Rearrange It!**, almost the day I put it up for sale in December, 2002. Since then it has undergone several revisions (and will always be a work in progress) to make it better and better.

From the day she read it, she and I have bonded and become good friends, even beyond our businesses. Teresa is one of those special entrepreneurs who is always willing to give back to help other people. It is no wonder she is such a success at everything she does.

Following is an interview I did recently with Teresa to share with you what she is doing in re-design since she works several different types of services together into a cohesive unit. She is an excellent example of someone who has genuinely made a success of her business is effectively using advanced techniques and is having a great time doing what she loves.

QUESTION:

Teresa, would you mind giving my trainees some background on what your business is all about?

I have an interior design/home staging business in Nashville Tennessee. This is my 4th year in business. I spent many years in the travel industry and after being laid off (best thing that ever happened) I started Changing Spaces.

QUESTION:

Can you tell us about how you first got started in re-design?

Since I have been doing this all my life in my own homes and others, I decided to follow my dream and just do it!! Luckily I had finally married at the ripe old age of 40 and was able to have my husband pay all the bills so I could get it started and do what I love.

How has your business grown and expanded?

For the first three years it was touch and go...I learned lots of costly lessons on advertising!! Plus, in Tennessee it takes a lot longer than in major cities for new things to get off the ground....I was used to living in cities like Dallas, Chicago and New York!!......But now, I do not have to advertise....after doing many shows, many articles, and many presentations, I have plenty of work! I am now involved in restoring historical homes for investors as well....so that takes a lot of my time.

QUESTION:

What compelled you to take the plunge and start your own re-design business?

Tired of the corporate world.....Like previously mentioned, if I had not had a partner to take up the slack at first, it might have been different....I started out by remodeling house boats at my marina....it evolved into homes

QUESTION:

Where did you take your initial training?   Any follow up training?

Initial training was in Chicago......I have not gone back for follow-up...

QUESTION:

Can you give us some background on yourself?

(Teresa's Bio) Teresa's background includes 3 years as a high school teacher, 13 years as a corporate travel consultant and 3 years as a facilitator for the technology division for American Airlines. She was awarded "Circle of Distinction" in 1999 as one of the top 100 employees of the company.

Her love for decorating began when she was in grade school and painted all of her furniture bright yellow and made drapes with colored sheets. Through the years of extensive travel, she has had exposure to many types of cultures, architecture and design.

Left: Before Interior Shot; **Right:** After Interior Shot

NOTE: Teresa does more than just rearrange furniture for clients. This is an excellent example of offering some advanced re-design services, such as window treatments (not shown in before picture). However, you need to know what you are doing and be able to completely satisfy your clients.

Teresa has always had a flair for making spaces feel comfortable and inviting. As a lover of antiques, she also has become an expert at restoring wooden pieces to heirloom quality accessories for the home.

Being in the travel industry afforded her the ability to fly to various cities to decorate homes for weddings, holidays and other special occasions. She has lived in many cities including Dallas, New York City, Phoenix, Minneapolis, Shreveport and Chicago, where she received extensive training to gain her status as a Professional Re-Designer.

Teresa has staged many homes to appeal to prospective buyers. These homes range from modest homes to million dollar properties. She redesigns the rooms to make the best use of the space while clearing clutter and giving new life to existing furniture, artwork and accessories.

As an avid boater, Teresa also "stages" houseboats for sale, redesigning interiors and restoring vintage houseboats to their original beauty.

Teresa has also been featured in City Lifestyle in Nashville's City Paper, The Tennessean, as well as other local publications. She has also been featured on Nashville's Talk of the Town conducting room makeovers, and on Fox 17's Mornings with Charlie Chase and Kelly Sutton.

Teresa was saluted as one of Nashville's 32 Women Entrepreneurs for the year 2003. In her spare time, she and her husband are restoring a 1950's cottage near Percy Priest Lake in Nashville.

QUESTION:

So how much time and money did it take for you to initially get your business running?

$5000.00 for training, 3 months to figure out how to build a website and build it........3 years to make a profit without putting everything back into the business.

QUESTION:

You've been successful getting publicity for your business. How have you managed to do that?

I have emailed and called every major newspaper and local TV station......I have been persistent and did 4 segments for local TV and have had numerous articles in various newspapers.

QUESTION:

I know you have a website about your business. How did you start your website?

I searched and found the cheapest with Yahoo. Then for 3 months every nite I would try to figure it out. The great thing about Yahoo is that it is just $4.95 per month and you do not have to know HTML....So now it is easy to keep it updated.

QUESTION:

Teresa, who is your target market?

Everybody!! Just kidding. It was very hard at first to find that out. It seemed that those who could afford me.....thought "she is not a real designer" and those that wanted me and could afford me thought "she is too expensive".......So I found that if I charge by the day or half day......no matter what I do, it seems to work better and I have more business.

My business seems to be somewhat seasonal....not much business in the summer months until this year! I was swamped all summer!

I am doing a lot more staging by making friends with a few agents instead of targeting entire offices....then the word of mouth has worked. I do not spend anymore money on advertising.

I still do a few presentations here and there for women's groups and real estate offices.

Someone recommended me to some investors who did not have the time to rehab the historical homes that they were buying....so now I am managing the remodeling for them and working on 2 homes at a time. What fun!. Getting paid to spend their money while getting to design kitchens, pick out fixtures, knock out walls, and be as creative as I want!

QUESTION:

And where do you find this specialized target market in your part of the country?

I staged a home for an up and coming country music artist that had no time to get his home ready to sell.....After I finished it sold in one day and was not in the best area of town! The handyman that I hired to help me recommended me to the investors...so now business is where I want it to be.

Left: Before Exterior Shot; **Right:** After Exterior Shot

NOTE: Teresa was involved in repainting this home, adding some shutters and plants. It didn't take much re-design effort to make a dramatic improvement.

QUESTION:

Can you tell us how you structured your services to them?

The same way.....$250.00 per day and $35 per hour after 8 hours.....of course I am right in there with them, pulling down drywall, rotten wood, painting, putting up light fixtures, tiling countertops, and doing anything that I can do to keep the project moving along. I love the physical part of it...I have bright yellow coveralls that I wear all over town while driving my van with my signs. I also put up a sign in front of the homes that I am working on.

Did you prepare a contract?

NOPE I hate paperwork.......I keep everything in excel spreadsheets on my computer and email the customer if I can every week. If they do not have internet, I mail them copies with all of the receipts. I use out look for my appointments and how much I made on the job...then print the calendar out at the end of the year for taxes.

How did you determine what to charge?

I have found that if I charge $250.00 per day that I will be working most days of the week.

What kind of vendors, helpers, or labor do you use?

Luckily I know a lot of home improvement people that are independent contractors.

Where did you find them?

Believe it or not at the marina where I keep my houseboat......there is plenty of talent there!

What and how do you pay them?

I write them checks from my business account......I do not have employees on a payroll. I also have bartered with two real estate agents......I help them stage their listings, and they help me decorate and redesign other homes...

Left: Before Exterior Shot; **Right:** After Exterior Shot

NOTE: Again Teresa was involved in some repainting, and adding plants. The real estate agents she has worked for are very happy with her work and intend to keep on using her services. She is good at what she does and makes the services very affordable. This is a winning combination.

QUESTION:

What types of products do you offer?

None......although I do a lot of shopping for furniture and accessories for my customers....I pass my discounts on to them.....then they don't mind paying me the $250.00 per day for shopping When I drive by a place that says.....to the trade only.....I go in and sign up! Same with stores like Pier 1. I have an account with Pro-Source Floors for carpet, tile, and flooring, for $25.00 per year.

Are all your products from the same supplier?

No......I don't work on commission so I can use many of them.

QUESTION:

In order of importance, could you please tell us about the top five marketing strategies that you use on a regular basis?

I named my business something that sounds like a TV show! I have a marketing post card that I hand out to everyone that will take it....supermarket, garage sales, etc. . . I have a Changing Spaces sign on my van which starts a conversation everywhere....(are you from the TV Show) I wear this outrageous pair of coveralls everywhere I go!! I find a way to get on TV.....even if it's not pertaining to my business.... I preach to people why they need to fix things up to sell!

QUESTION:

What challenges did you face and how did you overcome them?

I spent lots of advertising dollars in various newspapers that were expensive and did not bring results. Most people that called wanted a job! I quit spending the money on advertising!!

QUESTION:

What kinds of results have you seen from your various marketing strategies?

I get lots of decorating jobs from garage sales! I act very excited about redesign and do some free stuff once a month.....I am presently working on a church.

QUESTION:

Do you do any other advertising in addition to the website and publicity?

Nope.

QUESTION:

Teresa, could you please tell us about four online or offline places that you've found to be powerful resources for marketing your business or locating e-business strategies and information... and how they've benefited you?

TV has been the best.....get on a local program and do a free makeover.....it has paid off for me! The Internet.....for research purposes. Your newsletters! (Ed. note: Thanks, Theresa) ...trends... HGTV website......Inspiration

QUESTION:

How many hours per week do you spending running your business versus growing it?

10 hours running it in addition to working 5 hours growing. By research, talking to people, entering contests, trying to get on TV! I really do not want to get any larger.....I am at a happy medium right now. As long as I am working most every day, and I can take off when I want....I am a happy camper.

QUESTION:

What unique challenges exist for re-designers in your area?

People still do not understand redesign and are slow to "GET IT" on the home staging.

What are some of the other challenges you have personally experienced building and growing your business?

On redesign, I find a lot of people did not give me recommendations because they wanted their friends to think that they did it themselves!

QUESTION:

What would you consider to be your major achievements?

Entrepreneur of the Year 2003 Nashville Women! and doing what I love to do...

QUESTION:

What do you think has helped to make your business so successful?

Sticking with it......there were times that I thought.....should I get a "real" job?? but then a call comes and I am off again..

QUESTION:

How do you keep your customers coming back -- do you have a unique customer satisfaction strategy?

I find a way to say YES.......I listen to what they want.....and find a way to give it to them.

QUESTION:

What is the biggest mistake you have made since you first launched your business?

Spending all that money on advertising!

QUESTION:

Could you tell us about a "light bulb" moment that you've had? A moment when you've thought to yourself, "If only I'd known that earlier..."

When I read your ebook.....**Rearrange It**.......Could have saved me lots of money!

QUESTION:

What major mistakes do you see other re-designers making?

Pricing themselves out of the market. $250.00 every day is better than $500.00 twice a month! Not leaving a house clean looking.

QUESTION:

Where do you see your business one year from now?

Hopefully, doing what I am doing now.....a variety of different things!

QUESTION:

What advice do you have for beginners who are interested in starting a re-design business?

Do not plan to make any money for the first three years.....Put everything back into growing your business.

QUESTION:

Finally, Teresa, how has running your decorating business impacted your personal and professional life?

Personally, my husband is glad that I am not redecorating our home every season!! I work longer hours but I am much less stressed out than when I was in the corporate world.

Advanced Redesign

Chapter 15
Offering a Home Staging Service to Help Homeowners Sell Their Homes Quickly and for More Profit

Knowing the ins and outs of getting your client's home ready for sale can make your life, and theirs, a lot easier - here's how.

The job of a re-designer is to assist the client to make all important decisions. Some of the decisions they will face appear to be automatic with a minimal amount of thought needed. But there are other decisions, the ones that affect their happiness, well-being and contentment, that will be more difficult. One of the most difficult ones is when to sell one's home.

In most cases, when a property is owned for 20, 30 or more years, a substantial increase in appreciation has taken place. But not just for the homeowner wanting to sell - all properties have increased in value.

I bought my home in 1975 for $65,300. Today, nearly 30 years later, my home is worth close to $1,000,000. Some of that appreciation is due to inflation. Some of it is due to the ever-decreasing undeveloped land in my part of the country. A smaller portion of it is due to improvements I have made through the years.

The baby boomer's home may be their most valuable single asset, and as they approach retirement it's value might be a determining factor in the quality of those leisure years.

When anyone decides to sell their home it is important to have accurate information about the value of their home and it's potential marketability. A good re-designer will suggest to the client the need for carefully assessing the true value and marketability of their home.

There are five basic factors that affect marketability of a home.

1) Market Conditions

During the years of low interest rates a booming real estate market existed. When interest rates decrease, the buying power of the consumer increases. When this happens people who already own a house, which may be mortgaged at a higher rate of interest, realize that they could afford more house for the same basic monthly payment, so they begin thinking about moving up. Some will simply refinance their current home to lower their payments.

Individuals who are renting can often buy a house and have a monthly mortgage payment less than that of their rent. With creative financing to help with the down payment, these individuals enter the home buying market.

Do people continue to buy houses when interest rates increase? Of course they do as people's lifestyles change. People get married. They get divorced. Their children grow up and move out and so they downsize. They have more children and need a larger home. They retire and want a home with less maintenance. They continue to buy and sell homes regardless of the interest rates, but the buying power of their dollar changes, that's all.

When the real estate market is depressed, home staging services are more needed than in normal, up-trending markets. Owners and agents must use every weapon in their arsenal to help their properties stand out from all the rest. Even the lenders who have had to take back foreclosures are in need of staging services. Local governments who purchase foreclosures are also a good target market for stagers. And the home owners who pull their properties off the market when times are tough, usually want to invest in the property for their increased enjoyment. They are prime candidates for a redesign service while they wait for better times to sell their home. So staging services and redesign services go hand in hand and should be offered simultaneously.

2) "Location! Location! Location!"

You have all heard that this is the most important factor in real estate, and one that we have minimal control over. With that said, please keep in mind, we are a diverse population with many different needs. Just because one person perceives a location to be undesirable, that does not mean that it will be undesirable for everyone else.

My office is located in my home, so location doesn't mean that much to me. However, my husband's company is a 45 minute drive from our home each way. Location is an important consideration for him. However, since the original printing of this manual, he relocated his business to our city and now he is only 10 minutes away from home. Location! Location! Location!

One concern that many homeowners have, however, is that areas that were previously more stable, do sometimes deteriorate, thus decreasing market values of the surrounding homes. Take the homes in Big Bear (a local mountain resort town). A drought caused a specific type of bug, I forget which, to eat the trunks of the trees and thousands and thousands of trees died and had to be cut down. Property values plummeted.

The homes at La Conchita, in the news as I write this, have plummeted in value in a single day when a mountainside collapsed, killing 11 people and burying a dozen homes.

Zoning changes can also affect the value of a property in a negative or positive way. A competent real estate agent can evaluate the location and market for qualified buyers.

3) Time of Year

Time of the year is another factor that is often overrated.

In the spring and summer, along with the flowers, sprout hundreds of real estate signs all over town. Granted many people choose to move in the summer for a variety of reasons.

Houses may look better when surrounded by green grass rather than brown. It's a better time to switch schools. Vacation time can be used to do the repairs needed to get the house ready to sell. Warm and dry weather doesn't present as many problems for moving furnishings as cold or wet weather.

The reasons go on and on. I want to emphasize however that spring and summer are not the only time houses sell. There are many other factors to consider.

Seniors more than any other group are probably less motivated by a seasonal factor. Often when they decide to sell, the time of the year doesn't play at all into their decision, probably because they will be less involved personally in the move, leaving that to the moving company.

4) A Home's Condition

Unlike the first three factors, the fourth factor is one the homeowner can take some control over. I cannot emphasize enough that homes that are in good condition with many updates are typically easier to market and sell more quickly at a higher price. In the United States we live in a credit rich, cash poor society. Combine that with the fact that one's time is a rare commodity. Many buyers are looking for a home that is in "move in condition". They have neither the time nor the money to make expensive changes to their new home.

Home staging is a popular concept in today's real estate world. This is the process of de-cluttering, removing excess furniture, neutralizing walls and floors of a home before putting it on the market. Buyers need to be able to visually place their furniture and items in the house before they will consider making an offer. Staging "sets the stage" for buyers to be able to do this. Staging increases the chances that the home will sell for more money in less time. Home staging, therefore, has a specific and direct affect on the firth factor, pricing.

5) Pricing

Pricing is probably the most important factor, and one which the homeowner can control. If the owner's house is *priced right* in the beginning, they are in the best position to attract the maximum number of buyers able to pay the price their home is worth - and to sell their home within their time frame.

The period of best opportunity for selling a home is in the first four weeks. Sellers often say, "Let's price it high, we can always come down."

This can be a crucial mistake, as the interested buyers will know that it is overpriced and will go elsewhere, or at the very least not bother to return when the price has been reduced. They might not even know the price was reduced.

A CMA (comparative market analysis) by a reputable realtor is the best way to insure that your client's house is priced competitively. The CMA will compare the location, style, size, condition, number of rooms, features, and amenities of their home with similar homes in the area that have sold or are presently on the market.

Only a professional market analysis can give the owner the accurate, reliable foundation they need to price their home correctly. Sellers will sometimes choose to sell their homes in their present condition without updating or making improvements. Consultations with the owner's realtor before beginning any improvements is a wise move to determine which ones will probably be most cost effective. Sometimes a little paint goes a long way to giving a home a fresh clean look, and it certainly is cost effective. De-cluttering is very effective and costs nothing except for your fee.

Selling a house is not simple. A realtor is trained to have important information on issues such as disclosures of defects, anti-discrimination laws, and zoning provisions. Ignorance of these, as well as other matters, could result in a costly mistake.

When the time comes for the owner to sell the residence, it makes good sense to analyze, evaluate, and seek a competent professional before making any decisions. Whether they're going to sell in six months or six years having a plan can make it so much easier. A good re-designer will ask to see the homeowner's plan, and if they don't have one, recommend they create one before anything is done.

Why Home Staging Services?

Home "staging" is probably one of the hottest trends in real estate today. Advocates say that redesigned or staged homes often sell faster and at higher prices than similar un-staged homes. So the opportunity for a re-designer to get in on this industry is wide open and very lucrative.

Staging, as I've stated earlier, is a process of clearing, cleaning, organizing, rearranging, updating and preparing a client's home for sale. Anyone who's ever had a home for sale, languishing on the market for weeks or even months, will probably be all for any process than can help avoid that situation in the future.

At its most basic, a home resale service may be as simple as performing some needed repairs, pre-packing and removing unneeded items and accessories, and bringing in some fresh flowers, some art and some plants. In other cases it might be as complicated as repainting, re-carpeting, rearranging furniture, bringing in rented furniture or replacing outdated light fixtures or window treatments.

But no matter how easy or complicated, the end result has only one goal: to show potential buyers the very best side of the client's home. After all, they'll be able to concentrate on picturing themselves in the home when they're not distracted by clutter, dirt, a style or colors that don't appeal to them or home maintenance problems.

Learn More About Home Staging Services

If you doubt that home resale services can help sell a home faster and you're not sure you can make money offering a staging service, then try to put yourself in the shoes of a potential buyer. Picture yourself shopping for a new home. The first home you visit is a brand new model home. The color scheme is coordinated and the furniture has been selected and arranged to show off the size of the rooms.

Kitchens and bathrooms are polished to a high sparkle and are artfully accessorized. Clutter is amazingly absent. The closets are organized and the garage is neat and looks spacious.

The next home you visit is only a year old and has a similar floor plan to the model you just saw. The owners, however, have moved from a larger home and their possessions are packed floor to ceiling in every closet, drawer and shelf. The kitchen and bathroom haven't been scrubbed in days, and there's so much furniture in the dining room that you can hardly walk around the table.

Several dead plants sit in the corner and the paint on the front door has been marred by the incessant scratching of the owner's large dogs. The garage is filled with toys, boxes and holiday decorations and a car can't be parked inside. Family photographs are strewn everywhere and there is dirty laundry on top of the washing machine.

Get the picture? You've probably guessed that in most cases the model home would sell ten times faster than the similar but cluttered, competing home. The model has been "staged" to show buyers the features of the home, the spaciousness of the floor plan, and the ample supply of storage. It is also depersonalized, having no family photographs sitting around.

What most homeowners need to understand, is that the way a home should be presented for resale and the way you live in a home are two completely different things. Most of us don't actually live our lives like a page torn out of *House Beautiful*.

Boxing up collections, freeing floors of throw rugs and area rugs, and editing a room's furnishings, can all combine to making a home seem more spacious and airy. A re-designer must always keep in mind that what the owner is selling is the house -- not its furnishings.

It's all about flow. The eye should move easily from room to room, reflecting on the best features of the home rather than on the possessions inside the home. As a re-designer, you really have to completely detach yourself from the client's possessions and look at their home like you're seeing it for the first time, just as a potential buyer would do. It will be easier for the re-designer to detach from the furnishings than for the seller.

Selling Homes Faster

Homeowners with an objective point of view may be able to clear out and rearrange by themselves. After all, they'll eventually be packing up all of their possessions to move, so boxing up unneeded items and clutter shouldn't be too much of a problem. Have them rent a storage unit for a few months and fill it with boxes of collectibles as well as sports equipment, holiday decorations, seasonal clothing and extra furniture.

However, if they find it hard to edit their own stuff then that's where you come in. They will locate you "much like they would find any other professional service." They will ask around and get referrals.

They will check with their real estate agent. Many real estate firms keep lists of professionals who can do everything from clean a home to repair a leaking kitchen faucet and should have information on you if you have done your marketing correctly.

They will probably interview two or three home stagers at their home. You'll need to tell them what you will (and won't) do, how long it might take, what your fees are, and how soon you might be able to start.

They will probably ask for references from recent customers, ask to see photos of your "before" and "after" homes, and get your opinion on what exactly needs to be done in their home.

Be sure to clarify what items in their plan that you will be responsible for (perhaps moving clutter to the storage unit) vs. what they will handle themselves.

You should be able to advise them about small improvements that will improve their home's re-sale value. You'll notice things a homeowner may overlook, like adding fresh paint and replacing worn carpeting. Pretty basic stuff, but it can make a huge impact on a buyer's first impression of their home. And likewise, what a seller feels may be a big drawback may not be a factor at all in the overall appeal of the home.

Tips and Advice for Resale/Staging Services

Packing It Up and Moving It Out
Have your client borrow a friend's garage or rent a storage area for a couple of months. Then begin to fill it with pre-packed items, boxes of garage clutter and items pulled from storage areas, including the basement and attic. The client will have to move it sometime anyway, so get some of it out of the way before you begin.

If their home is small or "cozy", it's possible to create the feeling that it has more space than it really does. Donate and dispose of the things they no longer want, and pack up the rest of everything for storage off site that's not essential to living right now. Here's what to look for:

- Pack up small photos, decorative items and refrigerator magnets. Clear off horizontal surfaces -- tables, window sills and shelves.
- Store all off-season clothing, shoes, boots and the like. De-clutter bookcases and built-ins and dispose of paperbacks and magazines.
- Clean and organize closets. They will look more spacious if they are relatively empty. Don't forget to paint closets when painting rooms. Leave empty hangers and open shelf or floor space. Suitcases make great places to hide clothes, bedding, etc.
- Remove excess furniture. One of the biggest mistakes homeowners make is having too much furniture in their rooms. When selling, leave no more in place than absolutely necessary and store the rest. Empty floor space makes the room feel bigger.

What Goes, What Stays?

Potential buyers like to look in kitchen cupboards, storage areas and closets to see if their belongings will fit. If your client's closets are packed to the brim it's time to weed through things. You want the storage to appear as generous as possible. They can either sell or give items away or pack them up for their next home. Every storage area in their home -- including display shelves -- should be neat, organized and clutter-free. Nothing should look crammed full. It should appear there is room to spare.

Boxing Up the Personal Pictures

Take down the client's wedding photos, the kids' school pictures and refrigerator art, including the magnets. A buyer needs to picture himself living in the house. Besides, these things usually add to the "cluttered" look anyway. That will be more difficult if your client's personal photos, awards and plaques are evident everywhere. It will only take a little extra time to box up these items and move them to the storage facility.

Stashing the Valuables

Carefully pack up any collections, artwork or valuables that might be damaged (or temptations for theft) by strangers coming into their home. They'll have potential buyers, realtor walk-thrus, open houses, inspectors, cleaners and handymen coming in, so it's a great idea to pack up their art glass collection in preparation for the move. Have the client remove all cash, financial records and such from the home entirely or put in a safe or safety deposit box.

Makeover Their Home and Sell it Faster

Make a List

Take the time to make repairs before buyers knock on the door. Ask your client to help you put together a list of items that need fixing. Look for the obvious such as loose door handles, burned out light bulbs, leaking faucets, or stained carpeting as well as less noticeable features such as slippery area rugs, dangling and dangerous extension cords, or a non-functioning burner on the stove. Remember, quality service is in the details of what you do.

Anticipate a Home Inspector

Look over a sample home inspection report to learn what areas of a home will be examined before the sale. You should be able to get one from your city hall. Whenever possible, anticipate and repair items that could be cited on the report. You'll probably not be able to anticipate every inspection item, but you'll have another chance to fix these later, after the report comes back.

Checking For Grout

Take a look at your client's kitchen tile and bathroom tile. Clean and bleach white grout to remove any stains. Scrape out and re-grout any badly damaged or mildewed. Caulk corners, cracks, and gaps around the sink and tub. If they are really in poor condition, suggest the owner hire a professional company to come in and refinish the tub/shower area. This can be a deal-breaker if not presentable.

Clean! Clean! Clean!

Now that you've got the clutter out of the way it's time to get down and dirty. Cleaning for home staging goes beyond a regular house cleaning routine. You'll want to really concentrate on bringing a sheen to every part of your client's home. Make a list and do the work yourself or hire a cleaning crew to come in after you've moved out the clutter -- and just before the home goes on the market. Check every surface including windows (inside and out), ledges, door knobs, paddle fans, mini blinds, ceiling and floor corners -- and make sure they are clean. If necessary tape up a list in every room and check off items as they are completed, or put neon colored post-it notes on items with special instructions.

Instruct the Client About These Issues: Be sure all major appliances, cupboards, heating units, air-conditioning vents and the like sparkle the entire time your house is on the market. All beds should be made every day. Replace shower curtains and liners and say goodbye to all that mildew. Have all windows professionally cleaned, inside and out, and don't forget any skylights. Everyday odors -- from pets, tobacco smoke and strong cooking -- can turn off potential buyers. Drapery and carpeting should be cleaned in every room where smoking occurs; once this is done, smoking should not take place anywhere inside the home while it is on the market. Remove, clean and store all ashtrays. Be sure to run the fan while cooking in the kitchen; if necessary, open the windows for a while, regardless of season, to clear out strong cooking odors. Have all wall-to-wall carpeting shampooed by a professional. If the carpeting is very old, consider replacing it with something in a neutral color. This is not an inexpensive step, but it will greatly improve your home's appeal to house shoppers.

Checking the Entry

One of the first things a buyer may notice is the front door and porch area. They'll generally be waiting there for a couple of minutes while the realtor locates the key, so it makes sense to spend some time sprucing up this spot. Wash, scrub, or repaint the front door so that it shines. Replace the door handle if it is weathered and unsightly. Clean any windows in this area until they sparkle. Add a fresh topiary or planter and keep it watered and trimmed. Put a pretty wreath on the door. Stand outside and look into the entry area. It will be the first thing buyer's see of the inside of the client's home. Is it welcoming, clean, uncluttered?

More Tips for Re-designers to Solve

Arrange and Accessorize - This is where you will shine. Your client has looked at their furnishings in a certain way for years. You will provide a fresh view of the situation and can rearrange and redesign their furniture for maximum impact during the time their home is listed for sale.

If the space is empty or barely furnished, you may have to rent some furnishings to place in the home. You don't need to fill it up - just enough to give it a slightly "lived in" look, while keeping each room as spacious as possible.

What to Charge - - You will want to charge anywhere from a few hundred dollars for one room to a few thousand dollars for an entire home, depending on the size and scale of the work involved.

Empty one room at a time, then begin to bring back the furnishings and accessories to make a more cohesive design statement. Do not bring back furnishings to the point where the home looks filled. That will make the space look smaller.

Accessorize - Rethink your client's accessories in every room. Repeat the mantra -- uncluttered, elegant, color-coordinated, beautiful. Less is more, so pare down and box up anything "extra" or unneeded. The goal is to "hint" at furnishing the space, not to totally furnish it.

Fresh Flowers and Plants - Cast a critical eye on your client's houseplants. If they're leggy, browning, yellowing dying or otherwise scraggly, pitch them. Start over with some new plants. There are some services in larger cities that will rent houseplants, so that may be an alternative to buying everything new. Be sure to place the plants in clean and attractive containers that will contain and reduce any problems from excess watering. You can also bring in artificial plants and flowers if need be.

Light It Up - Keep the home light and bright as dark areas are uninviting. You know this from your own home. Open the blinds, add lamps, increase bulb sizes, or replace dated light fixtures. Several inexpensive up-lights are another great trick. Use them in your own home between projects. Place them in corners, behind plants or on top of tall armoires to layer additional light into the rooms. This type of lighting will create a strong mood, but remember that most potential buyers will visit during the day, not at night, so don't go overboard.

Lighten Up - Prospective buyers will be attracted to a bright and cheery home. Start by removing heavy drapes to admit as much sunlight as possible. If the view from their home is beautiful, take full advantage of what Mother Nature offers; if it's less than ideal, consider adding sheers or blinds that admit light but partially obscure the view. Pay attention to how artificial lighting adds or detracts from the home's appeal. Keep several lights on at all times, especially in hallways, entryways and small rooms.

Make sure all closet lights work. Consider brightening lights by increasing wattage, but be careful -- don't exceed the capacity rating on the lamp or fixture. Re-arrange table and floor lamps to create an even distribution of light around the prospective buyers home as buyers frequently drive by properties being offered for sale in the evening just to get a look. Make sure all outside lights are on and several rooms are lit from within, even if no one is in them. A brightly lit home is a welcoming home. Space, or the perception of it, is important. You want to show off all the space their house has to offer.

Bathrooms - It is mandatory that these rooms be sparkling clean. Replace old grungy towels with new ones. Add an artificial floral and remove all personal care items from the countertops. Eliminate any dirty laundry and toss in the washing machine. The mirror should sparkle. Clean with glass cleaner for best results. A small lamp on a small table somewhere, if there is room, will add an extra glow to the room.

Make Sure Client Maintains Cleanliness - Don't let your client undermine your hard work by ignoring basic maintenance during the weeks their home is being shown. Stress the importance of keeping everything neat, orderly and very clean. Have them keep up on watering the plants, polishing the mirrors, dusting the front door and keeping clutter out of the home.

Managing Pets - Your client may love their dog or cat like a grandchild but a buyer might not share their sentiments. Have you client take their pets and the pet's belongings to a neighbor's or a relative's home or put with a professional pet caring company, if possible, until the house sells.

Go the Distance with Extra Touches & Appealing Extras

Aroma - Many realtors suggest baking bread or cookies to fill a home with a wonderful aroma. Practically speaking this may not be possible every day, but you might keep it in mind for open houses or repeat visits by potential buyers.

Buy some potpourri and refresher oil in a non-offending fragrance like cinnamon or vanilla. Add some of those room deodorizers, the ones with the night lights, in the bathrooms and kitchen. These are the rooms most likely to harbor odors.

Floor Plans - If you have a clear floor plan of your client's home (perhaps from their builder) it is often a great idea to include a copy of it on the back of their home information sheet. Buyers will be able to study it at their leisure and it can set their home apart from all the others they've seen. The plan should be professionally drawn, not just a hand sketch. Room sizes are also a plus, especially if they are generous in size. A photograph of the living room or some special feature in the home would be good too.

Table Settings - Get out the owner's prettiest dishes and centerpiece and create a beautiful table setting or make a centerpiece for them or get one from your floral vendor. This may not work in every home, but can sometimes give a homey feel to an otherwise cold dining room.

Designing Relaxing Areas - Think of each room as a "TV setting" that you can decorate any way you please to demonstrate your client's home as a place of warmth and order. Consider some of these ideas:

- Set up a tea service at a small table by a window overlooking a garden.
- Place an open book and cozy throw on the upholstered chair in their bedroom.
- Pile an attractive bowl with fresh fruit on the kitchen island.
- Display a vase of fresh (very fresh) flowers in the entry hall.
- Arrange some beautiful cookbooks on the desk in their kitchen.

Have some fun with a few accessories here and there, making interesting little vignettes that say " Welcome ". They could very well help sell the home in record time and for a higher price! After all, that is the goal and the whole point of why you were hired.

More on Designing the Home for Sale

Have you ever bought a book just because you liked the cover? Corporations spend millions of dollars creating the right packaging for a new product launch. Publishers spend top dollar creating provocative book jackets to help their titles stand out on the shelf. This is marketing at its most fundamental level, and the same principles apply when selling a home.

The first step in obtaining the best price for your client's home is to never think about it as their home. Instead, try to think about it as a product in a competitive market. You want their home to stand apart from the crowd. There are several very simple steps that can be taken to improve the prospects of selling their home.

While it may be too soon to start spring planting, it's not too early to welcome the brighter days by lightening up their environment. One of the quickest ways to accomplish this is by exchanging heavy winter drapes for light, airy sheers or lace panels. Simple, white cotton curtains conjure those lovely days when the windows are open to a breeze carrying the scent of newly mowed grass or the salt air. The last thing you want on days such as these is to block the sunshine!

Lightly colored curtains allow diffused light to filter into a space, making the most of available sunshine. Even the daylight coming through an early spring snowstorm will filter through white curtains in an attractive manner.

You can also brighten up their day quickly by choosing throw pillows, slipcovers or light blankets in colors such as cheery yellow, grass green or robin's egg blue. A pretty vase filled with daffodils or a bucket with a spray of forsythia blooms will lighten moods all around. Best of all, many of these suggestions cost very little or nothing. Remember, when you're helping a client sell their home, you're selling a fantasy.

Atmosphere - The temperature should always be comfortable during showings, so have them keep the heat on in winter and run the air conditioner during summer months. Have them bake cookies before an open house. This is so obvious as to be almost a cliché, but it's always a winner. Don't you just love the smell of fresh-baked cookies? Photos of family members, loved ones and good times will help buyers envision their own good times in the future but keep these to a bare minimum. If they've got lots of personal pictures framed and hung on the walls, reduce those on display to the best of the bunch and store the rest.

Additional Decorating Tips and Reminders - If their walls have seen better days, give them a fresh coat of paint and consider refinishing dark paneling or moldings if they are peeling, dingy or dated. Stick with neutral wall colors such as white, cream or light gray. Add new throw pillows in cheery colors to sofas and beds, make sure bathroom towels are clean and well coordinated and place scented candles or soaps in the bathroom.

Living-room and den furniture should be arranged to create conversation zones instead of focusing these rooms on the TV set. Replace switch plates, particularly ones made of brass that have seen better days. Add under-cabinet lighting in the kitchen and replace old, dated cabinet knobs and pulls in the kitchen and bathrooms. Place live plants and fresh flowers in the home; large houseplants can even be rented if necessary. Re-paint the front door and expose or refinish any hardwood floors.

Finally, play up all your neighborhood and region has to offer. If you're in a seaside community, coffee table books on the ocean and beaches will set a nice mood, as will magazine titles such as "Coastal Living."

Chocolate May Be One Answer

When it comes to marketing, attract more customers with sugar. Enterprise Rent-a-Car, a client of mine in my art consulting business, started out wooing body shops with a box of donuts to get them to recommend their company for rental cars when owners brought their cars in to be fixed after an accident. They also treated insurance agents to the same. Now they are the No. 1 rental agency in the world, built largely from donuts because they didn't start advertising to consumers until many, many years later.

Real estate professionals are bombarded with information and calls so you have to make your marketing materials more memorable. Take a folder to hold your brochure and references and a signature chocolate piece which features your company's distinctive logo. Drop the items off yourself, targeting top real estate agents rather than blanketing a large group.

Offer several services. Visit a client's home for a consultation for $300. Promise a report which includes room-by-room suggestions for improving the home's appeal. But do as much as the client would like you to do, bringing in workers to handle specific tasks such as cleaning or packing overflowing bookshelves. Charge the client $300-500 per day.

Often a homeowner may achieve a new look by rearranging or storing excess furniture or by making small, low-cost changes. But many aren't sure where to start without an objective and professional opinion, which is where you come in.

You need to be good at working with people. Honest but gentle. Seek ways to advise your client on the best and most prudent ways to spend their money so that their home will showcase the strengths of the home and neighborhood.

A Quick Review

It's a question of doing whatever is necessary to make a home more visually appealing. You want it to look like a model home and have people think, 'I could live here.'"

That includes adding plants or artwork, if the homeowner doesn't have those. A few pieces of furniture could improve the look as well, if the rooms are bare, so consider offering furniture rental as well, which will add a new revenue stream.

- Tidy the frontage and add such features as hanging baskets to increase drive-by desirability
- Clear out clutter as this is the first thing that people notice
- Ensure the hall is welcoming as first impressions count
- Banish pets and children during a viewing - in that order!
- Ensure paintwork is clean and get out the paint can if necessary. White paint work is preferable to dark wood
- Clean or replace carpets and curtains with economical alternatives
- Ensure there are no dark, unwelcoming areas and put on lights and lamps
- Give each room a specific purpose - for instance, ensure a dining room or office area is given one role
- Kitchens and bathrooms are the biggest selling points: replace flooring (economically) if necessary; clear surfaces (including children's artwork from the fridge) and ensure that the kitchen and bathrooms are spotless
- Ensure all cupboards are tidy as they will be opened!
- Stage the garden as an extra room
- Waft smells through the house such as coffee, baked bread, potpourri or just good old fresh air.
- Have owner host a garage sale before the home is listed. Get rid of clutter to allow the buyer to really see their home. Pack away everything you can and clean out items they won't need in their next home. Homebuyers will be expecting the occupants to be preparing to move, so a few packing boxes here and there can be used to your advantage. They could be a good visual stimulant to someone who is "on the fence;" they show that the owners are moving and are serious about finding a buyer.
- If at home, have owners welcome the buyer at the entry. Put out a new doormat, but avoid mats with cutesy sayings. Clean and polish the brass door knocker. Put potted flowers on the porch. Make sure the front entry floor is always sparkling clean and the porch and steps are always swept. First impressions count.
- Stimulate buyers' imaginations. Set the dinner table with your client's best dishes. Use the coziness and romance of the fireplace to advantage. Put a pair of wine glasses and a vase of flowers on the coffee table in front of the fire. Your goal is to set a scene that will encourage buyers to imagine their family living in the home.
- Be ruthless about odors. If there is a smell, their house won't sell. Use cleansers of all kinds to make the home smell fresh, from carpet freshener to potpourri. Have owners deodorize cat litter and scoop litter daily. Put cedar chips inside the closets. However, be careful when using room sprays as they can irritate allergies.
- Create a spacious feeling. Make sure that all doors, cabinets and drawers open all the way without bumping into anything or sticking. Clean out the entry closet and put only a few hangers in it, so that the buyer can visualize winter coats. Move oversized furniture to a storage facility. Make sure entrances to all rooms have an open flow.
- Make the most of views. Disguise unsightly views. Put a screen or a basket of flowers in front of a fireplace if it isn't in use. Let breezes move their sheer curtains at the window. Make sure the interior is visible from the street. All windows must be crystal clean and clear.
- Create counter space. Store away extra appliances. Put away dish racks, soap dishes and other clutter. Decrease kitchen clutter.
- Avoid eccentric decor. De-personalize their teenager's room, the game room or other areas by removing wild posters or any decorative item that could be construed as offensive. Remove decorations which might not appeal to the masses, from hanging beads in doorways to jars where their children store their spider collections.
- Let there be light. Increase the wattage in light bulbs in the laundry room, kitchen and bathrooms. For showings, turn on lights in every room.

- Show how the family made the house a home. Put photos of their family enjoying their home in at least three different places. (Keep this to a minimum, however.)

Interior Checklist Summary

- Remove all clutter from the house.
- Are countertops free and clear?
- Have you removed unnecessary furniture throughout the house?
- Remove the art gallery and coupon collection from the refrigerator.

- Check the bathrooms.
    - Are the surfaces clean and clear?
    - Are shower curtains and doors hung properly?
    - Is the flooring clean and fresh?
    - Are towels neatly hung?

- Check the walls.
    - Is paint and wallpaper fresh and clean?
    - Are the walls free from holes?
    - Are there any marks or objects on the walls that need to be removed?

- Check the floors.
    - Is the carpet clean and free from stains?
    - Are hard surface floors clean and free from stains?

- Check windows and window coverings.
    - Are all the windows clean?
    - Are draperies and blinds clean?

- Pet check.
    - Are there any signs that this is a pet's home? Be sure to clean and remove kitty litter, pet toys and bedding.

- How's the aroma?
    - Try to air out the home prior to showings.
    - If air freshener is necessary, use well before showings as a consideration to those with allergies.

- Set the mood prior to showings.
    - Open draperies and blinds.
    - Turn on the radio to a classical music station, set the volume on low.
    - If you have time, cook a batch of cookies to have the warm, welcoming aroma permeating the home.

Exterior Checklist Summary

- Inspect the outside grounds. Remove any building materials, scrap wood, discarded household items, etc. from the property. Store garbage cans in the garage.
- Check the home from the roof down.
    - Is the roof free and clear from obstructions and moss?
    - Are the gutters clear and neatly hung?
    - Are the windows clean and free from obstructions (such as overgrown bushes or trees)?

- ○ Are bushes, trees and shrubs neatly pruned?
- Inspect the condition of the paint or siding?
  - ○ Is it time to power wash the siding?
  - ○ Is touch up paint needed?
  - ○ Is the front door in good shape?
- Do flower beds need an upgrade?
  - ○ Are plants neatly pruned?
  - ○ Is the bed free and clear of weeds?
  - ○ Is the bed properly mulched?
  - ○ Are flowers in bloom?
- Keep the lawn neatly groomed.
  - ○ Is the lawn free from weeds?
  - ○ Is the lawn free from grass clippings?
  - ○ Is the lawn neatly edged?

Now, step back, stand outside the front door, as much as 30 feet away, and evaluate the feeling you get. Is the house warm and inviting? Does it feel like home? Then perhaps it will to buyers too.

All you have to do now is present your invoice to the client, pick up your check, send them a thank you note, and remind them that you'll be available to help them arrange the furnishings in their **new** space as soon as they are moved in.

Advanced Redesign

Chapter 16
Niches Within the Niche

I've given you many ideas so far about how to take your interior redesign business to the next level by offering your clients more than a simple redesign service. There are many businesses that make more money selling their "back end" products and services than they do selling their "front end" service. To have the best chance of taking your business from small to medium, and from medium to large or from large to super-large ($100,000 and up), you may need to offer a wide variety of products and services to your clients.

But let's take it a step further.

Whether you're strictly a re-designer, or whether you also offer home staging services or any of the other add-on services we've discussed already, or associated products and related services, your target market is still fairly broad. Virtually anyone, whether they own a home or are renting, is a potential client for your redesign and home staging services.

Virtually anyone who wants or needs to sell a home is a potential home staging client, but may also be a potential redesign client. And the buyer who purchases the home is also a redesign prospect.

But still the target is a broad niche market.

Consider defining and targeting an even smaller, more descriptive niche within the broader niche. By narrowing your marketing message even further, you could become **the** "go to person" in that smaller, more highly specialized niche.

Here's what I mean.

Suppose you decided to specialize in one or more of the following tighter niche markets:

- Yacht Staging
- Green Staging
- Travel Staging
- Business Staging
- Restaurant Staging
- Celebrity Staging
- Auto Staging

- Bachelor Redesign
- Art Gallery Redesign
- Vacation/Resort Redesign
- Hospitality Redesign
- Church Redesign
- Restaurant Redesign
- Store Redesign

Think about it for a minute. How many Mom n Pop **delicatessens or tiny restaurants** have you visited that looked like total dumps? They look so bad you wouldn't dare eat there? What about offering your redesign services to them? You know how much it will help them.

Or how about all those **churches** out there that are meeting in warehouses or store spaces that look terrible? A drive by will virtually tell you all you need to know. Many churches don't have their own building yet, but the temporary facility usually needs a lot of work. When you're working with a church (or any entity in a large facility) you've got to think BIG. Your scale will be quite different from a residential home, but the design concepts are the same. By sprucing up the interior space for the church, looking for ways to accommodate a larger congregation, you'll be helping that church grow and flourish.

Do you have any **stores** in town that are overloaded with merchandise everywhere? Do they need your organizational skills to help them sort and merchandise their products more efficiently? Can shoppers find what they are looking for easily? If not, they need your redesign and organizational skills to come to their rescue.

Many people own more than one home. They might own several **vacation homes** or **rental properties**. Or maybe they own a **time share**. Approach them with a redesign of their other properties. If they rent the property out during the year, a redesign will give them the opportunity to get better, more attractive pictures on the internet, which will in turn bring them more renters (and happier ones too).

How many **motels or hotels** have you stayed in that looked terrible? The beds were not in ideal places. The art was old, faded and hung way too high. Offer your redesign services to the management. Chances are the problems in one room will be repeated in all the rooms and you could make a nice tidy sum of profit redesigning the whole motel. The hotels and motels to target will be on the lower end of the scale as your 5-star facilities will already be utilizing the services of a full service designer.

Why not target **bachelors**? Bachelors usually know nothing about interior design, hate to shop, and make good money. Position yourself as the person who makes bachelor pads look fabulous, to not only meet the taste of the bachelor, but to be pleasing to the eye of everyone he brings to his pad.

Do you visit **art galleries**? Some of them are in dire need of a good re-designer to come in and re-hang all of their art. Usually galleries have no rhyme or reason to why and where they display the art they sell. Often times the frame samples are displayed in a disorganized fashion too. Look for galleries that have too much merchandise on display and work your magic to help buyers find what they're looking for more efficiently.

Do you live near the ocean or a large lake? People buy and sell **yachts** just like they do homes. Some of them are in dire need of a stager to help the sale of the yacht. Since so many parts of a yacht are built-ins, your services would no doubt be very simple, but for a reduced fee you could make a difference in how that yacht is marketed.

With the whole world getting on the band wagon when it comes to the environment, why not position yourself as a "**green**" specialist in your area. Home Depot now has "green" products available and a special section for them. When staging a home, think of how unique it will be to market it as a "green" home. As time goes by, this concept will grow. Why not be on the front end of a growing trend?

Large corporations that do business overseas usually own properties for their executives to live in. Market your redesign and staging services directly to the **executives of the company**. If you're willing to travel, you can carve out a very nice income for yourself as their "in house" re-designer or stager. Get them to put you on retainer. Then when they have a need, they just call you and hand you the ticket and away you go to work your magic overseas.

Or why not specialize in servicing **businesses that are for sale**? It's just as important for a business to look organized and fabulous to a potential buyer as it for the financial picture to look promising. Look for companies that specialize already in marketing businesses for sale. Suggest to them that they add your business staging services to their list of services. You might not get a huge number to do, but what if you got one or two per year? Business owners will be willing, usually, to spend a lot more for services than home owners, if for no other reason than that businesses are harder to sell than homes. Think about how you could position yourself as the leading "business stager" in your area.

Restaurants are notorious for having short lives. But instead of the **restaurant owner** losing everything and having to shut down totally, perhaps you could specialize in helping them sell the restaurant by fixing it up first. There are many reasons why a restaurant might fail, but it should never ever fail because it looked terrible and turned off potential patrons.

Do you live near Hollywood? Or do you live near Broadway? Or are you in or near Nashville? These are just a few of the places where a large assortment of **celebrities** live and work. But chances are few, if any, stagers or re-designers specialize in serving this targeted market. That usually is because they have a "star struck" mentality that prevents them from feeling comfortable with this group. Stars and celebrities are just human beings like you and me. They have the same wants and needs. Yes, they probably have more money to spend but they remain a largely untapped market.

Have you tried to buy a **previously owned vehicle** lately? Well, my son and daughter have. And I've been shocked to see the terrible condition that some of them are in and the owners expect to sell them that way. Now this is a really small space compared to a home, and you'd need some mechanical know how, but there could be an interesting market here for a very enterprising individual, particularly if you're of the male gender. Auto detailing usually limits itself to vacuuming, polishing and waxing. But what if an auto detailer also offered some creative ideas to enhance the automobile or van or truck or SUV to help it sell faster for a better price?

Which brings me to the subject of **mobile homes and retirement homes**. Typically mobile homes are bought or rented by senior citizens who have had to downsize from a larger home. Perhaps they just wanted to reduce their expenses, or perhaps there was a death or divorce. Going from a larger home into a smaller home is difficult for many reasons. Decisions have to be made about what to toss out, give away or sell. These kinds of decisions are often made by children or relatives, but often the senior citizen is alone with no one to help them. They are perfect prospects for your business. Why not specialize in helping **senior citizens**, whether they are downsizing or not. Everyone wants to enjoy where they live no matter what size the space is. As the baby boomers start to retire in droves, you could carve out a really targeted, specialized service that will take off big time.

Questions to Ask Yourself

In the final analysis, you need to ask yourself a few questions:

1. Is there an aspect of redesign or staging that I enjoy more than others?
2. Is there a group of customers that I would enjoy working with more than others?
3. Can the space be redesigned sufficiently to earn a good profit for me?
4. Can the space be staged sufficiently to earn a good profit for me?
5. Is the smaller target market sufficiently big enough in my area to support me?

If the answers are "yes", then carve out for yourself the smaller target market and go after it. Streamline your marketing message to fit this group. Don't try to be all things to all people. You may find it much easier to grow your business to the level you want if you fine tune it and market solely (or primarily) to a smaller niche. These aren't all the ideas out there. Always be open to new ones that come along and see where you can fit in and capitalize on up-trending markets.

Home Enhancement Check List/Estimator

By Barbara Jennings

Home Staging/Enhancement Estimator

SERVICE RENDERED   TIME/COST ESTIMATE

Interior De-Cluttering Services

Closets
- □ Remove and pack or store extra items
- □ Clean and paint interior
- □ Organize clothes by color and arrange shelves
- □ Group clothing and hang in same direction
- □ Organize linens, towels neatly
- □ Organize athletic gear, store extra items
- □ Arrange shoes, remove old ones and pack and store

Bookshelves
- □ Remove, store and organize extra items
- □ Leave best on shelves but don't fill them up

Collections
- □ Pack and store for protection

Tools, Shop and Laundry Areas
- □ Remove and store extra items, organize
- □ Leave detergent out, hide the rest

Garage
- □ Organize tools and gardening equipment
- □ Label all boxes
- □ Move as much to storage as possible
- □ Sell as much in garage sale as possible

Children's Play Areas
- □ Pack and store extra toys and games, organize

Kitchen
- □ Clear counters, put away small appliances
- □ Remove and store accessories
- □ Remove and pack and store extra dishes
- □ Remove and pack and store extra pots, pans, bowls and so forth
- □ Consolidate duplicate food items
- □ Remove notes and magnets from refrigerator
- □ Organize silverware, utensils
- □ Clean out junk drawers
- □ Organize and consolidate under sink items
- □ Clean or paint flooring under sink
- □ Remove, pack and store any items which could be dangerous for children
- □ Replace drawer and shelf paper liners

Interior De-Cluttering Services Continued

Bathroom Vanities, Medicine Cabinets
- ☐ Remove, pack and store extra items, organize
- ☐ Remove and replace stained or torn paper liners

Living Areas
- ☐ Remove papers, mail and magazines from all rooms
- ☐ Remove extra furniture and extra items hanging on walls
- ☐ Rearrange furniture but not around perimeter
- ☐ Remove extra or unhealthy plants

Exterior De-Cluttering Services

Lawn and Garden
- ☐ Fertilize, mow, trim, weed, water & re-sod
- ☐ Remove lawn ornaments, gardening tools
- ☐ Clear all walks, steps, driveways of items/weeds
- ☐ Remove all debris from pet areas
- ☐ Remove all vehicles from curb view
- ☐ Remove excess ornaments/furniture from decks
- ☐ Remove excess ornaments/furniture from patios
- ☐ Remove all debris, wood, garden stuff, toys and sports equipment from yards

Interior Cleaning Services

Floors
- ☐ Remove old wax, scrub and wax and buff to shine

Carpet
- ☐ Clean thoroughly. Use professional service.

Walls
- ☐ Remove fingerprints, marks, cobwebs

Woodwork
- ☐ Clean and polish with scratch cover

Drapes and Curtains
- ☐ Launder or dry clean

Lighting Fixtures
- ☐ Clean and polish, wash or replace bulbs and covers

Windows, Mirrors, Glass Cabinets
- ☐ Clean to sparkle with glass cleaner/paper towels

Doorknobs, Handles and Pulls
- ☐ Clean and polish

Kitchen
- ☐ Clean and polish cupboards (inside/outside)
- ☐ Clean and deodorize vents, exhaust hoods
- ☐ Clean appliances thoroughly (inside/outside)
- ☐ Clean and polish and clean sinks, remove stains

- ☐ Clean and deodorize garbage areas
- ☐ Use garbage disposal freshener (baking soda)

Bathrooms
- ☐ Clean and polish vanities (inside/outside)
- ☐ Remove stains and mold (sinks, tubs, showers)
- ☐ Clean grout
- ☐ Polish mirrors and chrome to sparkle

Basement, Garage, Attic
- ☐ Sweep or vacuum floors and ceilings
- ☐ Wash down furnace, water heater, washer, dryer

Pet Areas
- ☐ Clean thoroughly and deodorize

Odors
- ☐ Scrub all hard surfaces
- ☐ Use odor neutralizer on upholstery, carpet, drapes

Exterior Cleaning Services

Windows
- ☐ Clean till they sparkle

Walks, Steps and Driveways
- ☐ Sweep and remove stains
- ☐ Rinse with hose

Siding, Brick or Stucco
- ☐ Hose off
- ☐ Use restoring product on vinyl & aluminum siding

Gutters and Downspouts
- ☐ Hose out debris
- ☐ Hose off as necessary

Decks, Patios and Backyards
- ☐ Use deck cleaner
- ☐ Hose off patios
- ☐ Rake fallen leaves and place in bags for trash pick-up
- ☐ Wipe down lawn furniture, grills
- ☐ Clean pool equipment and deck furniture
- ☐ Have pool cleaned professionally

Interior Repairs

Plumbing
- ☐ Repair leaks and make other repairs as needed

Mechanical Systems
- ☐ Have inspected and certified

Appliances
☐ Check bulbs and replace parts

Walls and Ceiling
☐ Patch cracks and paint as needed
☐ Repair torn wallpaper
☐ Remove wallpaper if busy pattern/poor color/poor condition

Windows
☐ Replace cracked glass, re-caulk as needed
☐ Hire professional to install new windows

Grout and Caulking
☐ Patch or replace as needed

Hinges and Knobs
☐ Tighten or replace as needed
☐ Use Wd-40 to lubricate

Flooring
☐ Repair or replace as needed

Light Fixtures
☐ Repair or replace if dated

Switch Plates and Outlet Covers
☐ Replace cracked or mismatched plates

Phones
☐ Check for static and service
☐ Repair lines if needed

Exterior Repairs

Doors and Windows
☐ Repair screens or glass, replace if needed
☐ Repair or replace door hardware
☐ Lubricate hinges

Sidewalks, Steps and Driveways
☐ Repair cracks as needed
☐ Remove stains

Siding
☐ Repair, replace or paint as needed

Gutters and Downspouts
☐ Repair or replace as needed

Decks and Patios
☐ Repair as needed

Fences
☐ Repair, replace or paint as needed
☐ Lubricate hinges and latches

Doorbells
☐ Make certain they are in working order

Alarm System
- ☐ Validate functioning

Mailbox
- ☐ Repair or paint if needed

Depersonalizing Interior

Wallpaper
- ☐ Remove if dated or worn or very busy pattern

Walls
- ☐ Paint a warm, light neutral color (not white)
- ☐ Use same color in rooms that flow together

Bathrooms
- ☐ Choose coordinating, warmer neutral color

Paneling
- ☐ Polish or remove or paint, if dated

Floors
- ☐ Replace warn or dated floors or carpeting

Artwork
- ☐ Remove distracting or bold posters and art
- ☐ Repair broken glass
- ☐ Replace buckled mats or chipped frames

Family Photos and Collections
- ☐ Remove extensive displays
- ☐ Choose a few happy photos to display discreetly

Basement
- ☐ Paint floors and walls

Ceilings
- ☐ Cover stains or soot with special coating
- ☐ Paint ceilings white for most open feeling

Depersonalizing Exterior

Siding
- ☐ Paint or touch up as needed with neutral color

Trim
- ☐ Paint or touch up as needed

Lawn Areas
- ☐ Remove any bold decorations

Lighting
- ☐ Replace old entrance light with new one

Creating Maximum Curb Appeal

- ☐ Set potted plants or small tree on stoop
- ☐ Add plants in hanging baskets for variety

- ☐ Flank front door with matching pots with plants
- ☐ Place new cushioned doormat at entrance
- ☐ Add new house numbers
- ☐ Add interesting door knocker or doorbell
- ☐ Replace doorknob
- ☐ Add new lighting fixtures
- ☐ Polish or paint front door
- ☐ Paint or replace garage door
- ☐ Add fresh layer of rock/bark over dirt in garden and around plants
- ☐ Plant new flowering plants/add artificial plants
- ☐ Replace or repaint mailbox
- ☐ Add window box with colorful annuals
- ☐ Keep lawn mowed, shrubs trimmed
- ☐ Remove all weeds
- ☐ Add solar lights to be seen from street

Creating Maximum Interior Appeal

Entry
- ☐ Showcase unique piece of furniture or artwork
- ☐ Group small table lamp with vase for elegance
- ☐ Add large beveled mirror to brighten entry
- ☐ Add drama with fresh flowers
- ☐ Add plenty of plants or a tree
- ☐ Add warmth and texture with an area rug
- ☐ Add dramatic new lighting fixture
- ☐ Add new switch plates

Kitchen
- ☐ Open colorful cookbook on a stand
- ☐ Group set of cooking oils next to cookbook
- ☐ Create neat, clean look with new burner covers
- ☐ Add cover to toaster or other small appliances
- ☐ Add new throw rugs
- ☐ Set decorative serving bowl with fruit on table
- ☐ Add blooming plant to counter
- ☐ Replace worn curtains with mini blinds/valance
- ☐ Paint worn cabinets and add new hardware
- ☐ Consider replacing dark countertops

Bathrooms
- ☐ Use plush new towels and rugs to soften hard lines
- ☐ Tri-fold towels; hang in layers on bars; tie off to keep fresh
- ☐ Stack guest or hand towels neatly in basket
- ☐ Drape bath towel over tub rim
- ☐ Place small bouquet of flowers on vanity
- ☐ Add new fabric shower curtain
- ☐ Highlight tubs/vanities with colorful bath oils

□ Add accessories: soap dish, vase, drinking glass; scented oils
□ Consider new towel racks or shelves
□ Keep new unscented guest soap on hand
□ Add a green plant or two

Bedrooms

□ Fold back plush comforter to show layers
□ Top bed with decorative pillows
□ Add curtains/valances to rooms without them
□ Add artwork for elegance
□ Add mirror for spacious feeling
□ Stack some books on nightstand
□ Add vase or photo and reading lamp
□ Place area rug for additional color/texture

Children's Rooms

□ Arrange stuffed animals
□ Display art materials, tea party, animal farm
□ Make cozy book nook
□ Consider adding new play rug
□ Add fun piece of art
□ Arrange athletic trophies, ribbons, medals

Living & Family Rooms

□ Drape afghan over easy chair or sofa
□ Add decorative pillows to sofas and chairs
□ Add fresh flowers or plant to coffee table
□ Stack interesting books on tables
□ Add art pieces to a bookcase for multiple use
□ Enhance cozy feeling with floor or table lamp
□ Neatly place family chess game or puzzle
□ Leave bowl of candy, fruit or chips for visitors
□ Place bean bag chair in front of TV

Showcase Fireplace

□ Place logs or unscented candles or plants on grate
□ Add artwork or mirror above fireplace
□ Place basket of birch logs on hearth
□ Update screen and tool set

Dining Room

□ Add dramatic bouquet of fresh flowers on table
□ Display interesting serving piece
□ Add candles or art piece on table or server
□ Add new table runner
□ If table is unattractive, add new table cloth or replace or refinish table

Backyard, Deck and Patio

□ Stage outdoor space to suggest leisure activities

- ☐ Place grill and lawn furniture for barbeque
- ☐ Set up lawn game: croquet, badminton, volleyball
- ☐ Group colorful potted flowers
- ☐ Display birdfeeder
- ☐ Add fresh layer of bark/rocks to gardens
- ☐ Add solar lights for dramatic effects
- ☐ Neatly arrange pool toys and games
- ☐ Add pot of bright flowers to tables
- ☐ Add outdoor lanterns for festive look

Basement, Laundry & Hobby Areas
- ☐ Add bright tablecloth to shelves/laundry table
- ☐ Face laundry supplies with labels forward
- ☐ Purchase new hangers
- ☐ Consider new ironing board or cover
- ☐ Add curtain or mini blind to window
- ☐ Add green plants or silk flowers
- ☐ Place stack of clean towels on dryer
- ☐ Brighten up with fun piece of art
- ☐ Add cushioned area rug
- ☐ Organize workbench or hobby area

Last Minute Open House Details

Interiors
- ☐ Vacuum, sweep, dust
- ☐ Empty wastebaskets
- ☐ Pick up dirty clothes; hide in washing machine
- ☐ Put away personal care items in bathrooms
- ☐ Clean all sinks and faucets with glass cleaner
- ☐ Make sure rugs are clean and straight
- ☐ Freshen carpets, drapes, upholstery against odors
- ☐ Clean pet areas and remove pets
- ☐ Open shades and drapes
- ☐ Set comfortable temperature on thermostat
- ☐ Turn on all lights
- ☐ Open windows to freshen rooms; add plug-in scented oils
- ☐ Arrange fresh flowers in key areas; get from yard
- ☐ Play soft easy listening music
- ☐ Turn television off
- ☐ Turn off all sounds of work (appliances)
- ☐ Remove all purses, wallets, financial records
- ☐ Final check of every room
- ☐ Welcome visitors with light refreshments
- ☐ Place floor plans & info near front door

Exteriors
- ☐ Pick up lawn tools and toys
- ☐ Pick up after pets and small children

- ☐ Remove obstructions from curb view
- ☐ Remove all trash cabs from view
- ☐ Clear driveways and walk areas
- ☐ Sweep or hose down entry walk and landing
- ☐ Store hoses neatly
- ☐ Remove all vehicle(s) from driveway and curb

Staging Consultations

The first step in the Staging process is to identify what needs to be done:

- **Initial Interview** - Conduct a telephone interview with the client to discuss objectives, and gather preliminary information. If the Home Staging is being done in connection with the sale of a home, a telephone interview should be conducted with the real estate agent responsible for the listing.
- **Property Tour** - Discuss the Staging opportunities, and if all parties agree to work together, walk through the house twice. First, ask client to provide a tour of the property so that you can discuss specific objectives. Then do a second walk-through yourself to take additional notes and photographs.
- **Staging Report** – Write up a detailed report describing the steps that need to be taken to stage the home. Use the checklist above to help you estimate pricing. Based on the situation, the report will identify things that should be packed, moved, painted or replaced. The report will also address where to place furniture and accessories and provide recommendations on acquiring accessories that will update the look of the home.
- **Staging Guides** – Using our staging guides (Home Staging for Yourself) saves you all the time and hassle of doing written reports. The 80-page booklet itemizes the most common tasks for every part of a typical home. All you have to do is circle the task to be done in each room or area of the home, writing on the blank lines any custom task unique to that home. When done, the booklet serves as your personal guide to completing the project or serves as a guide to the homeowner doing the labor of staging the property.

Sometimes your participation stops here, and the client will implement the recommendations in the Staging Report. At other times, you will stay involved as described below.

Fine-Tune Visit

A Fine-Tune Visit can be performed after the client has implemented the recommendations in the Staging Report.

During the Fine-Tune visit, make adjustments to further refine placement of furniture and accessories, and to make additional recommendations, if required.

If your help is requested with shopping for new accessories after the Staging Consultation, you can deliver those items during the Fine-Tune Visit. If you need professional help (such as a tree trimmer and landscaper) you can hire sub contractors to help you as was done here on this over-grown exterior.

Home Staging Implementation

Break down your services as follows:

- **Complete Staging** - A complete staging starts at the curb in front of the client's home. The home is assessed from every angle: the view from the street, every room in your home, the patio, the yard, even the closets. You can perform anything from a complete staging to staging only one or two rooms.
- **Staging Using the Client's Belongings** – You can stage the home using only the furniture and accessories the client owns.
- **Staging Using New Accessories** - You can stage the home using the furniture and accessories the client currently owns, and adding as many accessories as are required to achieve the desired effect.
- **Vacant Home Staging** - A vacant home for sale can be staged using rental furniture and accessories to furnish the entire home, or just to provide "vignettes" inspiring the buyer to imagine how they would enjoy living in the home and using the space.

Forms Section

Disclaimer

This manual is sold with the understanding that the publisher and author are not engaged in rendering legal, insurance, tax or other professional advice or services beyond the scope outlined here. All attempts have been made to give accurate information based on the author's own experience and background only. If legal advice or other expert assistance is deemed necessary and desired, the services of a competent attorney, CPA, insurance agent or other professional person should be sought and is highly advised.

Neither the author nor the publisher can be held accountable for errors or omissions, nor similarities to other business books or training programs. Some of the information regarding actual clients has been altered because of privacy issues. Any resemblance to actual persons or businesses is, therefore, purely coincidental. Standard business practices, marketing techniques and management philosophies, common to other consultants and other types of businesses, have been discussed and presented. The author and publisher further accepts no responsibility for inaccurate or misleading information, nor omissions of any kind, particularly with regard to training using hazardous materials or tools or where services or products may involve risks of any kind.

All readers of this manual are forewarned to use discretion and take all security and safety measures possible, paying close attention to all instructions given by various manufacturers for their own products.

These forms are free for your personal usage in your business as a re-designer, home stager or consultant, but are not to be used for training purposes or resale for profit under any condition.

Estimate

CLIENT NAME _____ DATE _____

ADDRESS _____ TIME _____

CITY _____ STATE _____ ZIIP _____ NEAREST CROSS STREETS _____

DIRECTIONS TO HOUSE _____

_____

_____

QTY	SERVICES PERFORMED/PRODUCTS RECEIVED	REGULAR PRICE	SPECIAL PRICE

Invoice

CLIENT NAME _____

DATE _____

ADDRESS _____

INVOICE NO. _____ TIME _____

CITY _____

STATE _____ ZIIP _____ NEAREST CROSS STREETS

DIRECTIONS TO HOUSE _____

_____

_____

QTY	SERVICES PERFORMED/PRODUCTS RECEIVED	REGULAR PRICE	SPECIAL PRICE

Subtotal _____

Sales Tax _____

Delivery _____

Total _____

184

Control Form

CLIENT NAME _____ DATE _____

ADDRESS _____ SIDEMARK _____

CITY _____ STATE _____ ZIIP _____ NEAREST CROSS STREETS _____

□ Redesign Services
□ Paint/Color Consultation
□ Home Staging
□ Holiday Decorating
□ Exterior Holiday Decorating
□ Home Shopping Services
□ Relocation/Move-In Services
□ Blended/Downsized Services

□ Public Speaking/Workshops
□ Floral Arrangements
□ Artificial Plants
□ Live Plants
□ Custom Framed Art
□ Custom Throw Pillows
□ Custom Area Rugs
□ Custom Candles

□ Reorganization
□ Exchange Program
□ Refinish Furniture
□ Re-upholstery
□ Restoration Services
□ Other_____
□ Other_____
□ Other_____

RETAIL SALES	SALES TAX	SHIPPING	DELIVERY/INSTALL	TOTAL SALE
$	$	$	$	$

Vendor/Suppliers/Labor Used

NAME OF SUPPLIER	WHOLESALE AMT	FREIGHT/OTHER	DATE PD	CHECK NO.	AMOUNT	BALANCE
_____	$	$		#	$	$
_____	$	$		#	$	$
_____	$	$		#	$	$
_____	$	$		#	$	$
_____	$	$		#	$	$
_____	$	$		#	$	$
_____	$	$		#	$	$
_____	$	$		#	$	$

Due Date_____ Delivered On _____ Invoice No. _____

Deposit Rec'd_____ Amount $_____ Balance Due $_____ Completed □

NOTES_____

Independent Contractor Agreement

Agreement is made this _____ day of _____, _____(year).

The following outlines our agreement:

_____
_____
_____
_____

You have been retained by _____,
as an independent contractor for the project of

_____
You will be responsible for successfully completing said project according to specifications stated below.

The project is to be completed by _____.

The cost to complete will not exceed $_____.

You will invoice us for your services rendered at the end of each week □ or month □.

We will not deduct or withhold any taxes, FICA or other deductions. As an independent contractor, you will not be entitled to any fringe benefits, such as unemployment insurance, medical insurance, pension plans, worker's compensation insurance, or other such benefits that would be offered to regular employees.

During this project you may be in contact with or directly working with proprietary information which is important to our company and its competitive position. All information must be treated with strict confidence and may not be used at any time or in any manner in work you may do with others in our industry.

Please submit information regarding:

Worker's Compensation Insurance Policy for Employees (Name of Company, Phone and Policy No.)

_____

Liability Insurance Policy (Name of Company, Phone and Policy No.)

_____

Signatures:

Independent Contractor_____ Date_____

Company Representative_____ Date_____

Change Work Order

Hirer: _____

Contractor: _____

Contract Date_____

1)   The Hirer authorizes and the Contractor agrees to make the following work changes to the above dated contract:

_____
_____
_____
_____
_____
_____
_____
_____
_____
_____
_____
_____
_____
_____
_____
_____

2)   The agreed additional charge for the above change(s) is:
$_____.

Dated: _____

_____
Hirer

_____
Contractor

Authorization to Return Goods

Date_____To_____

Please allow this letter to acknowledge that we shall accept certain return goods for credit. The terms for return are:

1. The aggregate cost value of the goods subject to return shall not exceed $_____.

2. We shall deduct _____% of the cost price as handling charges to process the return goods, crediting your account.

3. All return good shall be in re-salable condition and represent goods we either currently stock or can return to our supplier for credit. We reserve the right to reject non-conforming goods.

4. Return goods must be invoiced and are subject to inspection and return approval before shipment to us.

5. If good are shipped via common carrier, you shall be responsible for all freight costs and risk of loss in transit. Goods shall not be considered accepted for return until we have received, inspected and approved said goods at our place of business.

6. Our agreement to accept returns for credit is expressly conditional upon your agreement to pay any remaining balance due on the following terms:

_____
_____
_____
_____
_____

You understand this return privilege is extended only to resolve your account balance and is not necessarily standing policy. Thank you for your cooperation in this matter.

Very truly yours,

_____
Company Representative

_____
Company   Address

_____
City   State   Zip

Consulting Services Agreement © 2005 Barbara Jennings

The parties to this agreement are as follows

_____
Consultant

_____
Client

The Consultant will consult with and advise Client in the following matters:

FEES & EXPENSES:

The consultant's fee for the above services is $_____ based upon an estimated duration of _____.

A retainer (if any) of $_____ is immediately due and payable.

Future payments will be made upon completion of this assignment or as stipulated below:

_____

_____

Expenses will be reimbursed upon receipt of the invoice.

Signed this _____ day of _____, _____(year).

_____

    Consultant Signature   Client Signature

_____

Date

Conditional Sale Agreement

The undersigned Purchaser hereby purchases from

_____

_____
(Seller)

the following goods and/or services:

_____
_____
_____
_____

Sales Price $_____

Sales Tax (if any) $_____

Finance Charge (if any) $_____

Insurance (if any) $_____

Shipping/Freight/Delivery/Installation $_____

Other Charges (if any) $_____

Total Purchase Price $_____

      Down Payment $_____

      Other Credits $_____

Total Credits $_____

Remaining Balance $_____

      Annual Interest Rate _____%

The amount financed (if any) shall be payable in _____ installments of $_____ each, commencing _____ from date hereof.

Seller shall retain title to goods until payment of the full purchase price, subject to allocation of payments and release of security interest as required by law. The undersigned agrees to safely keep the goods, free from other liens and encumbrances at the below address, and not remove goods without consent of Seller.

(Continued on Page 2)

CONDITIONAL SALE AGREEMENT CONTINUED   (2)

Purchaser agrees to execute all financing statements as may be required of Seller to perfect this conditional sales agreement.

At the election of Seller, the Purchaser shall keep goods adequately insured, naming Seller loss-payee.

The full balance shall become due on default; with the undersigned paying all reasonable attorneys fees and costs of collection. Upon default, Seller shall have the right to retake the goods, hold and dispose of same and collect expenses, together with any deficiency due from Purchaser, but subject to the Purchaser's right to redeem pursuant to law and the Uniform Commercial Code.

THIS IS A CONDITIONAL SALE AGREEMENT.

Accepted:

_____   _____
Seller   Purchaser

_____
Address

_____
City   State   Zip

Release of Mechanic's Liens

FOR GOOD CONSIDERATION, the undersigned contractor or subcontractor having furnished materials and/or labor for repairs, additions or construction at the premises known as

_____,

standing in the name of

_____do
hereby release all liens, or rights to file liens against said property for material and/or services or labor provided to this date, with it acknowledged however, that this discharge of lien shall not necessarily constitute a release or discharge of any claim for sums now or herein after due for said materials and/or services, if existing.

This release shall be binding upon and inure to the benefit of the parties, their successors, assigns and personal representatives.

Signed this _____ day of _____, _____
(year).

In the presence of:

_____   _____
Witness   Company Name

_____   _____
Address   Contractor/Subcontractor

_____   _____
City, State, Zip   Address

                                 _____
                                 City, State, Zip

Client Billing/Time Summary

Year: Date/Time	Staging/Redesign Client Name	Activity	Time	
			Hours	Minutes

My Appointment Schedule

Date:

	Redesign/Staging Appointment	Notes
7:15		
7:30		
7:45		
8:00		
8:15		
8:30		
8:45		
9:00		
9:15		
9:30		
9:45		
10:00		
10:15		
10:30		
10:45		
11:00		
11:15		
11:30		
11:45		
12:00		
12:15		
12:30		
12:45		
1:00		
1:15		
1:30		
1:45		
2:00		
2:15		
2:30		
2:45		
3:00		
3:15		
3:30		
3:45		
4:00		
4:15		
4:30		
4:45		
5:00		
5:15		
5:30		
5:45		
6:00		
6:15		
6:30		
6:45		
7:00		

7:15		
7:30		
7:45		
8:00		
8:15		
8:30		
8:45		
9:00		

Year at a Glance Sheet

January	February	March
April	**May**	**June**
July	**August**	**September**
October	**November**	**December**

Additional Products Invoice

From _____   Invoice # _____

Address _____   Invoice Date _____

_____   Phone _____

To _____   Ship To _____

Address _____   Address _____

_____   _____

Phone _____   Phone _____

QTY	Unit	Item #	Price	Discount	Extension
___	___	_____	_____	_____	_____
___	___	_____	_____	_____	_____
___	___	_____	_____	_____	_____
___	___	_____	_____	_____	_____
___	___	_____	_____	_____	_____
___	___	_____	_____	_____	_____
___	___	_____	_____	_____	_____
___	___	_____	_____	_____	_____
___	___	_____	_____	_____	_____
___	___	_____	_____	_____	_____
___	___	_____	_____	_____	_____
___	___	_____	_____	_____	_____
___	___	_____	_____	_____	_____
___	___	_____	_____	_____	_____
___	___	_____	_____	_____	_____
___	___	_____	_____	_____	_____

Taxable Sales $ _____

Nontaxable Sales $ _____

Total Sale $ _____

Sales Tax $ _____

Other/Labor $ _____

Balance Due $ _____

Thank You!

Expense Budget

	Month Ending:			Year to Date		
	Estimate	Actual	Difference	Estimate	Actual	Difference
Fixed Expenses						
Your Draw						
Partner/Assistant						
Payroll Taxes						
Employee Benefits						
Travel & Entertainment						
Equipment/Computers						
Insurance						
Rent						
Depreciation						
Taxes						
Legal & Professional						
Repairs/Maintenance						
Furniture						
Utilities						
Contributions						
Warehousing Costs						
Costs of Goods Sold						
Subscriptions/Dues						
Miscellaneous						
Variable Expenses						
Education/Workshops						
Advertising						
Website Fees						
Travel & Entertainment						
Telephone & Fax						
Office Supplies						
Furniture/Accessories						
Postage/Freight						
Contributions						
Office Equipment						
Miscellaneous						
Other:						
Total						

Concluding Remarks

Tying It All Together . . .

I trust you have found more than enough ideas, concepts, strategies, procedures, tactics and intriguing ideas to excite you and motivate you to pick a few of them to add to your business products and services.

Building a six figure income is not easy. It will take much perseverance, effort and time. But you've got to first set your goal of achieving $100,000 or more firmly in your mind – then $200,000 – then $500,000. And you've got to be dedicated to achieving that goal.

It doesn't matter what type of personality you have. Seven figure success stories are everywhere – in every conceivable type of business – and each person has a different, unique personality. But one of the things they all have in common, is that they believed they could do it, they set the goal to achieve it, they put a time limit on achieving it, they remained optimistic no matter what was going on in their lives, and they did it. You can too.

I believe if you have thoroughly read this manual and you understand the premise that I am proposing to you, that you will find more than enough here to keep you busy and, most of all, profitable. There are NO limits on what you can earn. Every one of the add-on products and services I wrote about is related to decorating and design - a sister sideline, if you will. Each can become a stand alone business of its own or be coordinated perfectly into your re-design business. You probably don't have time to do every idea – at least not right away. But pick the ones that appeal to you the most and expand your opportunities to make money exponentially in the process. Not everyone will want their furniture rearranged - but they just might be interested in a beautiful work of art, or an old sofa to be re-upholstered, or have need of some good trees and so on. If you have it, you can sell it. If you don't have it, you're leaving money on the table.

Re-design, the basic premise of rearranging the furniture and accessories a client already owns, is a very simple, simple business. It really is.

It is so simple, in fact, I figured out in a matter of an hour just how I would go about getting my business started back in 1986. People want to make it complicated. It's not.

But here is the crux of what you have to understand. It's the **marketing** of the business, as it is any business you might choose, that separates the women from the girls, the dreamers from the doers, the rich from the poor, the $100,000+ achievers from the rest.

The opportunities are out there for everyone - but nothing good comes from fear and inaction. Nothing good comes from silence.

Now for Some Really Blunt Talk . . .

If you are now, after all of this, incapable of turning your goals and dreams into a profitable decorating business of some kind, the fault lies *solely* with you.

There is **no** magic formula **anyone** can give you.

The only sure fire magic formula in business is **hard work**, and a little luck or good timing once in a while is helpful, but you have no control over luck or fortunate timing – but you do have total control over how hard you choose to work.

Anyone who thinks a re-design or home staging business, or any other business, is magically just going to appear on their doorstep needs a reality check. It takes commitment and hard work.

Go to work now - and make it happen for you!

Contact Information

Barbara Jennings, Director, Academy of Staging and Redesign
Decorate-Redecorate.com
Box 2632, Costa Mesa, CA 92628-2632

Just as I have been teaching you to ask for referrals and testimonials, I myself would appreciate any testimonials and referrals you might share with me. Please write me and tell me what part of this manual has benefited you the most. If you are confused by any part, please let me know that too. And please tell your friends about Decorate-Redecorate.com. You will find contact information at this link: About Us (http://www.decorate-redecorate.com/about.html).

I've tried hard to give you the most complete training on the business side of advanced redesign you'll find anywhere. Your testimonials would mean a lot and I thank you in advance for taking the time to write me.

Warm regards,

Barbara Jennings

Appreciate Your Feedback

In our continuing commitment to improve the quality of our training materials, courses and tools of the trade, we would greatly appreciate your comments, thoughts, feelings or suggestions. Please feel free to write me. We value your opinions and will give thoughtful consideration to any comments you submit. Please use the form at this link to send your comments for on-line convenience:

http://www.decorate-redecorate.com/support.html

Resources

Additional Important Resources

Home Staging for Yourself

As you already know, home staging is a closely related business and one well worthy of your attention if you've only been doing or planning to do interior redesign. There is a dire need for staging services everywhere. Potential clients are real estate agents and brokers, home owners, lenders with REO properties and on and on. If you're interested in the finer details of operating a successful home staging business along side your redesign business, might I suggest you acquire my best selling basic business book called **Home Staging for Profit.** To read more about it, please visit my website for all the details: http://www.decorate-redecorate.com/home-staging-training.html.

Basic Interior Redesign Business

While some of this training will be naturally repeated in the redesign training I offer, I would highly recommend you get both of my ebook/manuals on starting, growing and managing an Interior Redesign business as well as what you have purchased here. You will find many similarities in staging and redesign, however there are some crucial differences you should know. Many strategies and tactics will work for both businesses, but you owe it to yourself to know all about that business as much as this one. I promise you that you will receive great training. This is my basic business training, but I also offer an advanced training as well. To get your copy of **Rearrange It!** visit this link at http://www.decorate-redecorate.com/redecorate.html.

Staging Luxurious Homes

One of the best overall marketing tactics is to concentrate a certain amount of your time and energy courting affluent homeowners and their agents. Why? Because they have the money to purchase your consultation services and your staging services. In addition to that, they are very busy people, usually concentrating more on making money than in selling their home, and they are naturally excellent candidate for a home staging service. I've written a one-of-a-kind tutorial that will teach you essentially everything you need to know to tap into this highly prized market and even specialize in staging wealthy homes – and explode your profits into a seven figure income. Get your copy right now. Visit: http://www.decorate-redecorate.com/staging-luxurious-homes.html

Staging Portfolio Secrets

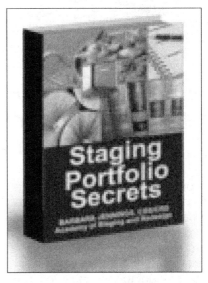

Once you've decided to start a business in staging, redesign or art consulting, you've got to create a visual portfolio to help clients understand how valuable your services are. You've got to highlight your personal strengths and define what makes you different from the competition. To help you achieve a powerful, authoritative portfolio to speak for you, I've written a book that thoroughly covers the subject from start to finish. I think you'll find it a valuable resource for this all-important part of your marketing efforts.

http://www.stagingportfoliosecrets.com/

Home Staging in Tough Times

During tough economic times, entrepreneurs often need to resort to more creative tactics and strategies to keep the profits coming through the door. Often times these tactics and business agreements do not involve cash, but something equally valuable. So to help readers acquire knowledge and skills in this type of business generating method, I wrote a book that covers the subject quite adequately. It's filled with practical forms, actual ads, the specific how-to, and much, much more.

http://www.decorate-redecorate.com/home-staging-in-tough-times.html

Getting Paid: Financial Strategies for Home Stagers

Home Staging is a more complicated business to run than a Re-Design business, So I felt it needed a specific guide on how to properly protect yourself against sellers or agents who might try to skip out on paying you after you've invested one or more days working on the home. This handy guide will help you learn great strategies to protect your business and make sure you get paid what you rightfully deserve each and every time. It also includes extra staging tricks of the trade you'll find very helpful.

http://www.decorate-redecorate.com/getting-paid.html

A Real Estate Agent's Guide to Offering Free Home Staging Consultations (or Advice)

For readers who aren't interested in starting a professional staging business but who already or are planning on getting a real estate license, you'll be happy to know we haven't forgotten about you and what you would need to authoritatively give great staging advice to your sellers. Now you don't have to spend upwards of $300 for a seminar or class. My newest book covers the subject thoroughly. It isn't meant to turn you into a professional stager, but it will help you advise sellers and, when necessary, point them to a professional local stager who can help them with all the fine details. It's great training, even if you aren't an agent.

http://www.decorate-redecorate.com/real-estate-staging-guide.html

Decor Secrets Revealed Ebook

For top notch training in all of the necessary interior design principles and techniques of professional designers, consider getting my electronic book of 25 chapters devoted just to these specifics. The ebook has over 600 color photos. It is an easy, breezy read and will teach you a lot about furniture and accessory arrangement design. Even if you've already got some design training, I've had full service designers with a 4-year degree tell me they learned from the training – or were reminded of concepts they had forgotten about. Please look on this as further investment in your success. Use this link to get your copy of **Decor Secrets Revealed** if you haven't done so already: http://www.decorate-redecorate.com/decor.html.

Arrange Your Stuff

Approaching furniture arrangement concepts from a slightly different angle, my 189 page soft cover (plastic comb binding) book of a wide range of sketched rooms, including the before sketch and then followed by anywhere from 1-4 sketches of how the room was and could have been arranged professionally. Lots of tips to help you immediately dissect any room and know how to solve it. Filled with the top and most common furniture arrangement configurations, you should find the answer to most rooms in these pages. Use this link to get your copy of **Arrange Your Stuff** if you haven't done so already: http://www.decorate-redecorate.com/arrange-your-stuff.html.

Wall Groupings! The Secret to Hanging Art and Photos

This is my soft cover book of 148 pages, giving you a huge array of ways to dress a naked wall. This book replaces my best selling book called *Where There's a Wall – There's a Way* which has sold out. However, the new book covers the same type of information but is now loaded with nearly a hundred photos of wall groupings designed by designers and re-designers. You'll love it. You're going to run into groupings while you're out there. It also includes hanging tips and is the most detailed book of its kind on the market. You may read more about it here: http://www.decorate-redecorate.com/book.html.

Dual Certification Courses

The best place to see a quick overview of everything currently available is at this link: **http://www.decorate-redecorate.com/home-staging-redesign.html**. It's a chart and you can easily see all of our "a la carte" components and compare the Silver and Diamond Courses.

Courses have been designed for those unique individuals who are really serious about building a career level business, want everything all at once, and want to save money in the process. It is not particularly a route I recommend for everyone, particularly if you're only interested in supplemental income or you would be too strapped economically as a result. That's why I offer plenty of options in an "a la carte" fashion so you can tailor your training and any additional products you might be interested in to your personal timing and resource limits.

But for those that can jump into a course, it makes the most sense. Duo certification is guaranteed with a Diamond Course and single certification is guaranteed with a Gold Course.

The Diamond Course includes design training, basic and advanced staging and redesign business training, multiple types of promotional aids to help you launch and promote your business, tools of the trade to help you actually do your projects, certification, directory listings, a members only site (with lifetime membership and no annual fees like others charge), VIP status on advice, and a bunch of other goodies thrown in.

Diamond Standard, Deluxe and Ruby Combo Programs - Our most comprehensive training programs, the Diamond Standard, Deluxe and Ruby Certification Courses give you all of the design training and business training you'll ever need (both basic and advanced), numerous sales aids, some management tools of the trade, double guaranteed certification, custom stationery to effective launch your business, brochure webpages or websites, double business listings in our directories and bonuses, but you get two businesses instead of just one.

(Standard Course) http://www.decorate-redecorate.com/diamond-redesign-training.html

(Ruby Course – Best Value) http://www.decorate-redecorate.com/diamond-ruby-combo-course.html.

Deluxe Silver Combo Training - Get all of our two businesses plus redesign training in one easy package. This program does **not** include the "tools of the trade" – it is strictly training, but is all of our training ebooks and books for a packaged price for two businesses, not just one. For details: http://www.decorate-redecorate.com//silver-redesign-training.html

Additional Training Options

Great Parties! Great Homes! – Learn how to decorate for parties and social functions, how to be the perfect hostess and how to be the perfect guest. **http://www.decorate-redecorate.com/planning-parties** Great training for learning how to effectively promote your business and acquire referrals. Since most business in staging and redesign happens through face-to-face relationships, being active social is a crucial part of building your business.

Sales Aids and Tools of the Trade

Home Staging Powerpoint Presentation Slides and Script – Another great tool, this 65-Slide Presentation is great for use before real estate agents. It primarily promotes the services of a home stager, but ends with redesign as well. Comes with a script that you can edit for your own purposes. See **http://www.decorate-redecorate.com/home-enhancement.html**

Interior Redesign Powerpoint Presentation Slides and Script – Don't try to "tell" people what you do – "show" them with our exclusive 60-slide presentation. It comes with a full script which you can tailor to your situation. For use with Windows PC computers, whether or not you have PowerPoint. See **http://www.decorate-redecorate.com/redesign-slides.html**

Musical Slideshow Prospecting CDs – Don't try to "tell" people what you do – "show" them with our Before and After Musical Slideshow. It's the perfect way to turn a prospect into a client and makes it so much easier for you to sell the benefits of your services. Available in sets of 3, 6 or 12. For the Home Staging Slideshow CDs, please visit **http://www.decorate-redecorate.com/staging-for-sellers.html**

For Interior Redesign Slideshows, visit: **http://www.decorate-redecorate.com/get-clients.html**

Steel Furniture Lifter With Carpet and Hard Floor Sliders – Save your back. Get the furniture lifter that will help you move the heaviest of furniture by using the concept of leverage. We sell the lifter along with two sets of sliders (one for carpeting; one for hard floors). I don't sell them separately because you need both to do the job. I do sell sliders separately because you're going to want to have more than one set on hand to cut down on those back-breaking tasks. For the Lifter Toolbox Set, please visit: **http://www.decorate-redecorate.com/furniture-lifter.html**.

Furniture Sliders for Carpet or Hard Flooring – Don't hurt your back moving heavy furniture. Do it the easy, effortless way with furniture sliders. We have them for both carpeted floors and hard floors. See **http://www.decorate-redecorate.com/furniture-movers-carpet.html** or **http://www.decorate-redecorate.com/furniture-movers-hard-floors.html**

Decorating Organizer/Tote – It's hard enough to go shopping for your decorating projects and keep track of all your swatches and samples. We've got a very professional organizer/tote combination that makes it super easy. And you'll look classy too. This is a super organizing tool and I use mine all the time. See **http://www.decorate-redecorate.com/decorating-shopper.html**

Promotional Postcards – Use our colorful, professionally printed promotional postcards to get the word out about your services. Many styles to choose from. Cards are sold in sets. We have staging cards, redesign cards, staging & redesign cards, variety packs and a quick start promo pack. See **http://www.decorate-redecorate.com/postcards.html**

One of the Greatest Aids You'll Ever Find

The Home Staging for Yourself Checklist Guide is one of our newest tools for helping you make money on every appointment – whether you're a professional stager or a real estate agent advising your seller. You'll always encounter people who want to do the staging themselves or who just refuse to hire professional stagers or simply believe they can't afford a stager's services.

With this 105-page generic to-do list (professionally printed and bound in a 5x8 booklet), you can fill it out for them so they can follow the instructions and stage their own home. It's truly a no-brainer solution and is exclusively offered by us.

Each section or room of a home has bulleted lists of common tasks for that type of area or room, followed by blank lines so you can customize it for the seller right on the spot. When you've filled it out with your recommendations, you simple give or sell it to them. Eliminates having to go back to your office to create a report – what a waste of time and energy that is.

Buy them in small quantities at a wholesale price and resell to your clients. No cost to you and even becomes a profit center for you if you want it to be one.

You simply sell them the guide for a higher price than you paid (be sure to account for your shipping charges). Since the list is so exhaustive, it will silently urge them to possibly hire a stager instead. For more details: **http://www.decorate-redecorate.com/home-staging-for-yourself.html**.

Furniture Arrangement Kit – One of the best overhead furniture arranging kits. You'll get around 1600 furniture decals to apply to special grid paper so you can create a bird's eye view of any room in your home or for a client. The furniture comes in multiple styles and sizes and all decals are reusable. See **http://www.decorate-redecorate.com/furniture-arrangements.html** For an Elevations Furniture Arranging Kit, visit **http://www.decorate-redecorate.com/furniture-elevations.html**

Newsletters and Discussion Forum

Decorating Newsletter – While you're at it, sign up for our free Decorating Tips newsletter that comes out monthly. You'll find links on almost any page of the website or from the drop down menus at the top.

Redesign/Staging Newsletter – This newsletter is private and only available to those trainees that have purchased redesign/staging training. Write us for information on this if you did not purchase this manual directly from me.

Free Discussion Forum – Be sure to visit our free discussion forum and join. It's a place to share ideas, tips and thoughts and to ask questions. You'll be in a community of home stagers, re-designers and decorators from all over the country. Visit: **http://www.decorate-redecorate.com/smf**. Membership is free to all.

Certification for Those That Want It

Certified Staging or Redesign Specialist – Certification is not necessary for success, but some people really want that extra credibility so we have a private certification process for you. It involves an exam and submission of a portfolio to be judged which makes it one of the most prestigious offered anywhere. If you're up against competition that claims to be "certified" or a graduate of some entity or "accredited", doesn't it make sense to become certified yourself by the only organization that requires candidates be accountable for their knowledge and talent? If I were evaluating one or more stagers or re-designers for my project, I would much more highly value the person who passed an exam and went through a portfolio process than someone who merely attended a seminar, workshop or class without having to prove they even understand or remember what was offered. But that's just me. I happen to believe that true certification or designation that represents a person's skills should require much more than that. And the person I would hire would be the person that demonstrated a highly level of accountability for their knowledge and talent. You may apply for single or double certification. Application fee. Apply here: **http://www.decorate-redecorate.com/certified-redesigner.html**

Certification for Real Estate Agents

To apply for our new designation for real estate agents, please visit:

http://www.decorate-redecorate.com/real-estate-staging-guide.html

Musical Slideshow for Presentations

I've also put together a Slideshow of 71 slides put to music, an easy listening type of music. This slideshow is on a CD and allows you to loan it to prospective clients to take home, so that they have something to "show" the spouse. Many times a person you talk to becomes interested in your services, only to go home and discuss it with the spouse, who isn't the least bit interested.

So don't trust others to present your services for you. Give them a visual presentation that is thoughtfully prepared so they have something to look at. Most people are visual learners. Then need to see and don't fare that well if they just hear you talk. The great thing about this Musical Slideshow is that you make an appointment to pick up the CD from them in a day or two. This pick up appointment puts you in their home where you can see first hand what is wrong. That is the best place to turn the prospect into a client – in their home.

The slides themselves show several different homes of different economic levels that have been staged. Interspersed in the show are slides that point out the benefits of hiring a professional stager like you. It gives the homeowner a chance to really see the difference between a non-staged home and one that has been staged. A picture is worth a thousand words. So this CD does a very good job of showing the power of staging, not merely talking about it.

The slideshows are available for purchase in sets of 3, 6 or 12. The more you have circulating, the better for your business, so stagers are buying the larger sets. The more you get at one time, the less each CD costs.

For more information on these, please visit **Staging4Sellers** at http://www.decorate-redecorate.com/staging-for-sellers.html.

The Home Staging Showcase Portfolio Book

While the CDs are great to loan out to prospective homeowners, you're going to have plenty of opportunities that come your way where it would be great to have a book you can show people. With a book of staging examples and benefits, you can show it to any one, any time, at any place. It is the most flexible of all. When you're new to the industry, you probably don't have any pictures of your own to use as examples. So just like in the CD slideshows I just wrote about, I've put together a Showcase Book for you to acquire, if you like, which will professionally do the job for you.

Again, it's a series of many before and after pictures. Many of the examples shown in the book are homes that were staged by several professionals from California to New Jersey and parts in between. So the book has no geographical boundaries. All of the pictures are in vivid color printed on archival (acid free) paper, so it should not yellow on you over time. The book is hard bound and has a black linen cover. It consists of 28 pages. Long enough to make a compelling case for staging and hiring you, but short enough to quit while it's ahead.

I believe you'll find this book one of the best promotional tools at your disposal. It points out one benefit after another to your client base and consistently encourages them to use a professional stager rather than doing the work themselves.

Don't worry about the photos reflecting the work of someone else. Your prospects really won't care. Once you get plenty of your own photos, you can use them as supplemental examples of your talent or create your own

Showcase Book. I'm just trying to help you get started right out of the gates. And if you've been trained elsewhere and you bought this manual for supplemental training, don't fret. You can utilize this resource too. It is generic enough for any stager to use and keeps gently suggesting to the reader that they will benefit more by trusting the services of a professional stager than they will of they attempt the process on their own.

For more details about the **Home Staging Showcase Book**, please visit this sister site of ours: **http://www.homestagingshowcase.com**. Because these books are printed in very small quantities, the price points are stiff due to the fact the book is in full color and hard bound with a fabric cover. Regardless, the book has received high praise from stagers using it and I must admit, I'm pretty proud of it myself. One recently wrote this: "I received my book today, . . . The books are very attractive and "rich" looking! What a pleasure it will be to show these to prospective clients!"

Mini Staging Portfolios

As you go about your daily routine, it's always wise to have a handy portfolio ready to whip out to show people you meet. We've developed some great purse-sized portfolios you'll love to pieces. They are printed in

beautiful color. The Staging Portfolio is filled with powerful statistics you'll need to help you convince agents and sellers that staging is a vital tool to be used when selling a home.

For details on the Mini Portfolios: http://www.decorate-redecorate.com/mini-staging-portfolio.html

We offer a set of two hard-bound portfolios: one on staging and one on redesign.

We also offer a soft cover portfolio (slightly larger) on staging statistics, which is very powerful in convincing sellers that staging is a must before putting a property up for sale.

Staging and redesign are very visual businesses. It's difficult to explain what you do and how it can benefit a potential client. That's where portfolios are so important. It doesn't have to be examples of your own work to be effective. Prospects may assume the photos are yours. That's ok. And if they should ask, tell them the booklet shows generic examples so that people can really see how the service will benefit them. It is not unusual for salespeople to show home office company literature as part of their presentations. Don't be concerned. You can eventually create your own personal portfolio whenever you like. Use ours in the interim to help you get your business off to a great start.

NOTE: The prices for these full color portfolios may be higher than you expect due to the high cost of printing. But they are well worth the investment when you consider how handy they will be. Keep them in your purse or car always so you'll always have them ready for any opportunity that comes your way.

Other Training Available

Pro Art Consulting – I worked the residential market as well as the corporate market. However, in the business world I offered my services as a corporate art consultant, specializing in designing decorative art programs for business facilities. If you want to work with business clients as well, this is a very low risk service to add. Select ebook version or printed version. **http://www.decorate-redecorate.com/work-at-home.html**

Floral Design Training – One of the most exquisite accessories any home could have are beautiful floral arrangements, whether artificial or real. Even in your home staging business, don't forget about the importance of strategically placed floral arrangements. Want to learn how to create them professionally? Visit: **http://www.floraldesigntraining.com**

Just a Very Few of
Barbara's Unsolicited Testimonials

Barbara Jennings, CSS/CRS

"Things are definitely heating up...I had another home sell two weeks ago...sold in 2 weeks ...and I just got news from another Realtor that another home sold in Turtle Rock that we just finished on 3/15. So, I am very happy to have happy sellers and happy realtors! – Debbie Muccillo"

"Barbara, Thank you for the newsletters. They have kept me going while I am finishing up my Diamond Certification. I needed one more staging, and now I have 2! I purchased the program last Feb, but due to family crises that have been insurmountable. The newsletters give me a reprieve and keep me moving on. I have had many jobs for redesign . . . a home improvement company in our area picked me up as a designer to assist in picking tiles, color consultation, overall design work. It's been exciting . . . It's a great program, and the furniture rental company I use has also heard of your program too. With appreciation, Debi Wheatley"

"I recently purchased Home Staging for Profit, Rearrange It, and Advanced Redesign, which I am enjoying very much! . . . Also, wanted to let you know that last year I took an interior decorating class from an online college and received a diploma from them, but I must admit your books are much more informative. Thank you, Gayle Mitchell"

"It's been over a year since I first downloaded and read your Home Staging Training book. I wanted to thank you as it encouraged me to get into the decorating business I love, despite not having expensive training as a decorator. After reading your book I made my first call to a local Realtor and offered a free consultation - a year later I'm exhausted with the constant work and my husband is considering joining me! This is especially surprising since I thought the business would 'slowly' grow until my youngest was in school. I'm busy, clients are happy and as yet I'm getting all my jobs from website contact and Realtor referrals. Realtors love my economic service and it keeps me in demand. Thank you for your priceless, hard-core business information that made me feel prepared to compete with the Big Boys of staging in my area! I believe most arts (including decorating) are talent based, but your business information gave me critical information to provide professional services from the first day. Thanks! - Shannon, Artisan Home Staging"

"Hi Barbara, Thank you for this delightful course. I am enjoying all the materials. I have been studying staging for about 8 months and reading as many books as I could get my hands on! Even though I have a Home Economics degree and have worked in the home improvement industry for 17 years, I still needed something to help me with my confidence. With my husbands encouragement I decided that what I needed was a course and a certification. I'm very glad I chose yours because I believe that my philosophy of home design is similar to yours. . . . Thanks again and I look forward to many years of contact with you. Pam Elkins January 25, 2008 (Purchased course) Diamond Standard"

"Thanks sooo much Barbara, you all did a great job, I imagine my video will be up soon. . . . I am soooo excited, I have a women's networking meeting this morning and I can finally announce that I have a website, almost complete. I have also officially been asked to be the guest for the evening at an opening of a lovely very upscale store in Delray Beach on March 6th, and on the eighth of March the women's networking group is having a trade show. So as you can see I am on my way. Thanks again, Audrey (Runya's Redesign)"

"You are the best teacher. Just awesome. I took an expensive seminar. It was overcrowded, noisy and not very informative. I felt cheated. Thanks for offering such a great alternative. - Betty Unger"

CPSIA information can be obtained
at www.ICGtesting.com
Printed in the USA
FSOW03n0241270517
34522FS

9 780961 802653